The Grumbling Gods

the grumbling gods

A Palm Springs Reader

Edited by Peter Wild

THE UNIVERSITY OF UTAH PRESS
Salt Lake City

© 2007 by The University of Utah Press. All rights reserved.

 The Defiance House Man colophon is a registered trademark of the
University of Utah Press. It is based upon a four-foot-tall, Ancient Puebloan
pictograph (late PIII) near Glen Canyon, Utah.

11 10 09 08 07   1 2 3 4 5

LIBRARY OF CONGRESS CATALOGING-IN-PUBLICATION DATA
The grumbling gods : a Palm Springs reader / edited by Peter Wild.
    p. cm.
  Includes bibliographical references and index.
  ISBN 978-0-87480-899-5 (pbk. : alk. paper) 1. Palm Springs (Calif.)—History. 2. Palm
Springs (Calif.)—Social life and customs. 3. Palm Springs (Calif.)—Biography. I. Wild,
Peter, 1940-
  F869.P18G78 2007
  979.4'97—dc22

                          2007015086

Contents

Acknowledgments | ix

Introduction: Teetering on the Edge | 1

1. For My Own People | 11
   Stories and Legends of the Palm Springs Indians by FRANCISCO PATENCIO

2. Life from the Rocks | 19
   The Forgotten Artist: Indians of Anza-Borrego and Their Rock Art
   by MANFRED KNAAK

3. The Spanish Lewis and Clark: Into the Swallowing Wilderness | 24
   Anza's California Expeditions by HERBERT EUGENE BOLTON

4. We Took Our Bullets in Our Mouths | 29
   The Personal Narrative of James O. Pattie, of Kentucky by JAMES O. PATTIE

5. Stuck in the Yuma Dunes: A Sandstorm Envelops a Stagecoach | 33
   Six Horses by CAPTAIN WILLIAM BANNING and GEORGE HUGH BANNING

6. Seeing with New Eyes: William P. Blake, Geologist | 37
   Report of a Geological Reconnaissance in California by WILLIAM P. BLAKE

7. Steamboating across the Colorado | 43
   Report upon the Colorado River of the West by LIEUTENANT JOSEPH C. IVES

8. "Thou Brown, Bare-Breasted, Voiceless Mystery": The Desert
   as Urban Melodrama | 47
   "To the Colorado Desert" by MADGE MORRIS WAGNER

9. Seeing with New Eyes: John C. Van Dyke, Aesthetician | 49
   The Desert: Further Studies in Natural Appearances by JOHN C. VAN DYKE

10. More on Van Dyke: The Nasty Young Man on the Imagined Trapeze | 56
    The Desert: Further Studies in Natural Appearances by JOHN C. VAN DYKE

11. John Muir on the Colorado Desert: In a Flowered Bathrobe | 60
    "I Remember John Muir's Visit" by HELEN LUKENS GAUT

12. The Runaway River | 68
    The Water Seekers by REMI A. NADEAU

13. The Wonderland: Ghosts at the Well | 72
    The Wonders of the Colorado Desert by GEORGE WHARTON JAMES

14. Love along the Irrigation Ditches | 76
    The Winning of Barbara Worth by HAROLD BELL WRIGHT

15. A Treacherous Camel at the Train Station | 82
    Palm Springs: The Landscape, the History, the Lore by MARY JO CHURCHWELL

16. Out of Revolutionary Mexico: The Three Wealthy White Sisters | 84
    Palm Springs: The Landscape, the History, the Lore by MARY JO CHURCHWELL

17. Barbara Worth on the Rampage | 89
    "Imperial Earthquake, Million Damage Done"

18. A Desert Village | 94
    Our Araby: Palm Springs and the Garden of the Sun by J. SMEATON CHASE

19. A Desert Saint—With Cracks: Carl Eytel | 98
    "Of Such As These Is the Spirit of the Desert" by ELWOOD LLOYD;
    and Letters to Edmund C. Jaeger by CARL EYTEL

20. Just What Was Needed: Edmund C. Jaeger | 106
    The North American Deserts by EDMUND C. JAEGER

21. Two Wealthy Feminists from Cleveland: A Great Hole Full
    of Blue Mist | 122
    The White Heart of Mojave: An Adventure with the Outdoors of the Desert
    by EDNA BRUSH PERKINS

22. A Tiny Figure Wavering in the Blue Mists | 127
    California Desert Trails by J. SMEATON CHASE

CONTENTS

23. The Ansel Adams of the Desert: Stephen H. Willard | 137
    "Stephen H. Willard: Photography Collection and Archive"
        by CHRISTINE GILES

24. The Excitements of Celluloid: The Camel's Nose | 141
    Hollywood Saga by WILLIAM C. DEMILLE

25. The Excitements of Celluloid: The Camel Victorious | 146
    California: A Guide to the Golden State

26. After God . . . Gen. George S. Patton! | 149
    Patton's Desert Training Center by JOHN S. LYNCH, JOHN W. KENNEDY,
        and ROBERT L. WOOLEY

27. *Desert Magazine* and Marshal South: Living like Indians | 155
    "Desert Refuge" by MARSHAL SOUTH

28. Pegleg Smith: A Legend Found—Then Lost Again | 160
    "Black Nuggets in the Valley of Phantom Buttes" by JOHN D. MITCHELL

29. Sands that Blossom into Viking Ships | 167
    "Ships That Pass in Desert Sands" by CHORAL PEPPER

30. The Death of Chuckawalla Bill | 173
    The Man from the Cave by COLIN FLETCHER

31. Murder in Fru-Fru Land | 180
    Poodle Springs by RAYMOND CHANDLER and ROBERT B. PARKER

32. Consequences: The Sea of Poisons | 183
    Salt Dreams: Land and Water in Low-Down California by WILLIAM DEBUYS

33. The Preserved Lands: Ecstasy and Agony | 191
    All the Wild and Lonely Places: Journeys in a Desert Landscape
        by LAWRENCE HOGUE

34. Bighorn Sheep | 198
    All the Wild and Lonely Places: Journeys in a Desert Landscape
        by LAWRENCE HOGUE

35. In the Vineyards: "Tío, I Need Some Work" | 204
    Highwire Moon: A Novel by SUSAN STRAIGHT

36. Any August Day a Hundred Years Ago: In the Cool Pines | 212
Palm Springs: The Landscape, the History, the Lore by MARY JO CHURCHWELL

37. Palm Desert, Rancho Mirage, La Quinta, Las Mentiras | 216
Palm Springs: First Hundred Years by FRANK M. BOGERT

Epilogue: A Beam of Dawn Light | 221
"A Landmark Fades" and "The No-Girls Club" by ANN JAPENGA

Notes and Source Credits | 227

Bibliography | 233

Index | 247

Acknowledgments

A warm place in my heart is reserved for the many people who gave freely of their information and time, but, more importantly to me, of their warmth: Sally McManus and Jeri Vogelsang of the Palm Springs Historical Society; Shelly Thacker, Sastri Madugula, and Patti Hanley of the Palm Springs Public Library; Christine Giles and Michelle Gallagher of the Palm Springs Art Museum; Manfred and Betsy Knaak of the Anza-Borrego Desert Natural History Association; and Jon Fletcher, archivist at the Agua Caliente Cultural Museum. That's not to mention dozens of other people—rangers, local historians, and just plain old-time residents of the Colorado Desert—who gave me their time and their good talk.

With her usual cheer, Linda Dols, head of the Interlibrary Loan Department at the University of Arizona Library, kept me supplied with rare documents. Once again it was my pleasure to work with Peggy Flyntz in assembling the manuscript.

The Grumbling Gods

Introduction: Teetering on the Edge

One of the first things visitors to Palm Springs learn about is the story of old Tahquitz.[1] A spirit of pure evil, an absolutely black soul all the way through, he is responsible for all kinds of mischief and mayhem. He causes crops to fail, occasionally carries off beautiful maidens, and has been known, so it is reported, to eat his human victims. Worse than that, he lives close by, up the namesake canyon that opens like a huge maw almost into the heart of town. Oh, and he causes earthquakes, too. In fact, while browsing through the fashionable shops of Palm Springs, if you care to pause you might well hear his rumblings far up the canyon as he prepares the next human disaster.

Once told with genuine fear and trembling by the local Cahuilla Indians,[2] the tale was passed on to the whites, who, no doubt, elaborated on it a bit and now retell it for the amusement of tourists. Yet we should be careful not to chuckle too quickly on such matters. The story has a particular appropriateness for Palm Springs and its surrounding desert. Tourists may be pleased at their visits to this place of boutiques, golf courses, and the homes of movie stars and former presidents, all spun into a grand Elysium of upscale restaurants and mineral baths existing impossibly here on earth, but beyond the glittering surface are tensions, conflicts, and deep uncertainty about the future. In this land of earthquakes, unbearable heat, and shortages of water, we find a strange overlay of modern glitz. This is one of the fastest growing areas in the nation, boasting population figures that fill the believers in endless growth with buoyant pride. For instance, in 1890 the village of Palm Springs had a population of fifty people, most of them Indians. Thirty years later, with an influx of whites, that number had grown to a whopping seventy-five. However, the purveyors of real estate, overjoyed at that increase, had no idea what riches lay in their future. They must have gasped in utter disbelief when in 1940 the little desert town had zoomed to an incredible 3,434 souls. The astonishment of those selling town lots only reflects the limits of our grasp of possibilities. To comprehend what's going on, we need to understand that this is an area of impossible things made real. According to the last census, Palm Springs had a population of 42,807—a soaring increase in a little over a century from the fifty of 1890, and by a factor not of tens or hundreds, but of thousands.[3]

Yet on several counts this hardly is the end of the story. The desert invasion was no slapstick, tawdry laying down of ticky-tacky, with the salesmen quickly pocketing their dough and running off for greener climes. The change from raw desert has been immensely qualitative as well as quantitative. In one of the great success stories of modern culture and entrepreneurial genius, some decades ago the tinsel of Beverly Hills' Rodeo Drive was transplanted into downtown Palm Springs. There it took root and is now spreading in a seemingly endless surge of prosperity ever more rapidly in new towns over the whole valley eastward across the desert in a rampage of upscale condominiums and acrylic-green golf courses where movie stars frolic.

One need not be a moralist with a sad look and thick-soled shoes to ponder that the ancient gods are not necessarily happy about such changes. This raving success has occurred in a severe desert, in essence not a good place for human beings. The tribes the whites first encountered in the region were not in this sparse land by choice; they had been pushed out from greener places by more powerful tribes taking over their homelands. Admirable as their adjustments have been in the hard job of survival in a place of rocks and cacti and sparse rain, they did little more than survive. Their numbers attest to that. The land simply could not support a large population. Their settlements numbered but a few dozen individuals each, likely a fairly stable population reflecting the carrying capacity of the land, except, of course, when the rains failed and starvation started whittling down the numbers to a pitiful remnant.

But, hey, you say, look at what we've accomplished! Despite our urban orientation, the glory of our automobiles, the magical work of electricity, and the superabundance in supermarkets, we tend to be sentimental about nature as a benign force, a reservoir of goodness; yet in one essential way of looking at it, the story of human advance on the planet has been one of success in manipulating the environment. That ear of corn you chomp on at a backyard barbecue once was the seedhead of a grass no larger than your thumb; only through selective breeding over the centuries have we managed to produce a robust and juicy item that is almost a meal in itself and, to boot, far more nutritious than its ancestor. Even in the middle of the desert we expect that a thoughtless flip of a switch will command a blast of cool air, and with a turn of a faucet we presume that water will gush forth. Such genies would have flabbergasted Indians counting themselves blessed if after a day of slogging through sands looking for cactus pods to eat and lizards to gulp down raw they came to a waterhole with just enough muddy liquid in it to ease them through the night. Yes, we, indeed, have been successful. A flight over the Colorado Desert shows the proof: hundreds of square miles of shopping malls in new suburbs, each house with its aquamarine swimming pool.

I will go back on my intention and wax moralistic for one moment. By what right have we turned this land into something it was not, wrenched it out of its natural shape to suit our pleasure? What right have we to push out the bighorn sheep and rip up the cactus? It is the right of conquest, of doing what we can do. Surely the gods must be angry about that. Yet perhaps I'm getting cranky. Let's ask a related and far more practical question: How long can it last? Here we get into trouble. Thinking back on those figures, the growth from fifty to 42,807, we have managed to build a successful society on the desert, but it is a colonial society, far more imposed on the land than a part of it. Almost everything people buy on the Colorado Desert comes from somewhere else, and this means, especially, water, the key to everything on the desert. We're putting on a wonderful show right now. Yet even as we dance, the water table beneath our feet is falling at a tremendous rate, and the Colorado River, once thought the ultimate solution to all water problems, is overallocated, with cities and states squabbling over the bones of a diminished resource. Surely the gods of mathematics are waiting in the wings.

I fear I'm being too dismal. We tend to rejoice as long as we can keep the party going, with the faith that tomorrow will take care of itself. And maybe it will. Just maybe our technology that has served us so well will continue to allow us to thrive and grow in a land where the Cahuilla Indians hung on by their bare fingertips. Maybe I worry too much about the bighorn sheep. And maybe I worry too much that the transplanted Rodeo Drive that has most people dazzled in fact diminishes them, represents far less than they should want out of life, and that the original ideal of the village of Palm Springs, still remembered by aging residents, if never completely achieved nonetheless had something very important to say about what we could be as human beings.

As for now, let's consider where we are. We're in Southern California. That is, inland over the coastal mountains from San Diego and in the southeastern corner of the state. That's the Colorado Desert. And one rushes in, as just about everyone else who writes about it, to add that the name of this desert derives from the area's main watershed and geologic feature, the Colorado River, which neatly forms this desert's eastern boundary, and note that the name has absolutely nothing to do with the state of Colorado, which didn't even exist in 1853, the year that explorer William P. Blake gave the Colorado Desert its name. In any case, scientists continue to bicker about the fine points of what that territory includes, and as to the details of its extent, makeup, and natural history we are fortunate to have the overview of a foremost authority, Edmund C. Jaeger, appearing in Chapter 20. All niceties aside, we have no problem with a general definition. For our purposes, the Colorado Desert is that region in southeastern California bounded on the west by the coastal range, on the north by Joshua Tree National Park, on the east by the Colorado River, and continuing on south across the international border into Mexico.

All deserts are unique, just as all people are unique, and for this we might contrast the Colorado with its adjacent deserts. To the east, in Arizona, is the wetter Sonoran Desert (of which the Colorado often is considered to be a western subdivision), a desert typified by the saguaro, or giant, cactus. To the north of the Colorado is the Mojave Desert. It lies at a higher elevation and hence is a bit cooler in summer and considerably colder in winter. Whatever the comparisons, the Colorado Desert is a very barren and dry landscape of rocky mountain ranges trending north-south and alternating with flat desert sweeps of low shrubs and cacti. Lastly, the Colorado Desert is a low desert, much of it lying either near or below sea level. Within this expanse, as the following chapters will reveal, is an incredible variety, but for now it helps in getting our bearings to think of the region as divided into three main parts. The best-known and most populous area, in the northwest portion, is centered on Palm Springs, with new cities stretching southeastward across the Coachella Valley to the Salton

Sea. Farther to the southeast, there's the Imperial Valley, a region of intense agricultural activity reaching north from the Mexican border up to the Salton Sea. Lastly, there's all the rest of the desert, that large part lying within the upside-down and reversed "L" formed by what we just described and consisting mainly of the Anza-Borrego Desert bounded on the west by California's coastal range. The center of this region is the little town of Borrego Springs.

As to history, at least since the coming of the whites to the desert, first there were the Spanish who, in the eighteenth century, began probing up from Mexico to find an overland route to supply their distant missions on the California coast. Soon after them came the Anglos, beginning with trappers from the Rocky Mountains looking for more beaver and good times on the Pacific shore. The main thing is that to such early people the Colorado Desert was one huge pain in the neck. To them it was a worthless and hideous expanse of sand and rock, a barrier to get across as fast as possible in order to reach greener places, such as the amenities of the coast. Then, in the 1850s a few stage stations took root, some of them becoming the nuclei of towns. In an age before antibiotics, people with nagging respiratory problems began discovering the curative effects of the dry desert air and started adding their numbers to the settlements. Their roots grew deeper when after the turn of the nineteenth century irrigation projects rapidly converted great swatches of the desert into vast fields of cantaloupes and alfalfa and endless groves of solemn date palms springing from the dunes. After that, especially with the improved roads and the blessings of air-conditioning coming around World War II, came the great spurt of growth represented by the rest of us—the tourists, retirees, and librarians making up the diverse mix of any community.

However, a combination of natural and cultural circumstances, together with that incalculable touch of human genius that often surprises us, made Palm Springs a special place. In contrast, most early towns across the Southwest were raw affairs. Often they grew out of the little clusters of houses that dotted the railroad tracks every few miles and served as maintenance stations. Often, too, they were mining towns or towns that supplied nearby mines, and sometimes a combination of the two. Either way, they were rough places; if the stereotype of the movie versions that would soon create our images of frontier towns with raucous saloons and bodies being dragged out by the hour exaggerated the facts, the pictures nonetheless captured the tone of prevailing crudeness. The railroad towns attracted transients often with devious intentions, while the mines lured in adventurers who, without the civilizing influences of women, might come to town and stay drunk for days at a time. Adding to the mix were soldiers from nearby military forts bent on soaking themselves to forget the hell-holes of military life. Cowboys fought with miners, miners fought with soldiers, inspired by demon rum but also simply because a good bout of fisticuffs and hooting and a free flow of blood was a lot more exciting than the boredom of desert life.

Uniquely, Palm Springs suffered almost none of these things. It was six miles from the railroad, far enough to discourage the attention of the wandering riffraff. Mining in the area was listless, and there were no nearby military posts. What Palm Springs did have was, first of all, a spectacular setting. As visitors still gasp today, the town is backed right up against Mount San Jacinto, an eminence that soars right out of the parking lots behind Palm Springs' business district and shoots seemingly straight up for thousands of feet into a pine forest; for this the town remains something of a marvel, for one can take a few steps beyond the crowds of tourists and soon be scrambling up the steep slopes to be alone with nature. That nature included, as we've noted, deep canyons debouching nearby, and they held, besides disgruntled gods, the marvels of palm trees and that wonder of the desert, gushing streams, one of them flowing right into town. Adding to the unique bounty were the nearby Indians, a small and peaceful group who herded cattle and tended their grapevines and olive orchards, and whose drums might be heard thumping softly on some nights in mysterious ceremonies.

In short, Palm Springs was a romantic place with a dramatic setting. And it had some of the amenities to lure in the less hardy. California was a boom state, and by the beginning of the twentieth century the booster mentality had crossed the coastal mountains to the desert at least in a sufficient dose to establish a modest inn or two. Who would be attracted to such a place? Artists, writers, and photographers seeking the romance they lacked in their urban lives. Palm Springs, with its cottages occupied by creative types scattered among the orange groves and pepper trees, was, indeed, an unusual and appealing village, a far cry from the rawness of most desert towns.

And then, added to this, there occurred the unpredictable, the alchemy already alluded to. Desert chronicler Ann Japenga puts it this way:

> Now and then a knot of like-minded artists and writers converges in one place and you get a Bloomsbury Circle or an Algonquin Roundtable. Such a confluence happened in Palm Springs early in the 1900s. But instead of paneled drawing rooms, the artists convened in a couple of oil can shacks beside the Tahquitz ditch, near where the Tennis Club is today.[4]

She is referring to Jimmy Swinnerton, George Wharton James, and any number of other devotees of the pen, brush, and camera, but especially to the triumvirate who came as close as anyone to forming a desert renaissance. First there was the painter Carl Eytel, a tubercular German who became a master at capturing the otherworldly presence combined with the aloof grace of palm groves. Second came J. Smeaton Chase, an Englishman and former orphan who would wander the Colorado Desert on horseback and make it famous to the nation with his writings. Joining the pair in 1915 to form an informal brotherhood was Edmund C. Jaeger. An early teacher in Palm Springs's one-room schoolhouse, he lived in a cabin near Eytel and eventually turned out the first reliable natural histories of America's deserts.

Despite their identification with Palm Springs, these men were not provincials, just as, remarkably, Palm Springs was not provincial. Furthermore, the three escaped the usual preciousness of small-town enthusiasts elsewhere by ranging far afield, taking in the whole fascinating desert for their territory, and they pondered what they saw and rendered it into art with an educated sophistication giving an analytical depth to their revelations. For these and other like-minded artists both then and in the decades to come, Palm Springs should not be considered as an isolated and circumscribed phenomenon, for, as will be seen in the following selections, it became a general influence spreading out and coloring the public's perception of the Colorado Desert, indeed of our entire Southwest. That's not to say by any means that what transpired in Palm Springs and vicinity was the sole inspiration for our coalescing views of the desert, but it was a large and vital influence whose subtleties often are missed. For instance, beginning in the late 1930s, *Desert Magazine*, with its lavish photographs and upbeat revelations of the desert's secret places, became one of the nation's main windows on the arid lands, and that the magazine eventually moved from El Centro, in the Imperial Valley, to build its headquarters in Palm Desert, just down the road from Palm Springs, likely was no accident but the desire of the editors to be part of the area's cultural milieu.

In exploring such aspects, I much prefer that the writings arising from them have the larger and more impressive voice. Some of the following selections are from desert classics, while others come from the almost unknown nooks and crannies of desert lore; all of the pieces, so it is my hope, reveal important forces in the dynamics of shaping our variegated and sometimes conflicting cultural views of the Colorado Desert. In offering what follows, my intent is to reflect what has transpired rather than to create a view of things from my own perspective. However, I admit to certain dispositions; having lived with the Indians of northern Arizona and over the years witnessed much devastation to our deserts, in my more oneiric moments I wonder if it might be best if all the Europeans went back home (as long as I were allowed to stay). That, of course, is an escape into a childish view, and as one who has done his share of slogging through sand and drinking infested water, I don't lightly depreciate the comforts those very Europeans have provided. So, I suppose as is true of most of us, my personal views are divided, and I hope that in the following I've hewn to the more intellectual goal of giving as inclusive and as varied a perspective on the issues as is possible. In line with this, the brief paragraphs introducing individual selections are meant to be informative as well as provocative in touching on complex and often unresolved issues.

It is impossible here, and perhaps not necessary, to give a detailed historical view of our deserts. It might help, however, to solidify a few essential points already touched on. Make no bones about it, deserts are rough places for human beings, and the pioneers, accustomed to landscapes of mooing cows knee-deep in grass, reacted appropriately when they first topped a ridge and gasped slackjawed upon the barren expanses lying endlessly before them. These, obviously, were hideous places, inhabited by scorpions, rattlesnakes, and wrathy Indians. They offered nothing but hardships, and sometimes death, in their crossing. Yet we are an optimistic people, and according to our national theology God must have made those places for some good reasons. Slowly, such reasons were discovered, and in the process attitudes changed. Irrigation made the deserts bloom, their healthful benefits were discovered, and, finally—Whoopeee!—treasures of gold were found out there in the sands. Then, in the way that wealth engenders perception of beauty, the deserts appeared lovely in themselves, an airy perspective helped along enormously by technological advances, by electric cooling and the conveniences of modern travel abrogating the earlier hardships. Think, for instance, of refined aesthete John

C. Van Dyke, an art professor from Rutgers College (now University) visiting the Colorado Desert in the late 1890s and now famous for describing the desert as a lovely dreamscape. Gliding across the sands in a plush Pullman car, mint julep in hand, he thought beautiful thoughts about the flowing shapes of the dunes he saw out the window—dunes containing the bones of the pioneers who had died there just a few years before. Compelling as his descriptions are, it is difficult to imagine they could have been written in the same lofty manner had Van Dyke been forced to cross the sands on foot.

So a great shift took place, from initial scorn to utilitarianism to aesthetic appreciation. This, however, was no simple linear movement, for it is in the nature of cultures that they can hold several different views, sometimes conflicting views, at the same time. Today, you almost never hear of desert haters; rather, the desert seems populated by "desert lovers," people enjoying the comforts of their modern homes and readily declaring the desert's beauty, while the next day they just as readily bulldoze it to build more subdivisions. As in so many other things in life, human beings are quite capable of adjusting their values to accommodate their psychic and financial interests.

One book will go far in making sense of these shifting and conflicting attitudes as they've developed in the nation over the decades. W. Storrs Lee's graciously written *The Great California Deserts* masterfully pulls together many cultural threads into a comprehensible pattern. More specifically, documented histories of Palm Springs and, more widely, of the Colorado Desert are yet to be written; a certain amount of caution, therefore, is in order when using the texts we have, some of them of great value but often penned by enthusiastic amateurs. In the meantime, we have a number of helpful works. Concerning the story of Palm Springs, one will find no more heartfelt and sometimes heart-wrenching yet authoritative probing of the town's charms and conflicts than *Palm Springs: The Landscape, the History, the Lore*. It was written by Mary Jo Churchwell, who, in the process of growing up there, lived deeply and sensitively with her shifting surroundings. Although I disagree with Frank Bogert on a number of his positions regarding the area's development, the early chapters of the former mayor's *Palm Springs: First Hundred Years* are a fine historical summary, one richly illustrated with rare, period photographs. Jack Nelson's four-part series of articles does a workmanlike job of detailing the cooperation and conflicts that over the decades went into the making of Palm

Springs. Patricia B. Laflin's *Coachella Valley California: A Pictorial History* shows the wider context, giving the background of the northwestern portion of the Colorado Desert and going into such solid details as the importance of the date industry in its development, while Jim Carr's *Palm Springs and the Coachella Valley* does something similar and, for those so disposed, celebrates the glitz that has recently overwhelmed the desert.

As to other areas, Otis B. Tout's *The First Thirty Years, 1901–1931* gives an insider's view of the burgeoning Imperial Valley during its formative years, while to the north William deBuy's solidly documented *Salt Dreams* investigates the poisonous consequences of successful agriculture. Diana Lindsay's books are the first place to turn for insights to the Anza-Borrego Desert. In *All the Wild and Lonely Places*, Lawrence Hogue takes us staggering under a backpack but rejoicing through the badlands of this extremely arid but also extremely beautiful place.

In addition to these, the bibliography that follows points the reader, chapter by chapter, to further sources. These include both readily accessible texts and, to add an extra depth, important local publications which can be highly useful but are easily missed. My hope is that, together, these will help general readers and scholars alike get a better grasp of a long-ignored land that only now, even while it is being ravished by development, also is beginning to be understood for its beautiful complexities. In this way we're teetering on the edge. It's a telling, if dangerous state, reminiscent of Hope's plight in the Pandora story. However valuable these books are, for now we plunge directly into the very substance of the Colorado Desert. Some of the following selections, such as the two excerpts from John C. Van Dyke's famous book, are fantastic flights, aesthetic pieces bringing sophisticated depth to a perception of the Colorado Desert. Others, notably Remi A. Nadeau's account of the Herculean Colorado River leaping its banks and sweeping in a tide of destruction across the Imperial Valley, are straightforward, journalistic reportage of dramatic events. All of the selections combine into an intricate tapestry of man and nature showing the struggles and joys, the beauty and the disasters, that have made the Colorado Desert an exciting and dangerous place—and perhaps, given the effervescence taking place there now, the bellwether of our civilization.

Lastly, to clear up any confusion, in 2005 the Palm Springs Desert Museum evolved into the Palm Springs Art Museum.

For My Own People

For at least two centuries, students of anthropology have puzzled over the meanings of the bizarre tales they heard from native peoples. Noble as such efforts are at ferreting out the truth, perhaps at heart the impulse is somewhat misguided. First of all, that an evil spirit would throw a deer high up into a tree or that a dog taking a bath suddenly changes into a young man is no more extraordinary than a snake tempting First Woman with an apple or Elijah whirled up in a glory of wind. What seems strange depends very much on one's perspective. Added to that, traditional myths from all cultures serve a variety of purposes, from filling the endless hours after the day's hunting is done to frightening children into desired behavior to giving at least the illusion of making sense of a world whose events often are arbitrary, defying humans' yearning for an explicable existence. Myths, then, whatever their content, allow us to function by giving us a grasp on what otherwise might keep us perpetually bewildered. Ah, yes, that's why the leopard has his spots. The matter is settled, and we can move on to the more important issues of propagating and getting food. And when such beliefs are shared by a group of people, all the more they are cemented into a community, for they are now agreed on the essential issue of how the cosmos works.

As we shall soon see in an initiation ceremony for girls made to lie in a pit on heated herbs, some of these tales are not really tales but part of a liturgy in performing an important social ceremony; for this, they likely had to be precisely told in order to gain the efficacy of the unseen but ever-surrounding powers. Other stories may be far more flexible in their telling, even elaborated according to the creativity of the teller. The evil spirit Tahquitz, who causes "the wrecks of trains and automobiles, and delights in everything that makes people trouble," here is responsible for the death of an innocent boy. Such maliciousness certainly is in character for this ogre, but the list of his depredations is limited only by his dark imagination.

Fanciful as such things may seem to us, often they are taken literally by their tellers, thus again relieving people of unsolvable conundrums. Beyond that, we might understand that such tales have come down through the uncounted centuries, told around camp fires from old to young for uncounted generations, and for that they only appear to have a stability when caught in print; likely, they were just as mutable over time as what occurs in our game of "gossip," and beyond the features mentioned have no innate or single, unshifting "meaning." Such is the nature of the mind constantly shaping the stories that in turn give it definition. What does surprise, however, is the resulting brightness of these passed-on and evolving tales, which, whenever caught in their continuing process of creation and however wayward in their events, often have a "rightness" to them. This we all have experienced in the odd convincing qualities of our own dreams. They can leave us at once awed but aesthetically pleased in ways we can't explain and with a sense of completeness rarely found in our daily lives.

As Chief Patencio makes clear, his hope was to revive interest in the old ways among his Cahuilla people, who for centuries had lived intimately with the desert. For the most part, it was a misplaced hope. Large land owners in booming Palm Springs, in recent years the Cahuilla have become involved in the glitter of real-estate and casino development, becoming one of the richest tribes in America.

Francisco Patencio, as told to Margaret Boynton, from *Stories and Legends of the Palm Springs Indians*

My friends have asked me many times to write the songs and stories of my people. This I have never done.

But now the older ones of our tribes are slowly passing away. The churches and schools of the new American people are teaching our children. We find that the beliefs of the Indian people are being forgotten.

Even now there is much that will never be remembered again; and so, before I, too, pass into the world of spirit which is around and about us, but which we do not often see, I now write this book for the ones who have interest in new things, for the ones who like to hear new stories, and for the men of science who study the world. But most of all I write the songs and stories for my own people, our children and our children's children, and those yet to come, that when the Indian customs are forgotten, they may read and know and remember in their hearts the ways and thoughts of their own people.

THE FIESTA FOR GROWING GIRLS

The people of the Sun Grey and Yellow Body gave a second fiesta for growing girls. This they did to teach them all the things that they should know about their own bodies. They were given a course of treatment which was to keep them from certain kinds of sickness which could come at the present time and in after years. They were given to drink of different kinds of bitter herbs.

The fiesta songs were all about how to take care of themselves to have good health. As the song continued about the shining earth, the ground was dug up with the shells of the land turtles, or by the baskets which they wore upon their heads. The ground was warmed by a fire of brush. This warm ground was then spread with green herbs, the girls were laid on this, and then more green herbs were laid on them. Then they lay in the steam of the green herbs for a few hours. This they did for three times, three days. They were not allowed to have salt or cold water, or fat or any meat during this time. One of the herbs used is called *Hoe bel*, another is called *Pa gu sish*, another is called *Hang all*. There are other herbs used, but these are for the girls only. However, if one has a bad cold, these are often used.

Now the people were thinking whom they would invite to this fiesta, and they decided to have *Tem al souit*, meaning Day Star Snake, who lived away to the south in the Santa Rosa Mountains. They sent a message by Wild Turkey, who could smell out everything, to notify this Day Star Snake. He went, but could not go near to him because of the strong whirling winds which knocked him over. The whirlwinds were made by the great snakes in those days, but now they are the spirits of the great snakes. Wild Turkey tried hard to get near, but he was blown all about by the winds. So he came back, and they sent a man called Crow, and he carried the message through.

Day Star Snake said that he would come in the morning and asked if there was a large place there. The Crow answered that they had a large fiesta house, and a large open space.

Now the Day Star Snake lived in a cave, and the Crow saw that he was large, and very, very long. When he came to the fiesta he did not crawl along the valley. No, he went up to the top of the mountain and came straight across from there.

The Day Star Snake was a long time coming, and he was making great coils all about to keep himself out of the way, but he was upsetting the Indians' houses, and pushing in the fiesta house, and yet he had not got all of himself off from the mountain. This made Scorpion, a man who lived in a cave nearby, very angry, and he went over and stung the Day Star Snake, who went away like lightning.

This spoiled the fiesta, and the three young girls who were covered up on the ground with the wild herbs turned to stone, and they are there yet, covered up by the sand. This caused the people all to move away from the place.

TAHQUITZ

The man Tahquitz (*Ta co wits*) was a man of great power. He was one of the first creators. But he did not do any good. He never tried to cure anybody, or do any good for anyone. So he did not have any friends among his people, and he knew that he did not deserve any.

He went up on one of the Moreno hills, and practiced flying over to the next one. This he did till he became powerful enough to fly. He became a very bad spirit. He lives in the world, and makes his home in the Tahquitz mountains. He speaks through the lightning and thunder, and is seen everywhere. He kills the people, also the spirits of the people. He kills the animals as well as the people, causes the wrecks of trains and automobiles, and delights in everything that makes people trouble.

Now in the early days, Tahquitz appearing in the dreams of some men of power gave them some of his power, so that they knew when Tahquitz had taken the spirit of some of the people and they had his power to make him drop them and they cured them.

There were two Soboba people, father and son, who were hunting in the San Jacinto mountains. They had killed a deer, and wounded another, when the father told the son to stay with the dead deer while he followed the other. While the young man was staying with the deer, Tahquitz appeared to him in the form of a man. He threw the deer up in the top of a high tree, and took the young man with him into his home in the mountain. The father came back. He could not find his son, or the deer. He looked everywhere around, and could find no trace of them. Then he went home, and the people came back with him to help find the boy, but none of them could find any trace of him.

After Tahquitz took the young man into the mountains, he tried to get all kinds of animals to eat him, but they would not do it, so he took him back to the place where he had found him, took the deer from the top of the tree, and sent him home, telling him if he told the people where he had been and what he had seen, before four or five days, he would get him again and make him just as bad as Tahquitz himself was.

The boy went back to his people, but would not tell them anything about where he had been, although they were asking him all the time. On the fourth day he built a fire and called the people around it, and then told them the story of where he had been. But Tahquitz had meant four or five years, instead of days, and next morning the boy fell dead.

THE DEVIL WOMAN

One of the head men of the Cocomonga Tribe went hunting. He shot a deer, but could not bring it home, because it had become near sundown.

Now these Indians had a summer home up near the foothills, and a winter home down the valley. These Indians were always bothered by a woman called the Devil woman.

As he could not get home that night, the hunter went to the summer home of the Indians, and slept in the fiesta house. He built a fire, and to keep away from this woman, he climbed up in the roof and slept there. As he lay there he had a terrible dream—all about what was some time to happen to his people. He saw himself come into the fiesta house and talk to other people, and he heard himself talking. And all the people came into the fiesta house, every one of them.

Next morning he went home and lay on the ground with his face on his arm, and did not move. His wife and family did not speak to him, as they thought he was only resting. But as the sun began going down they came to him and spoke to him. But he did not move or answer. Then the three head men, they came and talked to him. They talked about every thing, hoping to make him move.

Now among the Indians there is a friendship among the young people who have grown up together. They each share the same things, and never become angry with each other. Such a friendship this man had, so the head men went to him and brought him to his friend. He spoke to him, and then the young man answered him and got up.

He told them to call a meeting in the fiesta house, and he would explain the things that he had seen. So they did, and they all came in the fiesta house, every one of them. Then he told them what he saw: that he saw himself and every one of them, and that was what made him so quiet. He had never seen such things before. And this is what he told them in the fiesta house:

Near the Cocomonga Indians, called *Win e um*, lived a woman who was a bad spirit—the same as Tahquitz. This woman made the Indians lots of trouble, so much that mothers frightened their naughty children by telling them that the Devil woman would get them if they were not good.

Some of the Indians lived in houses that had doors. It happened that a little girl was crying, and would not be quiet, so her mother pushed her outside the door, telling her that the Devil woman could have her. Now the Devil woman was standing just outside the door and heard what the mother had said. She carried the child away, and she could never be found among her people any more. She took her to her home, and hung her up in a basket while she gathered food. She never had a fire, but ate everything raw. This went on for many years.

All of this time the child was growing up. When the Devil woman hung her up in a basket she had become so large that she climbed out to play. Living down the wash was an old woman called Gopher. The girl used to go to her place and talk with her. The Gopher woman told her not to eat the bad stuff that the Devil woman gave her to eat, but to dig a hole in the ground and cover it up. "She cannot see straight ahead, but she sees looking up, so she cannot see what you do with the food," she said.

The child did as she was told, and only ate what the Gopher woman told her. One day the girl saw a smoke across the valley, and asked the Gopher woman what it was, and she said, "That is the place where your people are living. Your mother and your father live there. This woman is not your mother. This is the Devil woman, and it is not good."

The girl was old enough to begin thinking about going home. So one day when the Devil woman was gone, the Gopher woman told the girl how to go home, and to go quick, because the Devil woman would come after her.

"When you get home, call a meeting in the fiesta house, and have them wrap you in tules (*Mic bot*). Then when the Devil woman comes and asks for her daughter, have the rock upon which the arrows are made straight, heated red hot," she said. All of which the girl did.

When the Devil woman came home, she could not find the child. She was running about, looking up and down. Then she went to the old Gopher woman and asked, "Where is my daughter?"

The Gopher woman said that she had not seen her for some time, that probably she was somewhere playing around. Then the Devil woman said, "No," and that if she didn't give up her daughter, she would kill her.

Now as soon as the child went away, the Gopher woman began digging holes all around to defend herself, because she knew what the Devil woman would try to do.

Then the Devil woman said to hurry and give up her daughter, or she would kill her.

The Gopher woman was making a basket in front of her home, and she did not even look up. She was not afraid.

The Devil woman picked up a big rock and threw it onto the Gopher woman, but the Gopher woman ran into her hole and came out another place, making the basket just the same.

The Indian women have a bone punch for making the hole to draw the straw of the basket through. They wet this bone, and it makes little squeaks every time it goes through. Every time the Gopher woman came out of a new hole she was still busy making little squeaks about her basket. Finally the Devil woman got disgusted because she could not catch her, and went away home.

The Indians use a round, flat, wide basket for separating seed, which they call *chip put al mul*. The Devil woman took one of those and threw it over to the south, but it fell over before going very far. Then she picked it up again and threw it over to the west, and it soon fell down. She picked it up and threw it to the north, and it rolled along the way the child went, and she followed it. The basket rolled to the fiesta house, and fell down in the door.

Then she asked for her daughter, and the people told her that they had not seen her. She went about the fiesta house, kicking at things and saying, "Here is my daughter. I know this is my daughter." Then she picked up the *mic bot* in which the child was hid, and killed her, too.

Then they told her, "All right, we will give you the child. Open your mouth," and she opened it. But they told her to open it more and more, because the child could not get in. She opened it wider and wider, till the people could see her heart. Then they pushed the hot rock down her throat.

When the Devil woman choked and found herself killed, she threw a handful of dirt both ways, which became poison and killed the people. Now an old woman was sitting on the ground, near the door, who had a big round basket. This basket she covered herself with, also her little dog that was curled up against her dress. In the morning she took the basket off her head and saw all her people dead. Also the Devil woman lying on the floor. She was very angry, and took the Devil woman and burned her separate. But her own people she burned with the fiesta house. When she had burned everything, she moved a short distance away from there, and made a little shack for herself and the dog. There she lived for a long time.

At harvest time, when the wild seed was ripening, she always went out early in the morning to gather it. She left her little dog at her place. Then she came home towards evening. This she did for many years. When the old woman had gone away harvesting, the little dog went hunting. One day he caught a mouse. He brought it back, and left it at the house. When the old woman came home, she saw it lying there, and she was very angry, because there was no one living there but herself. So she picked up the mouse and threw it away. The next day she went again, and the dog went hunting and killed a rat, and brought it home. When the old woman came home she was very angry again. She looked about, but could find no tracks. She thought someone was trying to tease her. She was grieving yet for her lost people, and did not want anyone near. Then, as she threw the rat away, the little dog began to whine.

Next day she went again, and the dog went hunting and killed four or five cottontail rabbits, and brought them home. Before the old woman came home, the little dog went to the spring and took a bath. Then, as he came up out of the water he was a young man. The old woman was coming home and saw him. Then she knew that the power had come. She dropped her basket of seed and went into the water herself, and came out a young woman again.

Among the Indian people no tribe is ever wiped out. The Power always saves two. If the people are all killed, there will be some away visiting, that keep the tribes. Then these two people, the old woman and the dog, they raised more people for that tribe. The people of these people are called the Dog Tribes. They are in many places now. They may have different languages, but they know that they are of that one Dog Tribe.

Life from the Rocks

It pays to keep your eyes open when hiking in the desert, not only for the rattlesnakes lurking camouflaged in the shadows of boulders but for treasures you and thousands like you may have passed many times.

Indian "art" doesn't refer to pleasant designs to hang on walls. True, much Indian art served a primarily decorative function, bright beads woven into clothes or patterns on baskets that delighted the eye. And sometimes it was used simply to make a pictorial record of unusual events. Yet as Ranger Manfred Knaak, the former archaeologist of the Anza-Borrego Desert State Park, successfully argues here, chippings and paintings on rocks often had a much more profound purpose, through the artists linking the people of the tribe to the powers of nature waiting all around them to be embodied by a skilled human hand. Thus, in this sense art served a similar role as did traditional stories, giving one a sense of control over the earth. Yet if this sounds a bit mystical, the Indians also were an eminently practical and observant people, taking advantage of every little purchase in a hard land in order to survive. This is illustrated in the last selection, concerning the turn of the cosmos at the summer solstice, marking the seasons and giving assurance that the old cycles of the seasons had not yet betrayed puny mankind.

—⁓⁓— **Manfred Knaak,**
  from *The Forgotten Artist: Indians of Anza-Borrego
  and Their Rock Art*

Rock art in the Anza-Borrego Desert is primarily symbolic art. Occasionally a rock art drawing depicts something less abstract, such as a rider on horseback, perhaps commemorating an historical event, but most are abstract illustrations that may represent visions or dreams of the artist.

Indian artists of Anza-Borrego used two different methods of drawing on stone. The first involved actually engraving the surface of rocks, resulting in designs known as petroglyphs. In the second and more common method, colored minerals were mixed with a binder. Designs were then painted on the surface of rocks. These are pictographs.

Carving or engraving rock surfaces is an ancient tradition and examples have been found worldwide. In Europe, petroglyphs date back approximately 35,000 years. In the United States, such art is located primarily in the Southwest and in the Great Basin, and approaches an antiquity of 4,000 years or more. Engravings were commonly made on volcanic basalt, sandstone, and granite rocks.

In making a petroglyph, the artist selected a fist-sized stone that fit snugly into the palm of his hand. He checked the rock for its hardness and shaped the stone into a blunted or pointed implement. He then carefully pecked or abraded his chosen design into the rock surface. For precise control, a hammerstone and a stone chisel were used to enhance the outlines and details of the drawing, producing a stark contrast with the dark patinated surface of the rock.

In the Anza-Borrego Desert petroglyphs are located predominantly in the north and are of rectilinear and curvilinear design with a few human-like drawings. Pictographs are most often found in the southern region of Anza-Borrego and are painted in four colors. The most commonly applied color was red, ranging from bright vermilion to dull brown. A large percentage of rock painting was done in black, and sometimes yellow and white appear.

In preparing red paint, the artist used hematite or red iron oxide and the oil of roasted wild cucumber kernels. The cucumber seeds were ground together with the mineral in a small mortar, with pitch from spruce or pine trees as the binding agent. To make black paint, wild cucumber seeds were roasted and charred on a piece of burning oak bark, then ground and mixed with manganese oxide or charcoal. Yellow paint was made from yellow ochre or limonite, and white came from deposits of gypsum and white ash. Often the mineral pigments were ground and molded into cakes and stored. If needed, they were reground and mixed. Other binding agents were employed such as animal and vegetable oil, blood, urine, and egg whites.

Once the draftsman had prepared the paint, it was applied to the rock surface by using pointed sticks dipped into the mixed pigments. Sometimes a brush made from long strands of yucca or agave fibers was used. Other times the artist simply used his fingers. It is likely that all three methods were practiced in Anza-Borrego.

For many interested in rock art, the question that may arise is why primitive man drew on rocks. Certainly, stones were a readily available material. More important, rocks were enduring and were considered permanent geographical features.

It was in caves and among large rock piles that the supernaturals dwelt. Certain boulders and outcrops were endowed with religious or magical powers. They were identified as sacred places and often revealed their location to persons with a knowledge of the supernatural, especially to the shaman in his dream time.

To primitive man anything could take on symbolic significance, including the sun, moon, plants, animals, rocks, and even man-made abstract forms on boulders. The artist sought to reveal the spirit of the rock and he was able, through his art, to make that spirit visible.

As difficult as interpreting rock art is, dating it, despite the wide variety of methods employed, is equally difficult.

Radiocarbon dating, the most accurate in establishing a relative age, has been of little help. Items such as fossilized vegetation, bone, and charcoal, necessary for this type of analysis, are seldom recovered at sites with petroglyphs or pictographs.

In Anza-Borrego, cultural remains such as stone tools, necklaces, and pottery have been found at abandoned village sites and have been dated from approximately A.D. 1000 to historic times. Encampments where such material has been recovered are often near rock art sites, and a maximum age of 500 or 1000 years for these rock art drawings is a reasonable proposal.

Superimposition and patination are other methods used by archaeologists to date rock art. Petroglyphs, either pecked, abraded, or scratched, expose the original lighter color of the desert-varnished stones. A black or brown patina of hydrous iron and manganese oxides generally starts to form on the exposed surface. The theory is that the darker the stain, the older the figure. A later superimposed drawing would be of a lighter patina and would indicate that it is more recent than the other drawings. Studies on accurately estimating the age of desert patina are continuing.

Superimposed pictographs are difficult to analyze and their age is often judged on fading and weathering of colors. Calcification from trickles of water and the exfoliation of rock material are also sources of reference. What makes pictographs especially difficult to date is that the original drawings may be quite old, but the designs may have been repainted by the Indians to retain the magic of the symbols.

Dating subject matter in petroglyphs or pictographs is equally challenging, and their meaning and age are very uncertain.

Two uncommon paintings, men on horseback, draw attention to a rock art site at La Puerta Real de San Carlos. December 26, 1775 was a cold, rainy day at La Puerta. The de Anza expedition of 240 men, women, and children, with cattle, mules, and horses was settling down for the evening. The worst was over. They had conquered the inhospitable Colorado Desert, trekking from marsh to waterhole. The windy stretch through Coyote Canyon was miserable. It had started to rain at nine o'clock in the morning and relentlessly pelted the wet and half-frozen expedition. They were now on the high route, and tomorrow they would begin to weave through the coastal foothills to the San Gabriel Mission.

Not far from La Puerta the Mountain Cahuilla had also bedded down. They had known for some time that a collection of animals accompanied by a couple of hundred people were trespassing on their land. The Cahuilla were a peaceful people. They wanted no confrontation or quarrel with these newcomers. One thing they noticed were men riding on top of stately horses. They also noticed a man in a long robe carrying a wooden staff shaped like a cross.

These newcomers left La Puerta the following day and are remembered in the annals of history as one of the boldest expeditions ever to cross the Colorado Desert. These emigrants later founded a village which would become the city of San Francisco. Their leader, Juan Bautista de Anza, became a recognized figure in the Spanish Empire.

Not far from where these emigrants slept, history may have been recorded as pictographs in A.D. 1775, commemorating the journey of this expedition through Cahuilla land....

In addition to direct observation of the stars and the sun, solstices could be seen indirectly by the way the sun struck an object or rock painting, or the way it cast a shadow on a fixed landmark. Such indirect observations have been made at famous sites in the Southwest including the Casa Grande in Arizona and Hovenweep Castle in Colorado.

In the Viejas and Cowles mountains in Kumeyaay territory, Ken Hedges has observed the rising sun at winter solstice in relation to a cross-shaped rock alignment and a bisected circle.

This author observed the first recorded summer solstice in Kumeyaay land on June 21, 1982. A combination of both direct and indirect methods was used. A small nodule on top the Fish Creek Mountains serves as a permanent geographical marker. The sun rises directly over this point at the summer solstice. As the sun continues to rise, a beam of sunlight falls through the small crevice of a rockshelter, illuminating the inside and lighting up a prominent anthropomorph painted on the cave's ceiling. The high degree of accuracy in this observation is achieved only if the viewer is sitting directly beneath the anthropomorph and looking through the small crevice toward the Fish Creek Mountains.

3

The Spanish Lewis and Clark: Into the Swallowing Wilderness

In late October of 1775, nearly 250 settlers, soldiers, priests, and muleteers said their last good-byes in Tubac, in what is now southern Arizona, and started to march into consequences they couldn't even imagine. They were leaving the last outpost of civilization. Ahead of them lay the swallowing, unknown wilderness of the Colorado Desert.

At the column's head was Juan Bautista de Anza. His purpose was to establish an overland supply route to the chain of Spanish missions hundreds of miles away dotting the California coast and secure these outposts, perilously supplied by ships from Mexico, against Russian and English threats of colonization. In immediate terms, the expedition was a success, comparable to the continent-crossing nation binding of Lewis and Clark and, in Canada, of Alexander Mackenzie, for in June of 1776, eight months later, the newcomers stood triumphantly overlooking the grand prospect of San Francisco Bay, among the first Europeans to set eyes on that pristine sight. The human aspects, however, make quite a different story. In the course of things, these people, only vaguely aware of the bewildering jumble of snowcapped peaks, deserts, and lush valleys they were entering, would be almost run into the ground. In the course of things, they would suffer the ravages of dysentery, thieving from Indians, the stampedes of crazed cattle, and heat and thirst. Especially heat and thirst. The expedition's route lay north to Tucson, arced across southern Arizona to Yuma, across the Colorado Desert northwest to Borrego Springs, and thence up Coyote Canyon out of the desert and over the mountains to the mission of San Gabriel, in the Los Angeles area. Then with buoyant steps they marched up the California coast, through the

San Joaquin Valley to the day of victory when they gazed down on the magnificent bay. All these names, however, except for San Gabriel and those of other missions visited along the way, did not exist in Anza's time. For the unschooled settlers and soldiers, this was a new land, with all the hopes and fears a new dreamland can conjure for the uninitiated.

It was their good fortune that the worst came first—the crossing of the Colorado Desert. It helps if settlers are steeled in advance to the sufferings ahead, and no doubt, since Anza had reconnoitered the route the year before, they expected to endure a certain amount of hardship as they slogged across the sands. What these people from Mexico's warm climate were totally unprepared for, and what nearly did them in, in addition to the debilitating heat, thirst, and dysentery, was a long spell of freezing and crippling cold. Animals, similarly weakened, went to their knees by the score, and the starving people watched bewildered as their traveling food supply died before their eyes. Miraculously, only one person was lost, a woman in childbirth (the baby lived). As the band made its way on shaking legs up steep Coyote Canyon and out of the Colorado Desert into a greening landscape, they may well have sensed that they were at once entering a blessing and leaving behind a phantasmagoric hell with teeth of both heat and cold tearing at their flesh, a searing memory that would, this being in the nature of things, become an endless source of tales to astound their bewildered grandchildren.

⟋⟋⟋⟋⟋ Herbert Eugene Bolton,
from *Anza's California Expeditions*

Thursday, December 14. As soon as day began to dawn it commenced to snow with fierce and extremely cold wind, which continued the entire day, and for this reason it was not possible to march. And since it is probable on account of the snow that on the next journey, to San Gregorio, there will not be such a shortage of water as we have assumed, I have decided to wait in this place for the two divisions which are following me.

At twelve o'clock the cattle arrived. As I have said, they came by a different route from the rest of the expedition, and in bringing them we lost ten head which became tired out. These animals, notwithstanding that they had not been watered for four days, needed so little in this present season that even when they were taken to the verge of the water most of them preferred to eat rather than drink.

The second division did not put in its appearance during the whole day, although it ought to be here, and for this reason I conclude that it encountered the same storm as ourselves and was prevented by it from marching. At eleven o'clock at night it stopped snowing, but the mountains and plains continued to be so covered with snow that it looked like daylight, and there now followed a very severe freeze, as a consequence of which this was a night of extreme hardship.

Friday, December 15. At daybreak it was very windy, and the snow which had fallen the day and the night before was very hard from the freezing weather which had preceded, as a result of which six of our cattle and one mule died. At a quarter past twelve the second division began to arrive, in charge of the sergeant. The people were crippled by the storm, which overtook them midway between Santa Rosa and here. In spite of all their efforts to reach here yesterday they were unable to do so, and on the way several persons were frozen, one of them so badly that in order to save his life it was necessary to bundle him up for two hours between four fires. As a result of these inclemencies, five saddle animals died in their divisions. But aside from these there were no disasters on their march, and, indeed, because the division was slower than the first and came by a made road, with wells open, it was more conveniently supplied with water than the former division.

Saturday, December 16. I remained in this place awaiting the third division. This morning four of our cattle died from injuries and cold because of the severe freezing weather. At eleven o'clock they informed me that when they were looking for some saddle animals which had disappeared from sight, they found that they were being driven off by four of the heathen who had come to see us. I therefore ordered the sergeant and four soldiers to go and follow them, with orders that if they should overtake the thieves in the open or in their villages they should three times require them to deliver the stolen animals, giving them to understand that if they did this again they would feel the force of our arms, but that they were not to punish them with weapons except in case the Indians by force of their own arms should attempt to retain the saddle animals or refuse to deliver them. At seven o'clock the sergeant returned with the report that he found the mounts in two different villages, distant about four leagues, where not a single man was to be seen, but he gave the women who were there to understand what his orders were, so that they might report them to their men.

Sunday, December 17. Since the third division did not appear yesterday, at seven o'clock in the morning I sent two soldiers to meet it with twenty saddle animals, in order that they may have new mounts to replace those which may be tired out or made useless because of the cold.

At half past three in the afternoon the third division arrived at this place in command of Alférez Don Joseph Moraga. His forces were in worse condition than the two earlier divisions because the storm of snow and cold had caught them in a more exposed position, and as a result several persons were frozen to the point of being in danger of death. From the same cause six saddle animals were left by the wayside and four others died. In attending to his division, providing fire for them, and in other services for their relief, this officer so exposed himself that he contracted very severe pains in his ears, and although these have been cured, the weather is so bad that he has been left totally deaf in both ears. Today two more of our cattle have died as a result of injury and cold....

Monday, December 18. Notwithstanding the care which we have tried to observe with the cattle, it has not been possible to keep down the mortality both from the cold and from injuries. This morning two of them were found dead and five others it is thought will not be able to go forward from this place. We have made such use of them as has been possible, making of them jerked beef and salting it well, but even so it is unpalatable because of its scent, color, and taste.

At half past one in the afternoon we raised our camp in order to set out and shorten the next journey. Going west, with some turns to the west-northwest, over level country, we traveled about three and a half leagues in as many hours, until we came to the first pasturage and firewood that was found in a wide valley, where a halt was made for the night [in the Borrego Springs area]. All the sierras which we have seen today in all directions have appeared covered with snow except those along the line of our route. Today's march has been made with some comfort, because the weather has been quiet and the sun shining, this last being a blessing which we have not enjoyed for the last six days. After nightfall the cattle arrived at our camp, having been made to march since ten o'clock in the morning, in order that they might make some stops, but this precaution has not been sufficient to prevent the loss of five head from weariness and injuries.

Tuesday, December 19. At nine o'clock in the morning we raised our train and began the march toward the west, with repeated turns to the west-northwest, over sandy country with bad footing. In this direction we traveled four leagues in a little more than four hours, and at the end of this time we came to the site of San Gregorio. This watering place appeared at first to have enough water for our saddle animals, but within two hours after we had halted we were left without any, and nearly half of the animals were still to be watered, notwithstanding that for greater economy we had led the first ones by the halters to drink. Being informed of this lack I went personally to have some wells opened, which was done in various places, digging them to the depth of more than an *estado* [a man's height]. In all of them water was found, but it flowed so slowly that we concluded that we should not be able to achieve our purpose during the whole night, which in fact proved to be the case.

After nightfall the cattle arrived, and although they had taken all day to accomplish the journey, this was not sufficient to prevent the loss of four head. The same thing happened with three mounts, for these animals, like the rest, have become so scrawny and lean that they have no resemblance to those which started on the journey, especially those not accustomed to the cold, which is true of many of them. But of the few which come from the presidios, notwithstanding that they are the ones which have done double work, not one has been lost. On leaving this place we begin the crossing of the range which runs from the Peninsula of California, which gives the appearance of having fair openings through which to go out to the port and mission of San Diego, not only from here but even from below Santa Rosa de las Lajas.

Wednesday, December 20. This morning it was so frigid and the night before was so extremely cold that three saddle animals and five head of cattle were frozen to death, and the weather was so hard on our people that almost none of them slept, for they spent the night occupied in feeding the fires in order to withstand it. At seven o'clock I was informed that for the reasons given, and on account of the thirst which the cattle of necessity felt, many of them had escaped into the darkness of the night from the men who were watching them.

We Took Our Bullets in Our Mouths

Despite Anza's bravery, in one large sense his expedition failed. The Colorado Desert presented such a hideous barrier that neither the Spanish nor the Mexicans coming after them developed it into a regular route. Less stymied by bureaucracy and given to jubilant risks, the laissez-faire American trappers, however, already used to confronting grizzly bears and wrathy Indians in the Rocky Mountains, eyed the hellish expanse as but one more deathsome challenge to overcome and plunged in anyhow, for on the other side lay lush treasures, not least of which were the sloe-eyed señoritas, of the California coast.

One might dip into trappers' diaries and find pretty much the same accounts of the crossings. The swollen tongues blackened by thirst, the bullets put in the mouth to raise saliva, the drinking of urine, although heartfully told and individually suffered, became standard fare in the recitation of tortures endured on the Colorado Desert.

Specifically here, in the 1820s a brash young adventurer, James Ohio Pattie, along with his equally brash band of Kentuckians, dodged a nearly constant hail of Indian arrows as they trapped beaver westward across New Mexico and Arizona. Now they were in a bind. Having reached the edge of the California desert, they had no wish to turn around and pass through that gauntlet again, which likely would be far worse now that the Indians were stirred up and eager for their return. Before the trappers lay an unknown desert with, they knew vaguely, the green blessings of San Diego waiting beyond. In this sense, they had no choice. They simply kept walking westward.

In general, Pattie's diary is the rollicking account of a headstrong youth who often puts himself at center stage of heroic exploits. Whenever there's a beautiful young maiden carried off by Comanches, it's James Ohio who saddles up, rides out howling for revenge, and rescues her from their clutches; grizzly bears defy him sometimes in whole herds, but he soon teaches them a lesson. Here, however, on the Colorado Desert a certain sobering humility takes over as Pattie finds himself in circumstances totally beyond his control, in which his innate bravado is utterly useless.

~~~ **James O. Pattie,**
from *The Personal Narrative of James O. Pattie, of Kentucky*

We attempted to chew tobacco. It would raise no moisture. We took our bullets in our mouths, and moved them round to create a moisture, to relieve our parched throats. We had traveled but a little farther before our tongues had become so dry and swollen, that we could scarcely speak so as to be understood. In this extremity of nature, we should, perhaps, have sunk voluntarily, had not the relief been still in view on the sides of the snow covered mountains. We resorted to one expedient to moisten our lips, tongue and throat, disgusting to relate, and still more disgusting to adopt. In such predicaments it has been found, that nature disburdens people of all conditions of ceremony and disgust. Every thing bends to the devouring thirst, and the love of life. The application of this hot and salt liquid seemed rather to enrage than appease the torturing appetite. Though it offered such a semblance of what would satisfy thirst, that we economized every particle. Our amiable Dutchman was of a sweetness of temper, that was never ruffled, and a calmness and patience that appeared proof against all events. At another time, what laughter would have circulated through our camp, to hear him make merry of this expedient! As it was, even in this horrible condition, a faint smile circulated through our company, as he discussed his substitute for drink. "Vell, mine poys, dis vater of mein ish more hotter as hell, und as dick as boudden, und more zalter as de zeas. I can't drink him. For Cod's sake gif me some of yours, dat is more tinner."

Having availed ourselves to the utmost of this terrible expedient, we marched on in company a few miles further. Two of our companions here gave out, and lay down under the shade of a bush. Their tongues were so swollen, and their eyes so sunk in their heads, that they were a spectacle to behold. We were scarcely able, from the condition of our own mouths, to bid them an articulate farewell. We never expected to see them again, and none of us had much hope of ever reaching the mountain, which still raised its white summit at a great distance from us. It was with great difficulty that we were enabled to advance one foot before the other. A circumstance that added to our distress, was the excessive and dazzling brightness of the sun's rays....

With great exertions and infinite difficulty, a part of us gained the summit of the hill; but my father and another of our company, somewhat advanced in years, gave out below, though they made the most persevering efforts to reach the summit of the hill with the rest. Age had stiffened their joints, and laid his palsying hand upon their once active limbs, and vigorous frames. They could endure this dreadful journey no longer. They had become so exhausted by fruitless efforts to climb the hill, that they could no longer drag one foot after the other. They had each so completely abandoned the hope of ever reaching the water, or even gaining the summit of the hill, that they threw themselves on the ground, apparently convinced of their fate, and resigned to die....

Being satisfied by our consciences as well as by the reasoning of my father and his companion, that we could render them no service by remaining with them, except to increase their sufferings by a view of ours; and aware that every moment was precious, we pushed on once more for the mountain. Having descended this hill, we ascended another of the same wearying ascent and sandy character with the former. We toiled on to the top of it. The Eternal Power, who hears the ravens when they cry, and provideth springs in the wilderness, had had mercy upon us! Imagine my joy at seeing a clear, beautiful running stream of water, just below us at the foot of the hill! Such a blissful sight I had never seen before, and never expect to see again. We all ran down to it, and fell to drinking. In a few moments nothing was to be heard among us, but vomiting and groaning. Notwithstanding our mutual charges to be cautious, we had overcharged our parched stomachs with this cold snow water.

Notwithstanding I was sick myself, I emptied my powder horn of its contents, filled it with water, and accompanied by one companion, who had also filled his powder horn, I returned towards my father and Mr. Slover, his exhausted companion, with a quick step. We found them in the same position in which we had left them, that is, stretched on the sand at full length, under the unclouded blaze of the sun, and both fast asleep; a sleep from which, but for our relief, I believe they would neither of them ever have awakened. Their lips were black, and their parched mouths wide open. Their unmoving posture and their sunken eyes so resembled death, that I ran in a fright to my father, thinking him, for a moment, really dead. But he easily awakened, and drank the refreshing water. My companion at the same time bestowed his horn of water upon Mr. Slover. In the course of an hour they were both able to climb the hill, and some time before dark we rejoined the remainder of our company.

Stuck in the Yuma Dunes:
A Sandstorm Envelops a Stagecoach

After Pattie's era, travel, relative to the pokiness of the past, improved apace across the stumbling block of the Colorado Desert. In broadest terms, this was due to the rush of history. With American acquisition of much of the Southwest after the Mexican War of 1846–1848 and with the great influx of the Gold Rush of 1849, adventurers started pouring across the region from the populous, restless East. Just as the California coast was beginning Anglo development in earnest, gold was discovered to the east, across the sandy barrier in Arizona. Such things demanded the transportation of men and supplies both ways over the wastes. Answering the need were a number of stagecoach lines, the most famous being the Butterfield Overland, which, despite everything, bulled its way across the Colorado sands in 1857. Such formal routes, often constructed under government contract to carry the nation's mails over the continent, were a great boon to travelers generally. Their stations, although grimy huts built for the exchange of horses every ten to fifteen miles or so and backed up by the muscle of periodic military forts, provided the first places of refuge from Indians and bandits. Of far greater importance, the ragged little installations offered the first system of reliable, regularly spaced wells.

By comparison to today's ease of travel, conditions progressed only from the hellish to the purgatorial, and they wouldn't make a quantum leap to civilized ways until the railroad puffed across the desert between San Diego and Yuma in 1877. Travel remained only for the hardy and the resigned, along frightful routes studded with the skeletons of horses and mules, with a few human femurs and fibulae mixed in. That is, it remained a horror; but, most of the time, whatever the wear and tear to the dazed passengers staggering down after their bone-crushing nightmare, the stage at least got you there alive.

~~~ Captain William Banning and George Hugh Banning, from *Six Horses*

A gila monster, hissing from its purple mouth, pushed back beneath a stone. Hissing, too, was the sand in the spokes of the wheels. The hoofs of the sweating mules plunged into it, ankle deep. It spread out on all sides with its wind-worked ribs; it lay heaped in glistening drifts against the escarpments, half filling the arroyos, half burying the few wretched shrubs which had fastened themselves like leeches upon the naked anatomy of land. Lying fierce and defiant in its torture of heat, it was a desolation whose vastness was terrifying; whose bounding rim of slashed and broken hills seemed to hem in some mysterious menace, something that lurked above the silence—heavy and oppressive. There was a desperate urge to hurry, to get away; but the barrier of horizon moved on before the stage, the sand clung.

The soaked and frothy animals, spangled with its glistening particles, pulled heavily into their collars. The driver "touched up" his wheelers with the stock of his whip, while his swamper went stumbling along by the leaders, prodding them with a stick, though he could scarcely haul his own feet through the drifts.

The movements of the conductor were strange. His mood seemed to fluctuate between an utter lethargy and the most acute expectancy. Either he sat with his head buried in his arms, the back of his red, wet undershirt exposed to the burning sky, or he arose suddenly, as though some one had tapped him on the shoulder; he began staring about from his bloodshot eyes. Then mopping himself with a scarlet bandanna, he would grumble something to the driver and wilt forward again.

Even he was aware of something about to happen; but he left his passengers sweltering in their doubts. What could happen? Who cared if it did? Spared in the east by the Comanches, in the west by the Apaches, and throughout by all the worst of the elements, anything extraordinary now would be welcome indeed. These ever-dangling menaces were maddening.

But they were dangling nearer. The stage wagon had reached a point some fifteen miles beyond the dry well of Alamo Mocho, when the hot air grew definitely sulphurous; the low sun became dull and tarnished. A black cloud beneath it arose like smoke from the jagged edge of a crater. It covered the sun and became splotched with fire. Long shreds of it tore themselves from the mountains. A great yellowish shadow spread over the world; and a black one came waving like a blanket across the dunes.

Wind-storms were not of frequent occurrence on the Colorado desert; but they were listed no less among the potential furies, all of which struck rarely, but one breed or another of which was likely to attack in the course of so long a journey. Warning, on this occasion, had sufficed for some preparations; and the first hot draft found the animals unhitched, hobbled, and tied loosely together by their necks, so that, free of the wagon, they were yet unable to stray and could turn their tails to the first blast of sand.

When it came it was with a sound like the heavy back-sweep of a sea. It struck upon the vehicle like a burst of it, like the green-frothing body of it, breaker upon breaker. It smashed with a dull impact upon the leather of the high forward seats and glanced from the boots like driving hail. The wagon trembled and rocked, the stanch covering of its after-part bulging with the intermittent concussions that pressed in from both sides. The animals, with heads nearly down to their forefeet, the blown hair of their hides sticky with the drying sweat, remained as rigid as though made of wood. The gaunt world had turned to a golden yellow; the heavens deep red and gray, one blending into the other, into a sweeping mass, a whistling chaos.

Hours passed. Distant screams came down from forms that appeared and vanished through the blizzard-like waves. They were the forms of the bending mesquite, yet they appeared to be moving, to be stalking into the sand-blast. It was a land for all things unearthly. Yet it was California; the State of the journey's end!

Then night. There were stars, and the wind was gone. And a certain water-hole called Indian Wells had gone with it. So had the covering of the wagon, so had all vestige of road, all landmarks. Mountains would not be visible until daylight; then the hot sun would take its toll of that which the wind had parched. Indeed, if the stage were ever to reach the station at Carrizo Creek, there could be no rest through the night. The contents of the canteens had become precious stuff; there was no water at all for the team. The beasts slogged on over the dry and starry wastes, through hills of sand which had never existed before, over patches of gravel that were new, barankas [sic] that were filled, old banks smothered over, strange ones uncovered along with the skulls and bones of other beasts upon whom the sun had once risen too soon.

Carrizo Creek was not far away; but perhaps the stage was not bearing toward it. The conductor was visibly worried. He seemed to be staking all on a driver's "hunch"—

" 'Pears like I recollect that star."

Seeing with New Eyes:
William P. Blake, Geologist

Not everyone was cursing volubly as he plodded across the dunes. After all, California, whatever its uninviting expanses, was the booster state, a place where, fulfilling America's Destiny, at last both material prosperity and levity of the soul surely would come into full bloom. Imagining a parallel with the Children of Israel reaching the Promised Land, many newcomers believed this with a patriotic conviction reaching religious intensity. After all, a caring God would not have created these lands for nothing. The trick, then, simply lay in finding out His purposes for them.

Yes, they were multiple. In a few decades a huge shift occurred as people discovered that the desert was a refuge for those dying of nagging respiratory problems, that the sands could be coaxed into an empire for agriculture generating millions of dollars in fields of rampaging vegetables beyond the wildest dreams—in fact, not only that but, showing how beauty is the handmaiden of loot, that those sands themselves were a realm of perfect beauty. The great change from a ragged frontier to a land of hope and compelling whim-whams would not come all at once, and it would come perhaps far more than people cared to admit because a growing technology, such as railroads and much later air conditioning, increasingly abrogated nature's truly hellish realities. Nonetheless, it came. The desert would be a beautiful as well as a supremely useful place.

Enter young William P. Blake, fresh out of the Yale Scientific School. Signed up on an official reconnaissance, significantly enough, to find a route for the grand hope of a transcontinental railroad, in 1853 he beheld the desert as a fascinating place, as a wonderland. True, on the government payroll and relieved of the usual concerns by his association with the expedition, he could afford to rise above the ordinary travel worries. Yet what he wrote hardly was the frothings of an immature youth. The first to recognize the geologic importance of the Colorado River, he not only named the region after that grand stream; piecing things together, the youth first recognized an astounding thing, that over the ages the river had periodically changed course and rushed in to create a sea in the middle of the desert before turning around and once again following its old bed. He first pointed to the coming agricultural miracle of Imperial Valley by noting that the desert floor was not mere noxious sand but rich soil awaiting only the touch of water to bloom. And furthermore, clinching the vision, he pondered that a single cut into the river's bank would bring those waters rolling across the land in a liquid blessing—a rather elementary mechanical fact that his followers, not quite grasping the concept, as we shall see, nearly turned into a permanent disaster.

Meanwhile, there is an immediate charm to reading Blake for the freshness of a youth seeing everything as new. We meet him happily trekking eastward through San Gorgonio Pass, where thousands of cars now speed on Interstate 10, and thrilling at the weird rock formations etched by the famous winds of that area. Skirting Mt. San Jacinto (he calls it San Gorgoño), we travel with him southeasterly to share his astonishment at seeing a *palm tree*! wavering over a hot spring at, yes, the very site that now is Palm Springs; and next day proceed a few miles farther on our course to ruminate over a winding passage into the earth, the origin, we fear long forgotten, of the present city of Indian Wells, now chockablock with multimillion-dollar homes looking archly down on manicured golf courses.

William P. Blake,
from *Report of a Geological Reconnaissance in California*

It would be difficult to find a place where the cutting power of drifting sand is more beautifully and clearly exhibited than it is at this point. The whole surface of the rocks was smooth and polished, and even the limestone had a peculiar, rounded and smooth surface, which resembled that of partly dissolved crystals, or deliquescent specimens of rock-salt. Long parallel grooves, deep enough to receive a lead-pencil, were cut on the surface of the hard and homogeneous granite. But the most striking and interesting examples were the effects produced on the portions of granite that were composed of large crystals of feldspar, quartz, and tourmaline, and also containing small imbedded garnets. These masses of minerals, differing in their hardness, were unequally cut away. The feldspar, being the softest, was most rapidly acted on, and even the quartz and garnets were unequally abraded, the amount of wear on each mineral being in the order of its hardness. The masses of quartz, tourmaline, and garnet thus acted as protectors to the portions of feldspar behind and under them, while the exposed parts were most rapidly chiseled out by the sharp grains, leaving the harder minerals standing in relief, or with the feldspar standing even with their surfaces on the lee side only, thus forming, in miniature, a kind of tail, similar to the accumulations of earth and stones on the lee side of obstructions in a current of water.

The effects produced on the vertical surfaces of the rock exposed to the wind were, perhaps, the most curious and interesting, for here the hard minerals were left standing out in points, the softer feldspar being cut out on all sides. Masses of feldspar and quartz thus presented very rough and uneven surfaces....

Where the feldspar was charged with small garnets, and was directly in front of the wind, a very peculiar result was produced; the garnets were left standing in relief, mounted on the ends of long pedicles of feldspar which had been protected from abrasion under the garnets while the surrounding parts were cut away. These pointed masses or needles of feldspar, tipped with garnets, stood out from the body of the rock in horizontal lines, pointing, like jeweled fingers, in the direction of the prevailing wind. They form, in reality, a perfect index of the wind's direction, recording it with as much accuracy as the oak trees in the vicinity of San Francisco, where, if the wind reaches them, they are bent from the perpendicular in one direction only, or in some places lie trailed along the ground. All the little points of stone pointed westward in the direction of the valley of the pass, to which the wind conforms.

We continued traveling to the southeast, and downwards over the broad slope to the pass, following the shallow bed of a brook in which water was flowing rapidly, but without trees or much vegetation on its banks. It appeared as if it had been entirely dry for the greater part of the summer. On reaching the next extended spur of San Gorgoño, we camped on the eastern or lower side, in order to avoid the strong wind which continued to blow without cessation. A considerable quantity of sand was found here also, and on the lee side of the rocks. The point was long and low, and the rocks were perfectly bare and very much broken. It was composed of a succession of granitic, gneissose and slaty rocks, intercalated with limestone and quartz rock, similar to those before described....

The stream of water flowed at the base of the rocks in a shallow bed of sand and gravel, and not a tree or blade of grass was visible on its banks. A short distance below, it spread out over the gravelly surface, and became completely absorbed by the sand. Our camp was near the piles of drifted sand; and the wind continued to blow through the night, and brought with it the grains of sand, making a rustling sound as they poured over the rocks and settled in all the hollows and crevices which the wind could not reach....

The ground over which we passed was gravelly and sandy. The sand was coarse, for all the finer particles had been removed by the wind. A range of hills, at the base of the mountains on the left, distant about ten miles, appeared to be composed entirely of sand, its surface being drifted into ridges.

After travelling about seven and a half miles over these long and barren slopes, we saw a green spot in the distance, and soon came to two large springs of water rising in the bare plain, not far from the foot of the mountain. One of these springs is warm, and forms a pool nearly thirty feet in diameter, and three to four feet deep. The cold spring is not quite so large, and is only ten feet distant from the other. The water stands at the same level in each, and probably commingles, so that, on the side adjoining the warm spring, there is but little difference in the temperature, one being 120° and the other 82° F. A constant odor of sulphuretted hydrogen rises from the water, and pails painted with white lead were turned black by it.

This place was evidently a favorite camping-ground for Indians. When we arrived, many Indian boys and girls were bathing in the warm spring, and a group of squaws were engaged in cooking a meal for a party returning from a great feast held near Weaver's ranch, and now just terminated.

A growth of rushes forms a narrow margin of green vegetation around the spring and its outlet. Willows and mezquite bushes grow there also; and I found a young *palm tree* spreading its broad, fan-like leaves among them. The surrounding desert, and this palm tree, gave the scene an Oriental aspect; and the similarity was made still more striking by the groups of Arab-like Indians.

The ground about the springs was raised so that a slight bank was formed around them. This bank may have been formed by the accumulation of sand around the moist earth, and among the roots of the plants and grass; or it possibly was thrown up by the springs, or by the Indians in cleaning them out.

We encamped at this place, not knowing how far we would be obliged to travel before water would again be reached.

A slight dew was deposited on the blankets during the night, but this was probably local, and derived from the warm vapor of the spring. The water was covered with a cloud of condensed vapor, and its temperature at sunrise was only 86°, the air being 46°. It is thus affected by the changes in the temperature of the air, the supply not being very rapid. The barometer indicated an elevation of less than two hundred feet above the sea.

On leaving the green banks of this spring, we again traversed the bare and gravelly surface, and skirted the base of the mountains on the right. The rocks were much broken and piled together in confusion, the absence of soil and vegetation permitting every inequality to be seen. At one point these rocks were found to be composed of quartz, hornblende, and feldspar, in nearly equal proportions, forming a compact granite. The quartz and feldspar are disposed in small rounded grains, enclosed in thin films of mica. This gives a structural character to the mass, and determines a line of easy fracture. The trend of the planes of structure was northwest and southeast (magnetic).

The whole aspect of the landscape was peculiarly dreary, and but little or no vegetation was visible. Numerous varieties of the cactaceæ began to make their appearance, giving a peculiar tropical character to the scene. Some of these plants were tall and cylindrical, four or five feet high, and grooved longitudinally.

Several drifts, and broad thin layers of blown sand were passed. The accumulations vary in depth from a few inches to fifteen feet; and the surfaces are beautifully smooth and rounded, and generally covered with ripple-marks, similar to those produced under water. As we proceeded, we found this sand rising into high drifts, which bounded our vision on the left, while on the right, the base of the mountains was not far distant. A narrow, but nearly level valley was thus formed. The soil appeared to contain a large portion of clay mingled with the sand, and several low places, where water had been standing, were covered with a thin coat of fine clay, now cracked and curled up. Near one of these low places, we found the remains of an Indian bush-house, and the stubble of a barley-field. This barley had been raised at the foot of one of the highest sand-drifts. The sand was thus found to rest upon a substratum of clay, and beyond the field it was found to have a bluish-gray color, and to be very compact and hard.

The Indian guide conducted us over this surface of clay to "*Pozo hondo*," or Deep Well, a deep excavation in the clay made by the Indians to obtain water. It was at the base of a high sand-drift, and about twenty-five feet deep, but contained only a little water. It was wide at the top, but became smaller towards the bottom, being a funnel-shaped depression. The water obtained by means of steps cut in the sides of the pit, the clay having hardened by drying so as to become like stone.

Steamboating across the Colorado

Fortunately, not all travel was sand in the teeth and straining horseflesh. Some of it was downright lyrical, if not poetical. Take Lieutenant Joseph C. Ives—his very middle name was Christmas.

We've mentioned in passing military forts keeping the peace and gold mines in Arizona. Of gold there is no long history on the Colorado Desert. Given the region's skimpy resources, Indians were few, widely scattered, and thus of little threat. The exception was Fort Yuma on the west bank of the Colorado River. On its bluff opposite present-day Yuma, Arizona, it was built to keep the rambunctious river tribes, fat on the Colorado's bounty, in line. Also, Fort Mojave was eventually founded about 200 twisting miles upstream.

The diggings of mines were strung along the river in the wildness between the two forts; and, as far as transportation was concerned, both the prospectors and the soldiers who protected them needed transportation and supplies. Soon, an easier way was found than stagecoaching, although this, too, had its troublesome aspects. It was something of a Zen solution. Instead of flying in the teeth of nature, in the traditional way hauling wagons through the sucking sands, why not simply ride upon the back of the river forming the eastern boundary of the Colorado Desert? Hence, goods and passengers arrived at the mouth of the Colorado River and thence traveled upstream by small steamboat.

We meet Lieutenant Ives in the winter of 1857–1858, testing just how far north navigation could go up the Colorado, a temperamental river pesky with sandbars. In the process the floundering expedition provided a good deal of merriment to the Indians. However, despite the embarrassing performance, this will not be the last we'll see of Ive's brave little steamship.

~~~~ **Lieutenant Joseph C. Ives,**
   from *Report upon the Colorado River of the West*

Upon the establishment of Fort Yuma, it was found a measure of economy to supply the post by way of the Gulf and the river instead of by the overland route, and for a year or two freight was carried up in lighters, which were poled along or hauled up by hand. The rapid current, the shoals, the marshy banks, the unknown character of the country, and the presence of hostile Indians, were obstacles in the way of inaugurating navigation that few men would have successfully overcome. As business increased a small steamer was procured, but, owing to some defect in the boiler, blew up before it had been long in operation. Another was then built, and a short time ago a third and larger boat. The two latter now ply regularly between the head of the Gulf and Fort Yuma, and secure profitable returns to their persevering and energetic proprietors. These have the good will of the Indians, and by contributing a certain amount towards staying the cravings of their stomachs, are exempted from thefts and other molestations.

The steamboats brought down a fair stock of passengers of both sexes from the nearest villages. They were, as a whole, better looking than the pair we had seen. Several of the men had good figures. The women were rather too much inclined to embonpoint, with the exception of the young girls, some of whom were by no means ill-favored. Bright eyes, white teeth, and musical voices, they all possessed. In point of apparel they were about as deficient as the men, a very short petticoat, their only garment, taking the place of the strip of cotton. While the steamboats were unloading both males and females sat in groups about the decks, watching the hands at work, and having a good time themselves doing nothing.

The rumor of the preparation of an expedition to ascend the Colorado was long ago circulated among the adjacent tribes, and has occasioned much interest and excitement. I am told that curious inquiries have been made of the troops by the Indians about Fort Yuma as to the object of the enterprise, and the half understood replies have been transmitted, with many amplifications, up and down the river, occasioning all kinds of surmises concerning our purposes and probable movements. None of the Cocopas were disposed to cultivate us, nor was there much in the appearance of the camp to tempt them from their comfortable quarters on the steamboats. We could see, nevertheless, that our operations engrossed a good deal of their attention and conversation, and that nothing escaped their keen-sighted inspection. The size and appearance of our unfinished boat evidently disappointed them, and I think they regarded it, and the expedition altogether, as rather a poor affair, and derived much amusement therefrom. One or two long-legged fellows, the wits of the party, were foremost in facetious criticism. They seemed to be pointing out to their female companions our makeshifts and deficiency in numbers, and were, no doubt, very funny at our expense, for their sallies were received by the young belles with great favor and constant bursts of merriment....

It was the intention this morning to make an early start; but the last preparations, as usual, consumed several hours of time, and it was nearly 11 when all of our party were collected at the wharf, everything put aboard, and steam gotten up. Our friends at the garrison came down to see us off, and the sides of the bluff were lined with Indians—men, women, and children—assembled to witness our departure, and, in spite of their distrust, delighted to have something to see and talk about. The urgent request of Lieutenant Winder to the chief had not failed of its effect, and the latter engaged (though reluctantly) that two Indians should accompany us—an old Diegeno, by the name of Mariano, and a young chief who had signalized himself by escaping unhurt from a recent memorable conflict with the Pimas and Maricopas, and whom it pleased to be called the "Capitan." With an eye to theatrical effect, not all uncommon with their race, my two recruits delayed making their appearance till the latest moment. We had bidden our friends good-bye, the plank was about to be hauled in, and I had begun to believe that the chief had played us a trick, when they came stalking along, and entering the boat, seated themselves on the rail with an air of indifference that did not altogether conceal that they thought they were embarked in a rather doubtful enterprise. Their friends on the shore, being out of the scrape themselves, were naturally delighted at seeing others in it. The men grinned, and the women and children shouted with laughter, which was responded to by a scream from the *Explorer's* whistle; and in the midst of the uproar the line was cast off, the engine put in motion, and gliding away from the wharf, we soon passed through the gorge abreast of the fort and emerged into the open valley above. The river here spread out over a wide surface, and was, of course, shallow and full of bars and snags. The channel became at each moment more difficult to find, and when we had made but two miles we were brought to a dead stop by a bar. An anchor was put out ahead; but the bed being quicksand, it would not hold. It was necessary to lighten the boat, and finally most of the men got overboard, and having thus further diminished the draught, succeeded, after four hours and a half of hard labor, in forcing the steamer into the deeper water beyond the bar. The delay would have been less annoying if it had occurred a little higher up. We were in plain sight of the fort, and knew that this sudden check to our progress was affording an evening of great entertainment to those in and out of the garrison. As it was nearly dark when the bar was passed, after proceeding a mile we stopped at a point where there was wood, and went into camp.

"Thou Brown, Bare-Breasted, Voiceless Mystery": The Desert as Urban Melodrama

Even as the sky turned arterial red while travelers cursed and turned up their collars against yet another sandstorm, while elsewhere soldiers labored waist-deep in muddy water to lift their little craft stuck on a sandbar, another use was being found for the desert, one of the joys of horror.

Likely penned in the early 1890s, the following poetic gasp was by Madge Morris Wagner. She was the wife of Harr Wagner, the editor of *The Golden Era*, an upbeat literary magazine published in San Diego between 1887 and 1895. There's a definite urban, hyperfibrillating quality to this view of the Colorado Desert. It would be difficult to imagine some snaggletoothed old prospector with a knack for rhyme casting the desert in such terms; he would be on the trail of the troves of the gold and silver waiting out there for him, and, a man of practical purposes, he would have guffawed in embarrassment at the representation of the desert as a grand sexual object with the veils of the Victorian niceties of the day somewhat indelicately slipping off.

Still, the treasures waiting out there were an important part of the milieu. One can imagine Madge Morris Wagner rising out of the comforts of palmy San Diego to peer over the mountains and becoming excited at what she saw. To her, the desert was no mere wasteland, a factual pain in the neck for travelers, not even a mere monster. Paralleling the growing tales of the desert as a land of treasures, whether mineral or agricultural, soon to be discovered, the region was becoming a wonderland for the psyche, a romping ground for literary types with frothing imaginations where their fantasies (perhaps their repressed sexual fantasies) might be turned loose in a glorious play far more powerful and overwhelmingly orgasmic than anything they could hope for in their daily lives. Or so they imagined. Such would be exactly the excitements that in a few years visiting aesthetes such as John C. Van Dyke would seize upon for grand effect with their audiences back east.

~~~~ Madge Morris Wagner,
from "To the Colorado Desert"

To the Colorado Desert

Thou brown, bare-breasted, voiceless mystery,
Hot sphinx of nature, cactus-crowned, what has thou done?
Unclothed and mute as when the groans of chaos turned
Thy naked burning bosom to the sun.
The mountain silences have speech, the rivers sing,
Thou answerest never unto anything.
Pink-throated lizards pant in thy slim shade;
The horned toad runs rustling in the heat;
The shadowy gray coyote, born afraid,
Steals to some brackish spring and laps, and prowls
Away; and howls, and howls, and howls, and howls,
Until the solitude is shaken with an added loneliness.
The sharp mescal shoots up a giant stalk,
Its century of yearning, to the sunburnt skies,
And drips rare honey from the lips
Of yellow waxen flowers, and dies.
Some lengthwise sun-dried shapes with feet and hands
And thirsty mouths pressed on the sweltering sands,
Mark here and there a gruesome graveless spot
Where some one drank thy scorching hotness, and is not.
God must have made thee in His anger, and forgot.

Seeing with New Eyes:
John C. Van Dyke, Aesthetician

Unwittingly, young geologist William P. Blake had touched on a controversy that would plague the nation, becoming an ever-widening chasm into our own day. If the desert is useful, well, then, it should be used. Such is only logical and, furthermore, for those inclining to the geographic theology of the time, all but a mandate to follow divine instruction. For the Children of Israel to refuse to enter the Promised Land would be blasphemy, an insult to the very Creator Himself.

However, if at once the desert is useful and also beautiful, as clearly it was to Blake, what should be done, then? What right have we mere mortals to sully the Creator's intricate handiwork? Some years after Blake, John C. Van Dyke, a professor of art at Rutgers College (now University) was traveling about and saw that the desert is "the most decorative landscape in the world, a landscape all color, a dream landscape." With an earnestness equal to that of the utilitarians, Van Dyke stormed that to violate such beauty was an act of sheer vandalism. Perhaps for reasons of expediency, Van Dyke tried to put a logical cast to his position, arguing elaborately that the desert was a regulator of the West's climate that had best be left alone. However, beyond the appeal to people of a practical bent, at heart Van Dyke's justification is pure aestheticism: The desert should be preserved simply because it is a beautiful place. This was a somewhat odd, if growing, notion for the times. A follower of Art for Art's Sake and a member of the nation's toniest salons, the refined professor believed that mankind was pretty much doomed by its own wayward stupidities, but that appreciation of beauty, as a kind of temporal salvation, was life's highest good, raising people, at least those few people capable of such sensitivities, above the race's innate brutism.

It is tempting here to rush in and say, even as Van Dyke says, that the position was anathema to a dynamic country growing by leaps and bounds and whose heedless exploitation of resources was the very basis of its vaunted prosperity. True as this is, there's a larger truth beyond it. The hardest thing for humans to do is to do nothing. One strains, searching and searching in history for examples to the contrary. It seems that humanity lacks restraint: If people are capable of doing something, eventually they'll do it. Perhaps in this larger sense, Van Dyke was right in ways he did not even imagine. The extent that we can leave well-enough alone, whether it be the open space of a park or the intricacies of a wilderness area, enjoying such things for what they are, rather than for what we can turn them into, is a measure of our transcendence, of a humility reflecting a true but rare nobility.

⁓ John C. Van Dyke,
from *The Desert: Further Studies in Natural Appearances*

In the ancient days when the shore of the Pacific was young, when the white sierras had only recently been heaved upward and the desert itself was in a formative state, the ocean reached much farther inland than at the present time. It pushed through many a pass and flooded many a depression in the sands, as its wave-marks upon granite bases and its numerous beaches still bear witness. In those days that portion of the Colorado Desert known as the Salton Sea did not exist. The Gulf of California extended as far north as the San Bernardino Range and as far west as the Pass of San Gorgonio. Its waters stood deep where now lies the road-bed of the southern Pacific railway, and all the country from Indio almost to the Colorado River was a blue sea. The bowl was full. No one knew if it had a bottom or imagined that it would ever be emptied of water and given over to the drifting sands.

No doubt the tenure of the sea in this Salton Basin was of long duration. The sand-dunes still standing along the northern shore—fifty feet high and shining like hills of chalk—were not made in a month; nor was the long shelving beach beneath them—still covered with sea-shells and pebbles and looking as though washed by the waves only yesterday—formed in a day. Both dunes and beach are plainly visible winding across the desert for many miles. The southwestern shore, stretching under a spur of the Coast Range, shows the same formation in its beach-line. The old bays and lagoons that led inland from the sea, the river-beds that brought down the surface waters from the mountains, the inlets and natural harbors are all in place. Some of them are drifted half full of sand, but they have not lost their identity. And out in the sea-bed still stand masses of cellular rock, honeycombed and water-worn (and now for many years windworn), showing the places where once rose the reefs of the ancient sea.

These are the only records that tell of the sea's occupation. The Indians have no tradition about it. Yet when the sea was there the Indian tribes were there also. Along the bases of the San Bernardino and San Jacinto Ranges there are indications of cave-dwelling, rock-built squares that doubtless were fortified camps, heaps of stone that might have been burial-mounds. Everywhere along the ancient shores and beaches you pick up pieces of pottery, broken ollas, stone pestles and mortars, axe-heads, obsidian arrow-heads, flint spear-points, agate beads. There is not the slightest doubt that the shores were inhabited. It was a warm nook, accessible to the mountains and the Pacific; in fact, just the place where tribes would naturally gather. Branches of the Yuma Indians, like the Cocopas, overran all this country when the Padres first crossed the desert; and it was probably their forefathers who lived by the shores of the Upper Gulf. No doubt they were fishermen, traders and fighters, like their modern representatives on Tiburon Island; and no doubt they fished and fought and were happy by the shores of the mountain-locked sea....

When you are in the bottom of it you are nearly three hundred feet below the level of the sea. Circling about you to the north, south, and west are sierras, some of them over ten thousand feet in height. These form the Rim of the Bowl. And off to the southwest there is a side broken out of the Bowl through which you can pass to the river and the Gulf. The basin is perhaps the hottest place to be found anywhere on the American deserts. And it is also the most forsaken. The bottom itself is, for the great part of it, as flat as a table. It looks like a great plain leading up and out to the horizon—a plain that has been ploughed and rolled smooth. The soil is drifted silt—the deposits made by the washings from the mountains—and is almost as fine as flour.

The long line of dunes at the north are just as desolate, yet they are wonderfully beautiful. The desert sand is finer than snow, and its curves and arches, as it builds its succession of drifts out and over an arroyo, are as graceful as the lines of running water. The dunes are always rhythmical and flowing in their forms; and for color the desert has nothing that surpasses them. In the early morning, before the sun is up, they are air-blue, reflecting the sky overhead; at noon they are pale lines of dazzling orange-colored light, waving and undulating in the heated air; at sunset they are often flooded with a rose or mauve color; under a blue moonlight they shine white as icebergs in the northern seas....

Is there any beauty, other than the dunes, down in this hollow of the desert? Yes. From a picturesque point of view it has the most wonderful light, air, and color imaginable. You will not think so until you see them blended in that strange illusion known as mirage. And here is the one place in all the world where the water-mirage appears to perfection. It does not show well over grassy or bushy ground, but over the flat lake-beds of the desert its appearance is astonishing. Down in the basin it is accompanied by a second illusion that makes the first more convincing. You are below sea-level, but instead of the ground about you sloping up and out, it apparently slopes down and away on every side. You are in the centre of a disk or high point of ground, and around the circumference of the disk is water—palpable, almost tangible, water. It cannot be seen well from your horse, and fifty feet up on a mountain side it would not be visible at all. But dismount and you see it better; kneel down and place your cheek to the ground and now the water seems to creep up to you. You could throw a stone into it. The shore where the waves lap is just before you. But where is the horizon-line? Odd enough, this vast circling sea does not always know a horizon; it sometimes reaches up and blends into the sky without any point of demarcation. Through the heated air you see faint outlines of mountains, dim glimpses of foot-hills, suggestions of distance; but no more. Across them is drawn the wavering veil of air, and the red earth at your feet, the blue sky overhead, are but bordering bands of flat color.

And there you have the most decorative landscape in the world, a landscape all color, a dream landscape. Painters for years have been trying to put it upon canvas—this landscape of color, light, and air, with form almost obliterated, merely suggested, given only as a hint of the mysterious. Men like Corot and Monet have told us, again and again, that in painting, clearly delineated forms of mountains, valleys, trees, and rivers, kill the fine color-sentiment of the picture. The great struggle of the modern landscapist is to get on with the least possible form and to suggest everything by tones of color, shades of light, drifts of air. Why? Because these are the most sensuous qualities in nature and in art. The landscape that is the simplest in form and the finest in color is by all odds the most beautiful. It is owning to just these features that this Bowl of the desert is a thing of beauty instead of a dreary hollow in the hills. Only one other scene is comparable to it, and that the southern seas at sunset when the calm ocean reflects and melts into the color-glory of the sky. It is the same kind of beauty. Form is almost blurred out in favor of color and air.

Yet here is more beauty destined to destruction. It might be thought that this forsaken pot-hole in the ground would never come under the dominion of man, that its very worthlessness would be its safeguard against civilization, that none would want it, and everyone from necessity would let it alone. But not even the spot deserted by reptiles shall escape the industry or the avarice (as you please) of man. A great company has been formed to turn the Colorado River into the sands, to reclaim this desert basin, and make it blossom as the rose. The water is to be brought down to the basin by the old channel of the New River. Once in reservoirs it is to be distributed over the tract by irrigating ditches, and it is said a million acres of desert will thus be made arable, fitted for homesteads, ready for the settler who never remains settled.

A most laudable enterprise, people will say. Yes; commercially no one can find fault with it. Money made from sand is likely to be clean money, at any rate. And economically these acres will produce large supplies of food. That is commendable, too, even if those for whom it is produced waste a good half of what they already possess. And yet the food that is produced there may prove expensive to people other than the producers. This old sea-bed is, for its area, probably the greatest dry-heat generator in the world because of its depression and its barren, sandy surface. It is a furnace that whirls heat up and out of the Bowl, over the peaks of the Coast Range into Southern California, and eastward across the plains to Arizona and Sonora. In what measure it is responsible for the general climate of those States cannot be accurately summarized; but it certainly has a great influence, especially in the matter of producing dry air. To turn this desert into an agricultural tract would be to increase humidity, and that would be practically to nullify the finest air on the continent.

And why are not good air and climate as essential to human well-being as good beef and good bread? Just now, when it is a world too late, our Government and the forestry societies of the country are awakening to the necessity of preserving the forests. National parks are being created wherever possible and the cutting of timber within them is prohibited. Why is this being done? Ostensibly to preserve the trees, but in reality to preserve the water supply, to keep the fountain-heads pure, to maintain a uniform stage of water in the rivers. Very proper and right. The only pity is that it was not undertaken forty years ago. But how is the water supply, from an economic and hygienic stand-point, any more important than the air supply?

Grasses, trees, shrubs, growing grain, they, too, may need good air as well as human lungs. The deserts are not worthless wastes. You cannot crop all creation with wheat and alfalfa. Some sections must lie fallow that other sections may produce. Who shall say that the preternatural productiveness of California is not due to the warm air of its surrounding deserts? Does anyone doubt that the healthfulness of the countries lying west of the Mississippi may be traced directly to the dry air and heat of the deserts. They furnish health to the human; why not strength to the plant? The deserts should never be reclaimed. They are the breathing-spaces of the west and should be preserved forever.

To speak about sparing anything because it is beautiful is to waste one's breath and incur ridicule in the bargain. The æsthetic sense—the power to enjoy through the eyes, the ear, and the imagination—is just as important a factor in the scheme of human happiness as the corporeal sense of eating and drinking; but there has never been a time when the world would admit it. The "practical men," who seem forever on the throne, know very well that beauty is only meant for lovers and young persons—stuff to suckle fools withal. The main affair of life is to get the dollar, and if there is any money in cutting the throat of Beauty, why, by all means, cut her throat. That is what the "practical men" have been doing ever since the world began. It is not necessary to dig up ancient history; for have we not seen, here in California and Oregon, in our own time, the destruction of the fairest valleys the sun ever shone upon by placer and hydraulic mining? Have we not seen in Minnesota and Wisconsin the mightiest forests that ever raised head to the sky slashed to pieces by the axe and turned into a waste of tree-stumps and fallen timber? Have we not seen the Upper Mississippi, by the destruction of the forests, changed from a broad, majestic river into a shallow, muddy stream; and the beautiful prairies of Dakota turned under by the plough and then allowed to run to weeds? Men must have coal though they ruin the valleys and blacken the streams of Pennsylvania, they must have oil though they disfigure half of Ohio and Indiana, they must have copper if they wreck all the mountains of Montana and Arizona, and they must have gold though they blow Alaska into the Behring Sea. It is more than possible that the "practical men" have gained much practice and many dollars by flaying the fair face of these

United States. They have stripped the land of its robes of beauty, and what have they given in its place? Weeds, wire fences, oil-derricks, board shanties and board towns—things that not even a "practical man" can do less than curse at.

And at last they have turned to the desert!

More on Van Dyke: The Nasty Young Man on the Imagined Trapeze

In the popular mind, then, Van Dyke is the great hero of desert lovers. It is he who thundered, "Hands Off!"—that the desert should be preserved forever as one of our great natural legacies—a slogan often appearing in today's brochures and articles advocating desert preservation.

Literature, however, can be deceptive. The closer we study Van Dyke, the more intricate he becomes, and sometimes what he says, and especially how he lived, leads us into shocking places. Note that he says the desert not only is the most decorative landscape in the world but that it is a dreamscape. This led him to write a whole chapter on the most delicious aspect of the desert, the very crème de la crème of desert experiences, the mirage. Very well. The mirage, with its upside-down mountains, appearing and disappearing castles, and antelope with surreally long and dangling legs, is indeed a strange and fascinating phenomenon.

But why would it be the supreme experience? After all, you'd expect that a desert lover would love the desert for all its variety, for all its animals, storms, floods, sunsets, and other multiple desert thrills.

How bourgeois! Van Dyke would thump with a snicker. The mirage is the desert's richest fruit precisely because it is unreal. People with any brains know it is an illusion, and your camera won't record it. Why, the mirage is really not there at all. Then where is it? Van Dyke says that it is "only a dream," but we know from the context that he means something more than electrical firings in our heads at night. A nihilist first and a mystic second, to Van Dyke the mirage is an inexplicable and insubstantial entity all its own, very much like a mistress, as he repeatedly says elsewhere, who never gives us her real flesh but tantalizes us deliciously, leading us on only with the hope of getting what we'll never attain. In the salons where the professor lectured, one can imagine the wealthy matrons tingling with vicarious deliciousness at the notion, while their husbands, practical captains of industry, shifted uncomfortably in their chairs.

And there was more. It turns out that the enemy of the desert's delicacies were not only the developers with dollar signs in their eyes but the common herd with packs on their backs swarming over a landscape best preserved for the exclusive use of Van Dyke and his coterie of swooning ladies. The public, he sniffed to fellow art critic Kenyon Cox, "is a great ass of some booby" (Teague and Wild 108), and Van Dyke meant every nasty word of it.

In the world of illusions, all this comes nicely full circle in a way that must have given wily Van Dyke supreme satisfaction.

John C. Van Dyke,
from *The Desert: Further Studies in Natural Appearances*

The form of mirage that gives us the reversed image is seen on the desert as well as on the sea; but not frequently—at least not in my experience. There is an illusion of mountains hanging peak downward from the sky, but one may wander on the deserts for months and never see it. The reality and the phantom both appear in the view—the phantom seeming to draw up and out of the original in a distorted, cloud-like shape. It is almost always misshapen, and as it rises high in air it seems to be detached from the original by currents of air drifted in between. More familiar sights are the appearances of trees, animals, houses, wagons, all hanging in the air in enlarged and elongated shapes and, of course, reversed. I have seen horses hitched to a wagon hanging high up in the air with the legs of the horses twenty feet long and the wagon as large as a cabin. The stilted antelope "forty feet high and upside down" is as seldom seen in the sky as upon the earth; but desert cattle in bunches of half a dozen will sometimes walk about on the aërial ceiling in a very astonishing way....

The most common illusion of the desert is the water-mirage and that is caused by reflection, not refraction. Its usual appearance is that of a lake or sea of water with what looks at a distance to be small islands in it. There are those with somewhat more lively imagination than their fellows who can see cows drinking in the water, trees along the margin of the shore (palms usually), and occasionally a farm-house, a ship, or a whale. I have never seen any of these wonderful things, but the water and island part of the illusion is to be seen almost anywhere in the desert basins during hot weather. In the lower portions of the Colorado it sometimes spreads over thousands of acres, and appears not to move for hours at a stretch. At other times the wavering of the heat or the swaying of the air strata, or a change in the density of the air will give the appearance of waves or slight undulations on the water. In either case the illusion is quite perfect. Water lying in such a bed would reflect the exact color of the sky over it; and what the eyes really see in this desert picture is the reflection of the sky not from water but from strata of thick air.

This illusion of water is probably seen more perfectly in the great dry lake-beds of the desert where the ground is very flat and there is no vegetation, than elsewhere. In the old Coahuila Valley region of the Colorado the water comes up very close to you and the more you flatten the angle of reflection by flattening yourself upon the ground, the closer the water approaches. The objects in it which people imagine look like familiar things are certainly very near. And these objects—wild-fowl, bushes, tufts of swamp grass, islands, buttes—are frequently bewildering because some of them are right side up and some of them are not. Some are reversed in the air and some are quietly resting upon the ground.

It happens at times that the whole picture is confused by the light-rays being both reflected and refracted, and in addition that the rays from certain objects come to us in a direct line. The ducks, reeds, and tufts of grass, for instance, are only clods of dirt or sand-banked bushes which are detached at the bottom by heavy drifts of air. We see their tops right side up by looking through the air-layer or some broken portion of it. But in the same scene there may be trees upside down, and mountains seen in reflection, drawn out to stupendous proportions. In the Salton Basin one hot day in September a startled coyote very obligingly ran through a most brilliant water-mirage lying directly before me. I could only see his head and part of his shoulders, for the rest of him was cut off by the air-layer; but the appearance was that of a wolf swimming rapidly across a lake of water. The illusion of the water was exact enough because it was produced by reflection, but there was no illusion about the upper part of the coyote. The rays of light from his head and shoulders came to me unrefracted and unreflected—came as light usually travels from object to eye.

But refracted or reflected, every feature of the water-mirage is attractive. And sometimes its kaleidoscopic changes keep the fancy moving at a pretty pace. The appearance and disappearance of the objects and colors in the mirage are often quite wonderful. The reversed mountain peaks, with light and shade and color upon them, wave in and out of the imaginary lake, and are perhaps succeeded by undulations of horizon colors in grays and pinks, by sunset skies and scarlet clouds, or possibly by the white cap of a distant sierra that has been caught in the angle of reflection.

But with all its natural look one is at loss to understand how it could ever be seriously accepted as a fact, save at the first blush. People dying for water and in delirium run toward it—at least the more than twice-told tales of travelers so report—but I never knew any healthy eye that did not grow suspicious of it after the first glance. It trembles and glows too much and soon reveals itself as something intangible, hardly of earth, little more than a shifting fantasy. You cannot see it clear-cut and well-defined, and the snap-shot of your camera does not catch it at all.

Yet its illusiveness adds to, rather than detracts from, its beauty. Rose-colored dreams are always delightful; and the mirage is only a dream. It has no more substantial fabric than the golden haze that lies in the canyons at sunset. It is only one of nature's veilings which she puts on or off capriciously. But again its loveliness is not the less when its uncertain, fleeting character is revealed. It is one of the desert's most charming features because of its strange light and its softly glowing opaline color. And there we have come back again to that beauty in landscape which lies not in the lines of mountain valley and plain, but in the almost formless masses of color and light.

John Muir on the Colorado Desert: In a Flowered Bathrobe

Of the many celebrities, ranging from Albert Einstein to Prince Charles, who would visit the Palm Springs area, John Muir deserves special note, for there were unique qualities and a number of subtleties surrounding his stay. Most famous personalities would come to enjoy the lavish amenities and be seen hobnobbing with other famous personalities. The abstemious Muir, however, certainly didn't come for the luxuries, of which at the time the tiny settlement offered almost none. Nor did he come to see the sights. In fact, the famous conservationist, a lover of ice and Sierra forests, didn't even like the desert. He was there because his daughter Helen suffered from severe respiratory problems, and his hope of a cure for her in those parched lands, rather than the lure of natural attractions, illustrates a prime impetus for the desert's early settlement. J. Smeaton Chase, Carl Eytel, John C. Van Dyke, and other names now associated with the area as "desert lovers," in fact were there primarily in hopes that the region's dry air would heal their afflictions, in some cases allowing them to take their first full breaths in years. Love of the desert, if it came at all, came later.

As to Helen Muir, likely because of easier access by railroad, she would settle on the Van Dyke Ranch (a place owned by Theodore, a friend of John Muir and elder brother of John C.; so you see how many of those desert things connect) far to the north on the Mojave Desert. Meanwhile, whatever John Muir's aversion to the desert, he was no sulk; it's interesting to see him making the most of things, romping off early in the morning to discover the desert's plants and ponder Indian petroglyphs, in general appreciating nature in all its guises, even if they weren't the guises he preferred.

The following piece, transcribed in its entirety, comes with advantages to us other than enjoyable vignettes of the great mountain man on the desert. The chronicler of the visit, Helen Lukens Gaut, comes across as something of a hagiographic literary vulture, but nonetheless she has left us an invaluable legacy, one of the most detailed early accounts of village life and a renowned visitor—flowered robe and all.

~~~~ Helen Lukens Gaut,
from "I Remember John Muir's Visit"

In the summer of 1905, John Muir, famous author, discoverer of Muir Glacier, grand old man of forested mountains and alpine lakes, arrived in Palm Springs, a prayer in his heart that the health of his younger daughter, Helen, might be benefited by the hot dry air of the desert.

A telegram to Dr. Welwood Murray, relayed from the railroad station, informed him that John Muir and daughters, Wanda and Helen, would arrive on the afternoon train, and requested transportation and accommodations at his hotel which had been closed for the summer. The guest cottages were deep with dust from recent sand storms. Dr. Murray was in a dither of excitement. He ran his fingers through his tousled white hair and beard. Perspiration oozed from the age-deep lines on his troubled face. Then suddenly, himself a recognized scholar and philosopher, an eccentric blustering old Scotchman with the roar of a lion and the heart of a dove, went into action.

Mrs. Murray, handicapped by overweight and increasing deafness, was somewhere in the garden. She had never failed him in times of stress and anxiety.

"Elizabeth!" he shouted.

No answer.

"Lizzie!"

Still no reply.

Then "LIZ" in a thunderous voice.

With this final summons she appeared with a basket of freshly picked grapes and figs, her face a patient map of questioning. Explosively, he explained, "The Muirs are coming. Three of them. They're coming today."

"But we can't—" Dismayed at the prospect of house cleaning, of cooking and serving meals, Mrs. Murray, near collapse, deposited her 180 pounds on a bench, arguing against—but trying to plan.

For several days I had been camping on the bank of the zanja [irrigation ditch] in Dr. Murray's garden oasis. Having previously camped with the Muirs in Paradise Valley in the High Sierras, I was overjoyed with the prospect of seeing them again, and offered to help in any way I could. Dr. Murray accepted my offer, but rather dubiously, apparently doubting that a young woman writer could be of much use. It was only because of my father's (T. P. Lukens) notable work in reclamation and reforestation, that he tolerated my being there at all during the closed season. In his present dilemma, I decided, was my opportunity to win the approval of this old Scotchman.

In a paroxysm of haste he dashed across the road to the Caliente Reservation, returning speedily with Ramon, a stalwart young Indian, and Amada, gowned in a voluminous calico mother-hubbard. Given brooms, mops, buckets and soap, Dr. Murray ordered them to "exterminate the superfluous accumulation of dirt." One of his pet hobbies was to familiarize the Indians with the niceties of the English language.

I was told to ride with Marcus, a patriarchal Indian; grey as the sage, bronzed as the hills; to meet the Muirs at the station. The so-called stage— a rickety, heat-shrunken uncovered wagon, was dragged through the six miles of sand by two antiquated mustangs. The Muirs' luggage, along with boxes of freight billed to Dr. Murray, which I hoped contained provisions to supplement storekeeper Bunker's meager supplies, were hoisted into the wagon box.

Mr. Muir and daughter, Helen, climbed to the high seat beside Marcus, the hoary apostle of desert silence. Muir's blue eyes were bright with anticipation. His brown hair and beard were but slightly grey at 60.

Wanda and I sat on a board that rested precariously on the sides of the wagon box and away we went, the wagon creaking and swaying in the deep wheel ruts that marked the road through drifting sand. A desert wind, increasing in velocity, stabbed us with dagger-like pellets of sand. In the open-jawed spaces, outside shelter of Mt. San Jacinto, in an out-of-doors new and strange to him, Mr. Muir had the opportunity to compare this maniac wind with the clean crisp tempests he'd met with in his beloved forests. With the desert in a state of hysteria, talking was impossible, and so we sat huddled and silent until we reached the oasis of Palm Springs.

Guest cottages had been made ready; pitchers of fresh water, bowls, towels and soap on the wash stands; baskets of figs, grapes, oranges and grapefruit on small tables. Mrs. Murray had contrived a plain but appetizing meal to be ready on the long board table in the adobe dining room.

During the meal the two opinionated old Scotchmen had a lively talkfest, exploding their theories, sometimes in cordial agreement, sometimes in heated argument. Mr. Muir, naturally gentle, kindly, and unobtrusive, expressed, but definitely, his belief in Dr. Murray's theory of geological evolution. Dr. Murray's voice rose in a roar of disputation, banging his fist on the table until the dishes rattled. Finally peace was restored when Muir quietly remarked with his inimitable chuckle, "Rocks are rocks—no matter how they evolved."

Dinner finished, Murray glanced worriedly at the litter of dishes, then at his wife. "She hasn't been well," he said, "and…"

Wanda, young, strong, efficient in any emergency, said "Don't worry. We'll manage." She started clearing the table and went into the kitchen, from which came a terrified scream and crash of broken crockery. Rushing out we found her in the center of the litter, eyes budging [sic] with horror at crickets, big black ones, on the sink, others crawling up through the cracks in the old floor boards. Murray assured her they were quite harmless, while her father, with his inimitable chuckle, remarked "For shame! To think a daughter of mine could be scared and let out such a yell because of a few little beetles."

For several days, Wanda, in spite of her antipathy for the bugs, took complete charge of the cuisine.

Star-bright evening hours were spent in the palm-thatched pergola over the rugged pillars of which were vines heavy with clusters of purple grapes. The night air in contrast with the intense heat of day, was cool, and drifted with fragrance of oleander and orange blossoms. In this rare botanical garden were trees, vines and shrubs which had been shipped to Murray from far corners of the world for experimental planting in the desert.

Muir's contentment was evident. His voice was low, leisurely as a woodland brook, as he talked on and on of his adventures in the out-of-doors, weaving rare word pictures of rugged peaks, deep canyons, waterfalls, glaciers, wildflower meadows and cathedral forests.

One had only to press the electric button of his anecdote generator to make him drift into reminiscence.

Asked why he tramped alone into far-away wildernesses, he said, "Because of my reverence for God's country, for the wealth of beauty and perfectness I find there. When tired, I brew a cup of tea, nibble on crackers or dry bread, lie on a carpet of pine needles, a mossy bank, a flat-topped rock, or a slab of glacial ice—then feast on the scenery. Afraid? What of? I'd rather climb a mountain peak or scale a glacier in dead of night than cross a city street and dodge traffic in broad day. That's the only time I am really scared."

Muir was slender, almost frail in appearance. It seemed a gust of wind would blow him over. But he was like a reed—strong, capable of meeting any need for physical endurance. His shaggy beard, streaked with grey, gave him the look of an old-time school master. In conversation, as in all his writings, he believed in simplicity of expression. A spade was a spade, not an agricultural implement. He had a keen sense of humor.

One morning when hearing Murray instruct Ramon how to plant trees in language such as this: "You must make the excavations of greater radius at the lower extremities than at the upper, in order that the wide-spreading roots will have greater opportunity for expansion."

Muir chuckled with amusement, and said: "Murray's confusing that poor Indian with those big words. What in thunder does Ramon know about radius and extremities of expansion? Why not tell him to dig a hole. He'd understand that."

One day Murray broached the subject of ideals. "Ideals, fiddlesticks!" Muir exclaimed. "John Burroughs got off some foolishness about ideals. As for me, I just jog alone enjoying every sheaf of grass, every blossom, every sunbeam, every rain cloud."

For several days the thermometer ranged from 100 to 120. Wanda, burdened with her self-appointed task of cooking, along with her continuing antipathy for crickets, began to show signs of wilting. To make things easier for her, Murray suggested having picnics in some of the canyons, where cooling streams and deep shade would be respite from the heat. His plan was met with cheers of approval. So into the old wagon went a basket of provisions, along with pillows for Helen, for whom he'd taken a great liking. Nothing was too good for her. She must have every comfort.

Murray took the reins. Helen sat on the "prescribed" pillow between him and her father. Wanda sat behind on a board. With a flip of the whip to awaken the horses, with me astride an Indian pony, "Whirlwind," we were off for Palm Canyon, seven miles from the village. And what a road! Narrow, deep with sand in places, or punctuated with huge boulders over which the wagon wheels had difficulty in straddling. We hadn't gone far until Helen insisted on changing places with me. In spite of Murray's vigorous objections, his declaration that such violent exercise would be the death of her, she had her merry way—as she usually did, mounted Whirlwind and dashed ahead in a cloud of dust, while I took her place on the seat elbow to elbow with Murray, who for some minutes was too angry and frustrated to speak.

Muir thought the incident a huge joke and whispered to me: "Now's your chance to make him like you." As I had previously confided to Muir my failure to quite win Murray's friendship, he quietly voiced this advice. "You must learn how to approach a Scotchman. Why don't you exert your charming feminine ways? There is a lot of good—even in a Scotchman."

Reaching the mouth of the canyon, Helen dismounted, removed the saddle and led her horse to the stream to drink. She seemed in fine mettle after her invigorating ride. Muir was overjoyed at her improvement in health, and sprinted with youthful enthusiasm as Murray led us up a steep trail densely hedged with cacti, then down into the scenic rock-tumbled bed of the canyon.

Muir was more interested in this miracle nature growth [of palm trees] than in the excellent lunch Wanda had prepared. In answer to his questioning, Murray said: "No one knows their origin. They are believed to be hundreds of years old. The Indians regard them with reverence, and have woven many legends about them."

Returning, we circled around through the "Garden of Eden," where a few tumble-down shacks were all that remained of a fantastic dream of real estate promoters to develop and build a world-renowned city, even going so far as to run a street-car railway to connect their dream city with the railroad station ten miles distant. A long abandoned car half buried in sand, remained then as monumental evidence of the ill-fated project.

Our next picnic was held in Tahquitz Canyon beside a rainbow-misted waterfall, a gallant stream rushing down from the forested heights of Tahquitz mountain. The Indians, Murray informed us, believed this mountain to be the home of the devil, who, during an earthquake, would emerge in full regalia of stovepipe hat and tails and carry off their most beautiful maidens.

In the shadowy cool of twilight hours, Muir delighted in strolling through the meadow at the base of San Jacinto, along the stone-walled zanja which at that time supplied water for the Village and reservation. He'd stand in reverent silence beside the weather-scarred wooden crosses in the old cemetery. He found much of interest in studying Indian psychology when visiting the palm thatched fiesta hut on the reservation, where tribal feasts and religious ceremonies were held.

Wanda and Helen experienced many a thrill when bathing in the hot mineral spring that gurgled from unknown depths, its water so buoyant one had to cling to a wooden cross-beam to avoid popping up like a cork. The spring and rickety bath-house belonged to the Indians who charged twenty-five cents for a dip.

As a solution to Wanda's culinary difficulties Muir decided it would be a fine idea to leave the hotel and camp in one of the canyons during the remainder of their stay. Murray stubbornly opposed this plan, declaring that roughing it, sleeping on the ground, would never do for little Helen. Then, realizing Muir's mind was made up, that both Wanda and Helen were eager for a change, he suggested that Andreas Canyon, dense shaded with a running stream, and only three miles from the Village, would be an ideal location, and set about packing blankets, provisions, and pots and pans.

My father, T. P. Lukens, connected with the U.S. Division of Forestry, had arrived in response to an urgent telegram from Muir, requesting he join us in the outing. A young man employed by the Biological Survey in Washington, D.C., to collect desert specimens, had also arrived.

Old Marcus helped unload on the bank of a brave little stream that went singing through a tangle of wild grape vines, alders, cottonwoods, and a small isolated group of palms.

Immediately Muir stepped from the wagon, he was reverently, quietly in tune with his surroundings. For some time with hands clasped behind him—a characteristic posture—he studied the far-reaching vistas of sand wastes below us, where shadows and brilliant sunset colors mingled in kaleidoscopic confusion. Turning, he faced the canyon walls that soared to great height, where jumbled boulders gleamed like polished brass. Gazing at this nature phenomenon born ages ago, he remarked: "Definite evidence of glacial energy! I wish Murray was here with me. I'd prove to him..."

Meanwhile we spread blankets on the mattress-like layer of dry leaves, cleared space among the rocks for a camp fire, hung baskets of provisions to tree branches beyond reach of ants, and in a tin container anchored butter, eggs, bacon and cheese in the stream for refrigeration.

Six carefree days passed all too swiftly—evenings around the camp fire singing the old-time songs best loved by Muir, listening to his stories of travel and adventure, hearing my father tell of his work of reforesting our fire-denuded mountain slopes with young trees grown at the government station at Henniger Flats above Pasadena, while the "U.S. Bug Man," as the girls had dubbed him, recounted his trapping experiences, of feasting on woodchuck roast and rattlesnake fries.

Regarding clothes Muir was indifferent. Any old suit would do. Here on the desert he wore white linen or grey alpaca made from materials he'd bought in India. His one treasured garment was a long woolen bath robe splashed with gay-colored flowers. This he wore when chill evening winds came down from the high meadows. Having no worries about shaving, of the color of his neckties or the fit of his clothes, gave him leisure to enjoy nature, time to write the word-pictures of out-door beauty to be found in each and every chapter of his many books. In his self-effacement he eliminated the personal pronoun in his endless chain of anecdotes.

In contrast to his usual quiet calm, he did, one day, startle us with a blood-curdling yell, danced around and shook a big red ant out of his breeches instead of a centipede or scorpion he'd suspected was making a meal off his "hind leg," as he described his lower extremities. "That ant," he said with a chuckle, "knew I had no business here, so tried to scare me to death."

"To think," Wanda teased, "that a father of mine could be scared of a poor little ant."

He found many plants he'd met with in the deserts of Nevada and Utah while with the Geodetic Survey in 1876. He was greatly interested in studying Indian hieroglyphics on the rock walls of a nearby cave.

Muir was always first to get up in the morning, leaving quietly to avoid disturbing the rest of us, and climb to some rocky height to receive the benediction of the dawn. His was the wealth of the spirit, as it is with all great men.

The Runaway River

If character is destiny, geography is fate. That is, unless modified by an even more powerful force of dreaming that often ignoring reality has things going flat-out bust, but in the mathematics of such things sometimes resulting in phenomenal success.

The dream part in the settlement of the West was the old Biblical hope of making the desert "blossom as the rose." Time and again, that bright hope, flying in the face of nature's realities, was a dismal failure. Yet there were huge exceptions. In the early years of the twentieth century, engineers tapped the Colorado River, as geologist William P. Blake first had suggested, and sent irrigation water coursing across the desert sands into the bleak Imperial Valley west of Yuma. Settlers rushed in to claim an agricultural success that was near hilarious, beyond the dreams, even, of the wide-eyed developers. Then geography intervened. On his expedition of a half-century before, Blake had recognized that nature is not immutable. Crossing the desert, he saw that the Colorado River did not always follow the same old course southward into the Gulf of Mexico. Occasionally over geologic time, the great stream changed its own course when a buildup of silt at the river's delta reached a critical mass. That sent the river flowing in a radical new direction westward into the Colorado Desert, then northward to flood the low-lying area now known as the Salton Sea. Evidence of that was obvious, in the "bathtub rings" the ancient seas left behind when, once again, the river withdrew, returning to its former bed.

All that was forgotten, however, in the rambunctious success of the irrigated Imperial Valley—until geography reasserted itself. A year of unusually strong floods played tricks with that overnight achievement of the developers, sending the river, ironically following the new irrigation channel, racing once again westward in its ancient course. This time it did not speed across mere empty desert but inundated the vast fields of cantaloupes and destroyed the new towns to which they were giving birth. Once again in the history of mankind, the impossible was happening. Farmers and developers alike stood with mouths agape, seeing the miracle gutted before their very eyes.

Eventually, in a Herculean effort, the Southern Pacific Railroad managed to stop the wayward river and force it back into the channel it occupies today. The Imperial Valley was restored to its place as one of the richest agricultural phenomena in the world. Nevertheless, all this gives us pause. True, human beings achieve success largely through modifying nature to serve human purposes; however, it's difficult, given the titanic forces at work, and viewing the evidence of those bathtub rings we see today while driving along Highway 86, not to wonder how long this success will last before geography has its way once again, creating a vast sea in the middle of the Colorado Desert.

―᷍᷍᷍᷍᷍ **Remi A. Nadeau,**
   from *The Water Seekers*

O ut of the delta country below the border the floodwaters came hurtling into the valley through two ancient channels—the New River and the Alamo. At the north end the Salton Sea was rising seven inches a day, placing a salt refining works sixty feet under water by June 1906. Time after time the Southern Pacific found its tracks awash and hurriedly moved them to higher ground. Below the border its Mexican line was completely submerged for miles.

All at once the valley people discovered a new threat from the treacherous Colorado. As its volume rose to 70,000, then 100,000 second-feet, it began to gouge out more elbowroom in the channels. At every bend the silt-laden current struck angrily against the banks, undermining whole blocks of soft earth which cracked off and plunged into the roaring current.

Worse still, the flood in New River began to scour deeper into the bed itself. Starting at its mouth in Salton Sea, a cataract was formed in the stream bottom where the muddy water gouged into the silt. The cutting action against the lip of the waterfall forced it to move steadily backward and upstream, toward the Imperial farm settlements and border towns. Within a few days the cataract grew to twenty feet in height, at the same time widening the channel to massive proportions. If it reached the regular Colorado channel at the Mexican break, all hope of damming the madcap river would be lost.

Over on the Alamo channel the same appalling phenomenon had occurred. A waterfall was cutting southward at more than half a mile a day, and by early June was bearing down on the Southern Pacific railroad bridge east of Brawley on the Los Angeles line—the only remaining route out of the valley. Frantically the Imperial farmers turned to their ripening cantaloupe crops. If that destructive cataract destroyed the trestle before the melons could be harvested and shipped, financial ruin would be added to the threat of inundation.

On June 14, 1906, with the Alamo falls scarcely a day away from the bridge, every farm family in central Imperial Valley was in the field stripping the cantaloupe vines. From all directions a stream of wagons trundled into the railway station at Brawley, where busy packers loaded the melons into crates and filled the waiting boxcars. Next day, after working through a sleepless night, the people saw the last trainload pull out for the Alamo crossing. The cataract had reached the bridge, but Southern Pacific crewmen had braced it enough to stand the strain. Cautiously the final cars were shuttled over the torrent and sent safely northward to the Los Angeles market.

Farther south toward the Mexican break the rising floodwaters were even more threatening. Near El Centro the torrent broke through the levee of the Central Main Canal, putting the streets of Imperial town under water and drowning out the surrounding farmlands. Here again every family turned out—this time to fight the water itself. Crews of desperate men, working feverishly to dam the flood, threw sandbags and brush mattresses into the breach. When gunnysacks gave out, local merchants emptied flour and grain bags, and housewives sewed more out of any cloth available. After three days of battle they plugged the gap, forced the angry current back down the canal, and rescued most of the nearby farms.

At the border, where New River ran through the edge of Calexico and Mexicali, the monster was taking worse toll. With the river undercutting its banks and widening by the hour, it was soon threatening to engulf the very buildings of the towns. In Calexico the people threw up a sandbag levee and fought to maintain it against the flood. But in neighboring Mexicali, located on the very banks of the river, native families were already fleeing before the waters. By the last of June house after house was toppling into the current. As the river undercut its banks, great chunks of the soft ground broke off, carrying with them whatever structures they supported. Larger buildings were first undermined gradually, then, after teetering on the brink, would be shocked by a heavy wave and sent thundering into the maelstrom.

After the first excitement the townspeople turned to watch the river's advance with philosophical abandon. Standing near the edge of the bank, their view almost obscured by clouds of dust rising from the crash of earth, they watched with fascination while the brown serpent slowly devoured Mexicali.

With the Southern Pacific depot threatened, engineer Jack Carrillo hurried up from his losing fight to protect company tracks below the border; his first sight of the situation told him no human effort could save the town so long as the flood raged. From Los Angeles came H. V. Platt, general superintendent of S.P. lines from the coast to El Paso. Debarking at Calexico, he stroke across the line to find Carrillo lounging in the shade of an adobe wall, joining the rest of Mexicali in cool resignation. His nonchalance, even while the S.P. freight station was being undermined, infuriated the officious Platt.

"What the devil are you doing to stop this?" he demanded excitedly.

Carrillo lit a cigarette before answering. "Not a God damn thing. What do you suggest?"

A few moments later, while the S.P. superintendent watched helplessly, the building crumpled and slid over the bank. With a roar and a shower of water it struck the surface and floated onward in pieces.

13

The Wonderland: Ghosts at the Well

What would you expect of a defrocked Methodist minister cast out of his congregation as a result of a huge sexual scandal, who next ran his own Radiant Life Press, and at one point published a book called *The Story of Captain: The Horse with the Human Brain*? Who on top of that not only celebrated himself as a buoyant blend of Presbyterianism, Theosophy, and Buddhism, but also, mounting the soapbox for Southern California, loudly hailed the region's hygienic winds, whose beneficent electricity zapped germs right out of the air.

It is easy to see George Wharton James as the stereotypical Southern California kook, creating himself as he goes along and avoiding complete lunacy by hitching his wagon to an ascending star and becoming a barker of circus proportions, wild-eyed about his new home as an Edenic promise fulfilled. That would be an accurate assessment of James who, along with thousands of other unstable newcomers, managed to stay relatively sane by channeling his unpredictable energies into an effervescent boosterism wildly applauded by the public.

Fortunately, however, James was much more than that. If we can overlook the equine genius who tapped out "Nearer My God to Thee" with his musical hoof and generously wink past any number of the former reverend's strange effusions, we find a travel writer who also had the toughness to clap on his hat and sally forth into the wilderness of the desert and actually do the things he said he did. In essence, James, ever looking for new lands to extol for buyers of his books, took the growing and quite justifiable enthusiasm for Southern California's balmy coast and projected it eastward out over the mountains into the Colorado Desert. The result, if it came with a thrill on every page—sometimes two or three—nonetheless in its essence was accurate. The desert, where one might pick up obsidian arrowheads as one goes, even find a huge olla emerging from the sands for the taking, was a land with a haunting Indian past and, with bighorn sheep gazing down quizzically on the passing travelers, one with a vibrant present. It was just what the growing middle class, getting bored with their prosperity and yearning for romance, wanted to hear, and James gave them a surfeit of it. Few readers back in snowy Ohio or slushy Connecticut picking up James' desert work, backed by a prestigious publisher and presented in a handsome two-volume edition with hundreds of charming sketches by desert artist Carl Eytel, would not be convinced that they were indeed entering a Wonderland as they read through the pages—a word that after James was increasingly applied to a bright new region entering the nation's consciousness.

George Wharton James,
from *The Wonders of the Colorado Desert*

When spring comes and the happy note of the quail resounds in the valley, and the low, plaintive call of the wild dove is echoed from tree to tree, the Land of the Mesquite calls and we long to be in its embrace.

Where is this Mesquite Land, and what constitutes its charm? It is hard to tell to another the subtle sensations that compel one to affection, yet it seems that no one could see Mesquite Land in spring and not be enchanted by it. It is not a large country. It is merely the name we have given to that part of the Coachella Valley in the Colorado Desert that lies near the base of the Sierra San Jacinto. Properly the name might cover an immense region where the mesquite abounds, reaching south to the mouth of the Colorado River, north to the center of Nevada, and east into Apache Land.

In the very heart of Mesquite Land are the Indian villages of Torres, Martinez, Agua Dulce, and Alamos Bonitos. Many a mile have we tramped to and fro among the *kishes* and *samats* of these people. Torres is completely hidden in a dense thicket of mesquites. A lane of sturdy old trees, massive and gnarled like veteran oaks, leads us to a little adobe hut. We almost pass by ere we notice the form of a man inside, lying on the ground, a woman sitting by his side. We have come to the death-bed of one of the oldest of the Torres Indians, one who for many years has been chief of his people. The dying man speaks a little English, and as soon as he feels our sincere sympathy he opens his heart and speaks with touching sadness of his life. He tells of his people's coming here, in the long ago, and how, ever since he can remember, he has helped their descendants in their sickness and want, and rejoiced with them in their joys. "But now," he bursts forth, "all of them have left me, all! all! All have left me to die alone! Only my poor old wife remains with me. When I am dead they will cry and wail, but what will it matter?"

A week later a funeral takes place, and a sad old woman remains alone. There is a large funeral. Indians come from all parts of Mesquite Land and there is much show of lamenting and woe, but "what does it matter?"

Many deeply worn trails lead us from one mesquite thicket to another, and many a mile of fence is built by the Indians from its trunks and branches. The framework of many a *samat* is constructed of it, so that it affords homes and shelter against the sun and rain. In scores of places there is no pretense at building a framework. The tree is taken as it stands, the lower limbs lopped off to suit the convenience of the family, a few additional posts put in and the spaces filled up with brush, tules, arrowweed, and willows, and thus a primitive and reasonably permanent home is made.

Leaving Indio we are soon on the sandy road leading to Palm Springs. The feet of men and animals sink deeply and walking is hard. To the right and left of us are immense sand-dunes, looking like the white graves of men's ambitions. Here and there are mesquites completely buried in the sand, which has blown and drifted around them until nothing but the new shoots appear. To see these great balls of sand rise from the desert floor, bursting into rich foliage, is one of the always delightful surprises of the desert.

Here and there our eyes fall upon pieces of broken pottery, and the farther we go the more we see. If the casual traveler should become interested and seek more he might make a rich strike and find a whole bowl or olla buried in the sand long ago and now uncovered by the winds. Or he will probably pick up a few arrow-heads made of flint or obsidian, clearly telling of the days when the Indians hunted the deer, antelope, mountain sheep and other game in Mesquite Land with their primitive bows and arrows.

Here we are at Indian Well. It is a square, boarded-up well, with rope and buckets all complete, standing as one of the old landmarks on the old desert road, surrounded by hills covered with green mesquite.

Back of the road, on the south, a rotunda of saw-toothed mountains beckons to us. An old Indian had told us that there are caves in these low mountains in which the skeletons of men and women are to be found and that a great Indian village used to lie between them and the water of the prehistoric inland sea. We hunt around but can find neither caves nor skeletons. Only the broken pottery and arrow-heads speak of occupation in the past. The Indians believe the whole region to be haunted. They claim that in the night-time if a man dares to walk here a peculiar light will follow him, and he will hear voices singing and talking, but no human presence can be discovered. It is a lonely region and when night falls upon us, in spite of our disbelief in the stories of the Indians, we cannot deny that we are impressed by the spirit of loneliness which seems to possess it. Even the well, standing on the roadside, ready to cheer man and beast with its vivifying water, takes on the appearance of a scaffold, and we shudder in spite of ourselves.

14

Love along the Irrigation Ditches

If beauty is the handmaiden of wealth, the one lending the other a good deal of its aura, there can be a good number of other blithe figures in this entourage: patriotism, boy-meets-girl, and the happy belief in Progress blessing our late-Victorian ancestors. In *The Winning of Barbara Worth*, all these fine things come together in the perfect setting for the blending, the desert in the process of being reclaimed and coaxed into farms with mooing cows, yet still remaining the grand, mysterious desert which, for all its fructifying, always will be the limitless and mysterious desert, ever beautiful and desired, but ever beyond our grasp and ken. Just as is our heroine, the symbolic Barbara Worth.

All the boys want her, some of them not very nice boys. Others, supremely upright in their intentions, are manifestly virtuous, proven so because they are dedicated to the worthy cause of turning the desert into alfalfa fields and thus helping the nation achieve its Destiny. Oh, why can't one of them at last finally succeed in the parallel plot and help Barbara fructify, too? Yet virtue means far more than consummation, or so goes this rage novel of the desert. It is an intricate tale of feints, mistaken identities, and nuances freighted with huge import from a civilized period of meaningful gestures which in their delicacy are almost lost to us today; yet they were essential to the aura equally shared in that fictional time both by virginal Barbara Worth and the desert she loves. Or so the story goes.

Do not mourn this graciousness long gone or our own rude and unappreciative age. The ideal of Barbara Worth lives on! The book was so wildly popular that the heroine's name began popping up all over the map across the Colorado, from hotels and restaurants to tourist camps and saloons. Even today, long after that initial en-thusiasm has faded, you might wish to play a round or two at the Barbara Worth Golf Resort. It's not quite the same thing as engineer Willard Holmes imagining what it's like actually to hold Barbara's hand, but it's the best we can do in our brutish age.

Harold Bell Wright,
from *The Winning of Barbara Worth*

When Barbara had left the San Felipe trail and was riding toward the hills, the man's eyes were attracted by the moving spot on the Mesa and he stirred to take from the pocket of his coat a field glass, while at his movement the horned-toad and the lizard scurried to cover. Adjusting his glass he easily made out the figure of the girl on horseback, who was coming in his direction. He turned again to his study of the landscape, but later, when the horse and rider had drawn nearer, lifted his glass for another look. This time he did not turn away.

Rapidly, as Barbara drew nearer and nearer, the details of her dress and equipment became more distinct until the man with the glass could even make out the fringe on her gauntlets, the contour of her face and the color of her hair. When she stopped and turned to look over the desert below he forgot the scene that had so interested him and continued to gaze at her, until, as the girl turned her face in his direction and apparently looked straight at him, he dropped the glass in embarrassed confusion, forgetting for the instant that at that distance, with his gray and yellow clothing so matching the ground and rock, he would not be noticed. With a low chuckle at his absurd situation he recovered himself and again lifting the glass turned it upon Barbara, who was now riding swiftly toward the mouth of a little canyon that opened behind the hill where he sat.

Suddenly with an exclamation the young man sprang to his feet. The running horse had stumbled and fallen. After a few struggling efforts to rise the animal lay still. The girl did not move. With long, leaping strides the man plunged down the rough, steep side of the hill.

When Barbara slowly opened her eyes she was lying in the shadow of the canyon wall some distance from the spot where her horse had stumbled. Still dazed with the shock of her fall she looked slowly around, striving to collect her scattered senses. She knew the place but could not remember how she came there. And where was her horse—Pilot? And how came that canteen on the ground by her side? At this she sat up and looked around just in time to see a tall, gaunt, roughly-dressed figure coming toward her from the direction of the canyon mouth.

Instantly the girl reached for her gun. The holster was empty.

The man, quite close now, seeing the suggestive gesture, halted; then, coming nearer, silently held out her own pearl-handled revolver.

Still confused and acting upon the impulse of the moment before, Barbara caught the weapon from the out-stretched hand and in a flash covered the silent stranger.

Very deliberately the fellow drew back a few paces and stretched both hands high above his head.

"Who are you?" asked the girl sharply....

Barbara, seeing his embarrassment at her question, guessed a part of the reason and gently sought to relieve the situation. "I think we had better find my horse and start for home now," she said.

The thin, sun-tanned face of the surveyor was filled with sympathy as he replied: "I'm sorry, but your pony is down and out."

"Down and out! Pilot? Oh! You don't mean—You don't—"

Abe explained simply. "His leg was broken and he couldn't get up. There was nothing that could possibly be done for him. He was suffering so that I—It was for that I borrowed your gun...."

He had evidently ridden from the river, from his work. Did he know? No, she decided, he could not know yet. Then the quick thought came; he *must not know until*—until she herself should tell him. Quickly the young woman walked down the hill across the bridge toward the town.

Willard Holmes arrived at the hotel and, learning that Miss Worth was out, carried a chair to the arcade on the street to await her return. He had not waited long when a voice at his shoulder said with mock formality: "I believe this is Mr. Willard Holmes."

The engineer sprang to his feet. "Miss Worth! They told me that you were out. I was sitting here waiting for you."

"I was out when you arrived," she confessed; "but I saw you coming and hurried back pronto. I knew you had just left the river, you see. And of course," she added, as though that explained her eagerness to see him, "I wanted to hear the latest news from the work."

"There is no news," he answered as though dismissing the matter finally.

"And may I ask what brings you to Barba?"

He looked at her steadily. "You brought me to Barba."

"I?"

"Yes—you. I stopped in Republic on my way back from the city the evening of the day you left. I was forced to go on to the river, but took the first opportunity to ride out here, for I understood you expected to be in Barba several days. Surely you know why I have come. The work I stayed in the Basin to do is finished. I have another offer from the S. & C. which, if I accept, will keep me here for several years. I have come to you with it as I came with the other. What shall I do? Please don't pretend that you don't understand me."

The direct forcefulness of the man almost made Barbara forget the little plan she had arranged on her way to the hotel to meet him. "I won't pretend, Mr. Holmes," she answered seriously. "But—will you go with me for a little ride into the desert?"

Her words recalled to his mind instantly their first meeting in Rubio City, but Holmes was not astonished now. The invitation coming from Barbara under the circumstances seemed the most natural thing in the world.

The young woman went to her room to make ready while the engineer brought the horses, and in a very few minutes they had crossed the river and were following the old San Felipe trail toward the sand hills.

Very few words passed between them until they reached the great drift that had held so long its secret. Leaving the horses at Barbara's request, they climbed the steep sides of the great sand mound. From the top they could see on every hand the many miles of The King's Basin country—from Lone Mountain at the end of the delta dam to the snow-capped sentinels of San Antonio Pass; and from the sky line of the Mesa and the low hills on the east to No Man's Mountain and the bold wall of the Coast Range that shuts out the beautiful country on the west.

The soft, many-colored veils and scarfs of the desert with the gold of the sand hills, the purple of the mountains, the gray and green of the desert vegetation, with the ragged patches of dun plain, were all there still as when Willard Holmes had first looked upon it, for the work of Reclamation was still far from finished.

But there was more in Barbara's Desert now than pictures woven magically in the air. There were beautiful scenes of farms with houses and barns and fences and stacks, with cattle and horses in the pastures, and fields of growing grain, the dark green of alfalfa, with threads and lines and spots of water that, under the flood of white light from the wide sky, shone in the distance like gleaming silver. Barbara and the engineer could even distinguish the little towns of Republic and Frontera, with Barba nearby; and even as they looked they marked the tall column of smoke from a locomotive on the S. & C. moving toward the crossing of the old San Felipe trail, and on the King's Basin Central another, coming toward the town on Dry River where once beside a dry water hole a woman lay dead with an empty canteen by her side.

Willard Holmes drew a long breath.

"You like my Desert?" asked the young woman softly, coming closer to his side—so close that he felt her presence as clearly as he felt the presence of the spirit that lives in the desert itself.

"Like it!" he repeated, turning toward her. "It is my desert now; mine as well as yours. Oh, Barbara! Barbara! I have learned the language of your land. Must I leave it now? Won't you tell me to stay?"

He held out his hands to her, but she drew back a little from his eagerness. "Wait. I must know something first before I can answer."

He looked at her questioningly. "What must you know, Barbara?"

"Did you ever hear the story of what happened here in these very sand hills? Do you know that I am not the daughter of Jefferson Worth?"

"Yes," he answered gravely. "I know that Mr. Worth is not your own father, but I did not know that this was the scene of the tragedy."

"And you understand that I am nameless; that no one knows my parentage? That there may even be Mexican or Indian blood in my veins? You understand—you realize all that?"

He started toward her almost roughly. "Yes, I understand all that, but I care only that you are Barbara. I know only that I want you—you, Barbara!"

"But your family—Mr. Greenfield—your friends back home—think what it means to them. Can you afford—"

"Barbara" he cried. "Stop! Why are you saying these things? Listen to me. Don't you *know* that I love you? Don't you know that nothing else matters? Your Desert has taught me many things, dear, but nothing so great as this—that I want you and that nothing else matters. I want you for my wife."

"But you said once that you would never marry me," persisted the young woman. "What has changed you?"

"*I* said that I would never marry you? *I* said *that*? That cannot be, Barbara; you are mistaken."

She shook her head. "That is what you said. I heard you myself. You told Mr. Greenfield at my house that morning he came to see you when you were hurt. I—I—the door into the dining room was open and I heard."

The light of quick understanding broke over the engineer's face. "And you heard what Uncle Jim said to me? But Barbara, didn't you hear the reason I gave him for saying that I would not marry you?"

"I—I couldn't hear anything after that," she said simply.

At her confession the man's strong face shone with triumph. "Listen, dear, I told Uncle Jim I would never marry you because you loved someone else and that there was no chance for me."

Barbara's brown eyes opened wide. "You thought that?"

"Yes. I thought you loved Abe Lee."

"Why—why I *do* love Abe."

The man laughed. "Of course you do; but I thought you loved him as I wanted you to love me; don't you understand?"

"Oh-h!" The exclamation was a confession, an explanation and an expression of complete understanding. "But that"—she added as she went to him—"that *could not be*."

And then—

But Barbara's words, rightly understood, mark the end of my story.

Rarely is it given in the story of life, to those who work greatly or love greatly, to gather the fruit of their toil or passion. But it is given those others, perhaps—those for whom it could not be—to know a happiness greater, it may be, than the joy of possession.

15

A Treacherous Camel at the Train Station

Despite the sweetness and light giving birth to the airy and artistic Colorado Desert we'd like to imagine, the economics of a place forms its very basis, whatever the striving toward a desired aesthetic atmosphere. Ignoring sandstorms, earthquakes, and the lack of water, the booster mentality sweeping coastal Southern California almost inevitably swept out even into the desert. From those early days, the conflict has grown. Should such a unique place as Palm Springs remain a special enclave for the sensitive few, or was it yet another opportunity to turn nature into a cash register? Given the forces at work, the question was moot, the result in golf courses and glittering shopping malls perhaps unavoidable. Nonetheless, we can derive some chuckles from the bizarre guises greed can assume, perhaps no more bizarre, come to think of it, than some of the come-ons of today.

The nearest train stop to Palm Springs, by the way, was a tiny place out in the sand dunes about six miles north of the village. It's still there, moved down the tracks a bit and well worth a visit, for lacking even an attendant, the modern version is just as bewildering (even sans camel) in its weird desolation as it was back in the heyday of promoter McCallum.

~~~ **Mary Jo Churchwell,**
    from *Palm Springs: The Landscape, the History, the Lore*

But back to McCallum and his colony to be—Palm Valley it was now grandly called. He had a water supply, a general store, a post office, and a hotel. He was on a roll, burning up body and soul with plans: The

McCallum Land Auction Show. The clever man had worked it all out. He had seen to the distribution of flyers—Palm Valley, the Land of Purple Night and Golden Morning … Earliest Fruit Region in the State … Perpetual Water Rights. He had arranged for a special Southern Pacific excursion train to conduct the speculative hordes to the site. Done and done. Except that a misunderstanding on the part of railroad employees had the train leaving Los Angeles ahead of the advertised time. Hence the attendance from there was regrettably small. But this was a minor matter.

McCallum just didn't know when to quit! Had you descended from the train that auction day, first thing you would have noticed was his promotional stunt: the Indian Willie Marcus tricked out in Arabian robes, a heap of cloth piled on his head. Having thus been reduced, in the space of one event, to the level of sideshow freak at a circus, Marcus was trying his cheerful best to give the Seven Palms Station a weird and faraway association with the Promised Land. The camel he was perched upon in no way went unnoticed. In all his life, Marcus had probably never seen such a creature, let alone ridden one. Yet there it was beneath him, big boned and firmly humped, smelly and treacherously alive—although like the robes and turban, it had seen better days.

16

Out of Revolutionary Mexico: The Three Wealthy White Sisters

In one of those intricate phenomena more alchemical than measurable, Palm Springs manages to keep one foot in its inviting village past. Symbolic of this small-town warmth is the house of Cornelia White, preserved with its delicate artwork and quaint furnishings on the Village Green, an open space of grass graced by a Mexican fountain in the very heart of downtown. Here, one steps into an earlier, welcoming world, yet despite our longings for easy sentiment, one with its own set of telling complexities.

As we've seen, without the allure of mining bonanzas or the inevitable riff-raff moved by exploitation that comes with a railroad, people came to Palm Springs because they appreciated the loveliness of that particular place. There, far from that busyness that was rapidly overwhelming Southern California, they wanted to fulfill themselves, to seek, as we'd put it today, their personal growth. That meant, if you will, a healthy inflow of eccentrics, artists, writers, and photographers, often without pretension and pleased to live and let live as long as they could pursue their lives according to their own lights. Surely not all of them had the wealth of the three White sisters, originally from a powerful banking family of Utica, New York. Wealth, of course, did count for much, even in the leveling desert, allowing Cornelia White to romp off on long cattle drives with the local ranchers, while her sister Florilla, a medical doctor, strode the village streets in jodhpurs and pith helmet.

Yet there was a wonderful conventionality among the waywardness that fueled these refugees from the Mexican Revolution. As we walk through Cornelia's tiny but intimate home described below, we can imagine the slight but feisty woman devotedly studying her collection of Bibles as she drinks hot chocolate or Dr. Florilla in social obligation pitching in to comfort the distressed in the influenza epidemic of 1918, which reached out even to isolated desert communities. In such things lie true character. Evidence of this benefits us all today beyond the charms of Cornelia's preserved home, for in 1947 Cornelia donated the land for what has grown into Palm Springs' exceptional Art Museum.

Tantalizingly, some things are revealed while others remain shrouded in mystery, just as one might expect of sisters chastened in the crucible of revolution. There was yet a third White sister of Palm Springs, Isabel. The main thing we know about her was that she married the then penurious, but now famed, writer J. Smeaton Chase. It was a winter romance for both of them. Other than that, despite earnest pursuit, I have been unable to find out much more about this third gracious lady. Sometimes, however, the stymied scholar quits in joy. From the little correspondence that survives, it seems that, despite the economic disparity, Mr. and Mrs. Chase, enduring plaguing illnesses, were devoted to each other in the brief years of a marriage cut short by the husband's early death. Something also to ponder while touching the past at the Village Green.

～ Mary Jo Churchwell,
from *Palm Springs: The Landscape, the History, the Lore*

First-time visitors to the Little House (as we affectionately call it) enter with a sense of surprise and delight as they take in the cozy domesticity of the four small rooms, where Cornelia White closed out her days. Here is Miss Cornelia's gingerbread kitchen, the wood-burning stove, the pitcher pump, the butter mold, the "sad" iron, the meat grinder, and all sorts of cast iron cookware, everything in sight and ready to use, so unlike modern kitchens where everything is hidden in artfully designed cabinets. Here is Miss Cornelia's dining room, the four brocade-seated chairs waiting for her guests, the polished Duncan Fife table in whose center a vase with painted grape leaves holds a dainty spray of yellow asters, the year's brittle last blooms. Here is her bedroom, the old cherry-wood four-poster with flowers and leaves carved into the headboard, the hand-stitched quilt smelling of crushed lavender. Here is her living room, the braided rugs, the lace curtains, the faded settee wearing its doilies like snowflakes, the rolltop desk with the curved front that slides back to reveal useful-looking drawers and pigeonholes, the rocking chair where she read in the evening over a mug of hot chocolate. The curators have cleaned the lamps, snipped the wicks, and set out her Bibles.

On the east wall, framed in wood, is a painted Miss Cornelia, a wren of a woman, fine-boned, fine-skinned, her gray hair pulled back from a central parting to form an untidy bun. Even though the artistry is flat and amateur—simply dabs and splashes of color—it nonetheless captures the headstrong eyes, the determined set of the unrouged lips. So who was Miss Cornelia? The picture I have developed is a collage of images pieced together from the files our local historical society labors to keep in good repair. What I have found is something of a square peg, a woman who found her true identity in fringed jackets, riding britches, and the kind of jungle helmet that the adventurous wear. And indeed, in this era of stylishly dressed women, of high lace collars, floor-dragging petticoats, and preposterous, air-borne hats, Cornelia had an adventurous spirit, a story worth telling.

She was a child on a family farm in western New York State. After successfully defending herself against ten boisterous siblings, eighteen-year-old Cornelia toured Europe for a year, perhaps looking for a place of her own. She became one well-traveled woman. She went to the Pacific Northwest with a mining expedition. She went to the Arctic with her brother. She went to North Dakota and taught home economics, carpentry, and plumbing at the university there. And even that wasn't the end of it. Except that her next adventure, an undertaking of no small proportions, would be neither her best nor her wisest.

Because frankly, 1912 was not a good time to be packing off to Mexico, even though it seemed like all of North Dakota was doing just that. Picking up bag and baggage, Cornelia joined the migration amid the distraction of the Mexican Revolution, that is to say, while Mexico was being ravished by a number of different armies, those of Pancho Villa and Emiliano Zapata contributing more than their fair share.

Upon landing in Sinaloa, Cornelia settled down on a vast tract of wilderness that North Dakota Senator William Lemke had subdivided twenty years earlier. Here, among succeeding waves of revolution, a colony of perhaps two thousand Americans were trying to create a new social, economic, and political destiny for themselves. Invariably there would be a fragile interlude of peace; then the customary violence would begin again, making things impossible. Palm Springs pioneer Carl Lykken, who was also there at Sinaloa, gives us a glimpse of what it was like, a few short paragraphs of what could have been a darn good yarn.

Carl and Cornelia had known each other from the beginning. Having met at the University of North Dakota, they renewed their acquaintance in Lemke's colony, a tract that Carl himself had surveyed and mapped. "It was beautiful country," he told an interviewer, meaning Sinaloa. "And you can imagine how anyone from North Dakota would like that climate down there—it was like heaven."

In June 1913 the rebels took Durango, forcing thousands of panicky Americans to flee Mexico for good. Very few remained, Carl and Cornelia among them, huddled in their adobe homes, in a stillness of suspense. Then they, too, decided they had seen enough. "When the revolutionists stole all our horses, our only means of transportation, we knew it was time to get out and stay out."

All told, the little band of refugees numbered six: Carl Lykken, Cornelia White, Cornelia's sister Florilla White, and three other die-hard adventurers. It was eighty miles by handcar to safety, one jump ahead of the devil. And they didn't dawdle for a moment. "They'd burned all the bridges and there were no trains. We had a rough time getting our handcar over some of those places. The ties were all burned away, only the rails were left. We'd give the car a good shove and get over it."

Through the second night they crept, everybody taking turns pumping, convincing themselves that they did, too, know where they were going. The country had become so notorious a place for bandits, men who blandly shot people in the head, that no one in the party was surprised when they were flagged down and searched, their every bundle prodded and poked. And no one could believe their luck when they were sent on their way. Shortly after they reached the American transport ship waiting in Mazatlan—at which point they surely thanked God *that* was over— Sinaloa fell to the revolutionists.

Adios, Old Mexico. Done, but not forgotten. Although the White sisters, both on the verge of confirmed spinsterhood, could endure no more chaos and revolution, frontier life had not lost its appeal. After a hurried exit from San Diego, they migrated to Palm Springs, an obscure little village that Florilla had discovered quite by chance the year before. The place was wonderful, more than wonderful: the shifting light and color of the mountains, the canyons inviting adventure and exploration, the inexhaustible space, the ease and openness of life unconfined in gossipy parlors. If you lived in San Diego or Los Angeles, you had to fit yourself to the demands of your neighbors. You had to play by the rules. Here you were free to arrange the village snug around you, like a blanket. You could lead the good life, that is, your own life. It was no more complicated than that.

If Mexico was Paradise lost, then Palm Springs was Paradise regained. Luckily, the White sisters arrived long after Welwood Murray had decided to retire from the hotel business. For ten thousand dollars, they bought the Palm Springs Hotel. And while they were at it, they invited Carl Lykken, then working in Los Angeles, to share their place in the sun. "I accepted the invitation and never left."

Miss Cornelia's little house shares the Village Green with the venerable adobe home (venerable by Southern California standards) of John Guthrie McCallum, he who figures so conspicuously in the founding of Palm Springs. Brick by brick the adobe was dismantled by bare hands, moved from its original site in the Tennis Club area, and rebuilt with precision into the modest headquarters of the Palm Springs Historical Society, where, between the hours of ten and four, you are welcome to wander around for nothing more than a small admission charge and your signature in the visitors book.

Barbara Worth on the Rampage

Perhaps nihilist John C. Van Dyke was right: All is illusion. It turns out that those peaks and dunes and grand desert sweeps we observe with awe from a roadside vista, seemingly forever there and the very model of ancient stability before us, are but like the waves and troughs of the sea frozen in the frame of a movie. We blink, the movie begins again, and all before us starts to flow as it always has through the geologic ages.

If the fictional Barbara Worth is a Virgin Mary figure, a symbol of a beneficent desert that is all good things to all men of good will, what is the actual, rather than the fictively imagined, desert, really like? It turns out that at the core she is one rough gal, even tumultuous when she gets it into her head to throw a tantrum. Putting aside the obvious, that with her heat, dryness, scorpions, floods, and cactus spines she is no lover of men, so harsh, in fact, that desert Indians likely fled into the arid lands as a radical solution to saving their own skins from more powerful tribes bent on killing them, on top of that the desert is a woman of rambunctious movement, a fact you sometimes can witness yourself by comparing an old photograph of a landscape with the present scene. Things may be similar, but perhaps cliffs have fallen, boulders tumbled down. The earth has been in motion.

Violently so. If this were a slow process, few people would notice. But Barbara Worth as real desert is a woman who lies there in a torpid state for years, then, as the earth's tectonic plates shift, she writhes into paroxysm.

These upheavals likely made little difference to the Indians, who lived in brush huts and had no more than the bejeezies scared out of them in a sharp reminder that old Tahquitz was at it again. But in a society with a complex and fragile infrastructure of pipelines, aqueducts, and railroad tracks rather casually laid over the lace of faults running under the Colorado Desert, this can spell disaster. The earth has not moved today, and for that we have faith that it will not move tomorrow. It is a naive, misplaced faith. One need not be an alarmist to recognize that disastrous earthquakes have riven California in the past, as some of us have experienced; and we need not have the confirmation of the scientists who study such things to know that worse rendings of the earth lie in the future of the Colorado Desert—likely, given the statistics of it, not far in the future.

The day is coming, as it already has come to other parts of California, when trains will leap off tracks, freeway overpasses will dissolve into clouds of pulverized concrete, and homeowners will stand for their last few seconds absolutely astounded as their houses collapse around them.

Even the "magnificent new" Barbara Worth Hotel has felt that touch.

⁓⁓⁓ "Imperial Earthquake, Million Damage Done"

El Centro. June 22—Rocked in a succession of severe temblors practically every business building in El Centro was damaged tonight. The loss is estimated over $1,000,000. Although roofs fell and walls crumbled into rooms filled with people not one fatality resulted. Almost simultaneously with the first shock fire broke out to add to the roll of destruction.

Calexico, Cal., and Mexicali, Mex., on the international boundary, were also hit by the earthquake that began a little after 8 o'clock this evening. In Mexicali from ten to fifteen lives are reported to have been lost and a score or more persons injured. Calexico and Mexicali probably suffered worse than El Centro.

As far as can be learned, the shocks were severest down at the border and below the border and grew less and less the farther north it came, so that Calipatria and Niland appear to have been injured slightly; less than the towns in the south end of the valley.

The earthquake extended all the way from San Diego, Cal., to Yuma, Ariz.

At midnight El Centro is a darkened city. On either side of the business streets are ruined buildings, some completely razed, others opened by gaping holes. Broken glass of the display windows covers the sidewalks. In the gutter are the bricks and debris fallen from above. The streets are closed to automobiles, and pedestrians are warned to keep in the center of the street.

On the lawns in the residence district are the cots of residents with only the sky as the roof. In the industrial district the firemen are still fighting a fire.

The first shock came at 8:05. It was slow and prolonged. A moment later came a short and sharp temblor. Those outside heard a warning rumble, then the shocks, immediately followed by an explosion in the warehouse of the Delta Mercantile Company which lighted the entire countryside.

In the moving picture theaters a small panic ensued yet singularly no serious injury resulted. In the magnificent new Barbara Worth Hotel the glass and plaster crashed down. In the Baldridge drug store, the west side of the Security Savings building, a two-story structure caved into the drug store filled with people. All raced to the street. Every building was disgorging similarly. In the residences, dishes, cupboards and all movable furniture was tumbled down. In the stores shelves were dumped down, roofs caved, sides fell out and through the whole mass to the center of the street rushed inmates.

The interests of W. F. Holt are badly damaged. The Holton Power Company is damaged, one of the new gas tanks is leaning similarly to the Tower of Pisa. The Holt Ice plant is cracked. The side of the Holt plant is cracked open. The building of the Imperial Valley Baking Company, another Holt enterprise, is demolished. The warehouse of the Globe Mills, full of sacks of barley, burst its sides and the roof sagged. The Masonic Temple building is opened so that one may see through the roof and part of the floor having fallen.

The Calexico Cotton and Oil Company building is a wreck, the brick buildings of the Broadway Garage and Hermon Brothers buildings were shaken out. The roofs of the local newspaper buildings caved in and there is not a building but what received some damage.

With the first temblor attaches [*sic*] of the Sheriff's office rushed out into the open. Some of the walls about it were falling. Fearing for the safety of the jail, an old two-story brick structure, the deputies took out the prisoners under guard and transferred them to the City Jail, a safer building. Five chose to remain behind. Immediately following the first shocks Sheriff Meadows organized an armed guard. Five men were arrested for loitering. The guard is on all night.

In passing through the Courthouse, Mrs. Mary Smith, matron of the jail, was struck by a brick.

At Brawley the High School was slightly damaged. At Imperial one side of the McHenry Theater is leaning inward. It is reported here that the Globe Mills warehouse at Calipatria burned.

In Calexico the Daum Building collapsed, and every window in the town was broken. The City Trustees were in session in the Masonic Temple, and, when the earthquake began rocking the building they all rushed into the street. This building was badly damaged and will have to be entirely re-plastered.

At Heber the First National Bank and the Heber Hotel buildings were badly cracked. A moving-picture house was nearly totally wrecked, and Pearl Emery, one of the spectators, suffered a broken foot in the scramble to the street.

Just outside of Heber, on the ranch of L. A. Morgan, a wealthy capitalist, a lamp was overturned in the Morgan residence and the house was entirely consumed. The home of John Setta, near by, fell to the ground, but the occupants, as if by a miracle, all escaped injury.

In Mexicali a panic prevailed. Gamblers and the women who make up the greater portion of the population of the place rushed to the streets. The gambling-houses were deserted like magic and piles of gold were left on the tables, to be rocked off and mixed up with the debris of the buildings.

Most of the houses in Mexicali are of flimsy construction and offered but little resistance to the wavering earth. The soldiers on duty there were quickly assembled and martial law was declared. This had the effect of preventing anyone from crossing the American line, and tonight it is impossible to tell just how bad the place was hit. Reports, however, state that from ten to fifteen persons were killed and more than a score injured.

The temblor did no damage north of El Centro. Brawley felt it, but indistinctly. San Diego also felt two shocks, but no damage was done there. The first shock occurred at 8:05 and lasted about forty-five seconds. The second came about an hour later, but was less severe.

In this city the lights were all extinguished a second or two after the first shock, due to the breaking of the power lines to the Holton powerhouse. Every telegraph and telephone line into the city was torn down, and communication with the outside world was broken off for more than two hours.

One feature is the absence of any reports of breaks in the great levee system of the valley. These levees extend throughout the entire agricultural districts, or practically from Niland on the north, far below the Mexican line, but no one has reported any damage to them.

San Diego. June 22—An earthquake shock at 8:02 p.m. and another at 8:58 p.m. shook the china on the shelves of San Diego households and shook up the town generally, but did no damage. Reports here are that the quake hit the Imperial Valley hard. All communication between here and Imperial Valley was cut off after the first shock.

El Centro. June 22—At 2 o'clock this morning small shocks are still being felt. They have continued at sporadic intervals since the first shock. With each, persons who have ventured into buildings rush out. Those persons who slept in rooming-houses are stretched on the sidewalks tonight. Those in the residence section are sleeping out on cots. A small crowd is walking the streets.

San Bernardino. June 22—Two slight but distinct earthquake shocks were experienced here tonight after 9 o'clock, following the reported damage as the result of the temblor at El Centro. The Pacific Telephone and Telegraph Company, which sustained considerable damage at El Centro, will send a force from this city tonight to aid in repair work.

Calexico. June 23. 1 a.m. (from the manager of the Western Union office)—Martial law has been declared in Calexico and Mexicali. All is quiet and very few people are out. There was a veritable reign of terror from 8 p.m. to midnight.

American cavalry regulars are encamped here and patrolling the streets to prevent looting. Mexicali is being cared for by Villa troops. It is reported that one man across the border has been shot when caught looting.

Information from Mexicali is very meager, but the first refugees to arrive across the line stated to me personally that there were no less than twelve persons dead in Mexicali and many injured. I personally saw a child very badly hurt on this side of the line.

All brick buildings are deserted and most of them are in ruins or badly cracked. Two houses were destroyed by fire here. One business building was gutted. Hundreds of persons are sleeping in the open tonight.

18

A Desert Village

As seen in the introduction, when compared to the raw, ramshackle mining and railroad clusters typifying early desert towns, Palm Springs was unique.

There's nothing writer J. Smeaton Chase loved more than to return from one of his exhausting desert treks at evening, clomping on a weary Kaweah up the darkening, tree-covered lanes into his familiar village as in the cottages of fellow contemplative folks the lanterns winked on. No doubt, Chase's portrait here in sepia is somewhat idealized. Nonetheless, he helps us understand. Combining the charms of an English country village with the intimacy of a small college campus and the mystery of the desert, no wonder Palm Springs tugged at the heartstrings of creative and sensitive people as a refuge from the rushing world.

J. Smeaton Chase,
from *Our Araby: Palm Springs and the Garden of the Sun*

Village is a pretty word, though ambitious settlements are keen to disclaim the implied rusticity and to graduate into the rank of town or city. Palm Springs has no such aims, and is well content to remain far down the list in census returns. We decline to take part in the race for Improvements, and are (so we feel, anyway) wise enough to know when we are well off. Rural Free Delivery does not entice us: we prefer the daily gathering at the store at mail-time, Indians and whites together, where we can count on catching Miguel or Romualda if we wish to hire a pony or get the washing done. Electric lights? No thanks: somehow nothing seems to us so homelike for the dinner-table as shaded candles, or for fireside reading a good kerosene lamp: while if we want to call on a neighbor after dark, we find that a lantern sheds light where you need it instead of illuminating mainly the upper air. To us cement sidewalks would be a calamity: we may be dusty, but dust is natural and we prefer it. After all, the pepper- or cottonwood-shaded streets of our Garden of the Sun are really only country lanes, and who wants a country lane cemented? In fact, a little mistake was made when they were named. Cottonwood Row would have been better than Indian Avenue, and Hot Springs Lane than the commonplace Spring Street.

The Hot Spring is the outstanding natural feature of our village, though not so natural as when one took one's bath in the rickety cabin which antedated the present solid little bath-house. However, the Spring itself is as natural, no doubt, as any time this five or ten thousand years: and you may get as weird a sensation in taking your bath, and as healthful a result afterwards, as bygone generations of Cahuillas have enjoyed. The water, which is just comfortably hot and contains mineral elements which render it remarkably curative, comes up mingled with quantities of very fine sand. You may bask in the clear water on the surface of the pool, or, if you want all the fun you can get for your money, you may lower yourself into the very mouth of the spring where the mixture comes gurgling up. This will yield you (especially at night and by candle-light) a novel and somewhat shuddery experience, though one absolutely without risk; and you will come forth with a sense of fitness and fineness all over to which only a patent medicine advertisement writer of high attainment could possibly do justice.

Our village is bisected by the Reservation line, which thus makes a geographical division of the population. Only geographical, though, for, fortunately, there has never been anything but complete harmony between whites and Indians. Something more will be said about the Indians later: here I will only remark that I, for one, could not wish for better neighbors than our Indians: I should be pleased, indeed, to feel sure that they could say as much for us. They are but few in number, forty or fifty, for the Cahuillas are scattered in small *rancherias* over a wide territory. The white population is variable. In winter and spring, when the "Standing Room Only" sign hangs out, there may be a total of two hundred or more residents and visitors (the latter much the more numerous): in the hot months residents may number a dozen or two and visitors there are none. In desert phrase, the whites have "gone inside" (i.e., to the coast), an odd turn of speech but one quite appropriate to the point of view of the man of Big Spaces—"inside" where one is shut in and boxed up. You will understand when you have lived a little while in Our Araby.

For so small a place, the number of people who have fallen under the charm of Palm Springs, and their variety of class and kind, are rather surprising. You would agree as to the latter point if I were to begin to mention names. Wealth and fashion, as such, are not much attracted to our village: Palm Beach, not Palm Springs, is their mark: but among the fraternity of brains the word has passed about, and persons of mark are ever finding their way here, returning again and again, and bringing or sending others. But then, the importance of persons of mark in any community is apt to be overestimated; the important thing is the general quality, the average. The average with us is automatically raised by the total absence of any hooligan element, such as is sometimes in evidence on the sands of the sea-shore. To that class the sands of Our Araby do not appeal. On the other hand, the scientists, writers, painters, musicians, in fact, all kinds of people who love quiet, thoughtful things and whose work or enjoyment lies in natural instead of artificial fields, come and share with us the wholesome pleasures and interests that are inherent in a clean, new, unspoiled bit of this wonderful old world.

So much for the people. The village itself is a place of two or three score of unpretentious cottages scattered along half a dozen palm- and pepper-shaded streets. We don't run much to lawns and formal gardens: we live in the desert because we like it, hence we don't care to shut ourselves away in little citified enclosures. But the two or three old places which formed the nucleus of the settlement are bowers of bloom and umbrageous greenery. Gray old fig trees lean out over the sidewalk, while oranges, dates, grapefruit, lemons, and trees of other sorts for fruit or ornament flourish in tribute to the memory of that wise old Scotsman and pioneer, Doctor Welwood Murray, who had the courage to plant and the patience to rear them in the teeth of horticultural disabilities.

There remain to be mentioned our stores, inns, school, and church. Of these it is enough to say that they are well up to what would be expected in a community such as ours: though one of the inns might fairly object that this statement comes short of doing it justice. There are, further, a minute Public Library, housed in a quaint little hutch of adobe, which, half a century ago, was the Stage Station, and a tasteful Rest-house raised as a memorial to the old Scottish doctor, named above, who may fairly be termed the patriarch, well nigh the founder, of our village.

19

A Desert Saint—With Cracks: Carl Eytel

Rarely do artists live up to the personal lives we create for them. Their work may lift our spirits by teaching us to see the world in bright, new ways, but upon investigation artists often turn out to be just as grasping and mean-spirited as the rest of us—and sometimes more so.

The exception, as the first selection below maintains, was desert artist Carl Eytel. Without resorting to the crutch of sentimentalism, his canvases project the hint of a mysterious presence behind the desert palms and dunes he painted. Personally, he was the genuine item, a kindly man and a tough desert rat. He lived in a shack on what now are the grounds of Palm Springs' upscale Tennis Club, selling his paintings (now worth thousands of dollars) for a pittance to tourists and riding his horse, Billy, sometimes for hundreds of miles clear to the Hopi Pueblos of Arizona, returning from his excursions filled with ideas for still more paintings.

And yet, even the saint-like artist had his cracks. Fortunately for us, he was a gossip and somewhat of a churl—at least when he was writing his good friend and fellow desert rat Edmund C. Jaeger. Then, Carl Eytel's pen sails down the page, the threadbare artist unburdening himself of his melancholy and in the course of things giving us valuable insights into the dynamics behind the idyllic surface of life in the village of Palm Springs. His letters also reveal the intimate connections, sometimes endearing, sometimes acidic, among the village's residents. Irrefutable are the bonds that developed among the pioneer band of artists and writers best seen in the happy triumvirate of Eytel, Jaeger, and J. Smeaton Chase. Yet even this brotherhood had its rocky course. Clearly, Eytel became self-righteous about his poverty, and this began to fester. During World War I, the English-born Chase became a lightning rod for the frustrations of German-born Eytel. The Englishman, Eytel carps to Jaeger, has married into the wealthy white family to solve the problem of his own poverty. Eytel should have looked in the mirror; he seems to have forgotten that his own affections had been rejected by the daughter of another well-off local family. Yet it comes down to this. To his credit, Eytel eventually overcame much of his animosity toward Chase. In the meantime, we see that even mild-mannered and talented saints can have swampy places in their souls harboring nasty, if telling, jealousies.

In transcribing the letters below, for ease of reading I have corrected a few obvious errors, as in spelling, but in the main have retained the flavor of the letters and left them stand as written.

Elwood Lloyd,
from "Of Such As These Is the Spirit of the Desert"

One time I asked Carl Eytel why he stayed so many years in the Palm Springs area. He replied: "Just so I may learn to paint, some time, one tiny bit of its spirit, its peace."

Almost 40 years have come and gone since Carl taught me the first of many important lessons. It was in Tahquitz canyon, where he wanted to show me the hidden waterfall. The floor of the canyon was, and still is, covered with great boulders.

In those days there were many wildlife denizens of the desert in the neighborhood of Palm Springs. The little spotted skunks were particularly plentiful. They were playing and frolicking in and out around the boulders over which we climbed. Those were the days when I thought hunting of wild things was a prime sport, and considered a pistol as necessary equipment for a rural hike.

One of the little spotted skunks ran into a tiny opening between two great boulders. I crouched down, pulled my pistol from its holster, aimed carefully, and fired. Then I called, "Come here! Look! A clean hit! I got him!"

Carl slowly bent down on his knees and peered into the crevice. Then, over his shoulder, said to me, "Yes. You did. What will you do with it?"

"Nothing," I answered. "There isn't anything I can do. Those rocks are too big to move. I couldn't get at it even if I wanted to try. I was shooting just for practice."

"So-o," mused Carl, "but what are you going to do about giving back that life you took from him? It was giving him joy but it gives you nothing. Alive he did no harm."

The holstering of my pistol was the only answer I could make, but Carl did not press for further reply.

Years later, when we had grown to know each other better, Carl invited me to accompany him on a little sojourn in China canyon, where we made our frugal camp beside the spring amid the palms. One day we were sitting on the ground with our backs against the same palm trunk—Carl making a sketch of the dunes and serrated mountains across the valley—I, a quarter way around the tree, making notes of local color for a story. We were both quiet for a long time, for we had reached a stage of acquaintance where conversation was not often necessary.

In his low, hesitating voice, Carl said to me, "Ach, Elwood, we have a visitor."

Following his gaze I looked, and there near us, close against the base of a palm, a coiled rattler was enjoying the morning sun and the beauty of the day. Quietly we continued our occupations. After a while Brother Diamondback uncoiled and lazily slithered away toward the cool shadows of the underbrush.

Carl's canvases fairly exuded the desert atmosphere and fragrance. They were more than pictures. They were bits of real desert. One day I remarked on the fidelity of his colorings, particularly the tinting of the sands.

At this Carl gave a whimsical chuckle and said, "Yes, the sand! Fourteen years I could not get the sand right, no matter how I try. Then one day a little breeze blew my canvas from the easel and it fell upon the sand—but not with the wet paint down, I am thankful to say. Instantly I discovered my trouble, when I saw the sand coloring of my painting lying flat upon the real sand. Such a simple thing. Always I had been seeing it from the wrong angle. Just like life, the wrong angles make wrong colors and spoil harmony."

One time—it was when Carl was very poor, financially—he received a commission to paint a desert mural in one of the new state buildings at Sacramento. Without explanation he declined the commission. Knowing his economic need, I questioned him about it and twitted him about being afraid of the noise and crowds of the city.

"No," he remonstrated in his gentle manner. "It is not that, although

I should not enjoy being in a city so long. But if I took the commission I would want to do the best work I could possibly accomplish. If it was good, as I should like to have it be, it would, perhaps, make other people want to see the real desert here. Then, perhaps, they would come here and ask me to show them the scene from which I had painted. That would bother me. I am too happy here as I am to have time for bother."

Not long before Carl went to his long rest in the Indian burial ground—where he had asked to be placed among its close friends—we were sitting, chatting, in the gloaming, and I questioned him. "What was the biggest moment of your life, Carl?"

"The biggest moment of my life? Ach, yes, Elwood, I will tell you.

"One day, just a while ago, I am at the edge of the desert painting, with the canvas on the easel before me. On my head I have my stiff brim hat to shade my eyes from the sun. In my left hand I have my palette, with my thumb stuck through the hole, holding my brushes.

"Not far is a creosote bush and in the bush a little bird is hopping from branch to branch. He flies from the bush and lights on the rim of my hat. He jumps down on my shoulder and my arm. He perches on my thumb stuck through the hole in the palette. Then he sings a song right in my face!

"Ach, yes, Elwood! That is the biggest moment in my life. I know I am in harmony with all things."

And of such as these is the Spirit of the Desert.

—ww— From Carl Eytel, letter to Edmund C. Jaeger, April 16, 1917

Palm Springs, April 16th, 1917
Dear Edmund:

Thank you very much for your welcome letter with the sentiments expressed within it. Surely hatred and insanity is rampant through the world and it is simply astonishing how the reign of terror has unbalanced even minds which professed religion and the love of the Lord. But their eyes seem to be blinded to the punishment which is meted out to them openly before their very eyes: famine and the revenge of the poor who are starving right now. To us there is nothing left but to retire into the solitude—a hard matter for you whose work has to be done in the open and before the public—easier for me who can retire into the wilderness.

Just a few minutes ago when I was at the Post Office 7 o'clock in the morning I met Pester [a local hermit] who shocked me with the news that the Palm hut in Chino Cañon burned to the ground and Prof. Lass barely escaped being burned. All his belongings were destroyed. Contrary to Pester's warning he kept a fire in the stove inside of the cabin and the wind did the rest. Poor man! A few days ago he wrote to me that he intended to travel by burro wagon to Arizona and New Mexico and he asked me about roads and distances. This will tear his plans to pieces.

Also this morning I received a letter from Mr. Hallett stating that he and the painting are safely home and adding: I hope it will find some one that admires it as much as I do and who will purchase it. According to this the sale is doubtful and perhaps the very reason is that I put too cheap a prize [sic] on it. You are perfectly right. I ought to have asked 100 or 200 or 300. Otherwise rich people think it isn't worth it....

I sold my favorite painting: the snowcapped San Bernardino Mtn. with the blue sky and the sunny foreground for 25 Dollars instead of 50. Also the Painted Hills of the Mecca for 25 Dollars, both to a very nice gentleman of Kansas City more in order to please him than anything else. I am glad I am a failure when it comes to the point of commercialism and I suppose this is one of the reasons I was not permitted to get married. In that case the wife makes the prices. If I ever get married however I choose a woman who will not interfere with my work nor with my sales. Surely it won't be an American woman with modern tendencies and high flyerism.

Tomorrow Mr. Chase is to be married in Pasadena. Mr. Saunders [writer Charles Francis Saunders] acting as "best man." Mr. Chase don't need to worry any more about the filthy lucre. He will be *worth* about 50,000 Dollars, owner of several houses in Palm Springs, and part owner of 17 collie dogs. Well, I am not going to steal his bride....

Well, I won't take your time away any longer. I believe I shall start on my journey from Pasadena, not from San Bernardino and so I hope to see you at Saunders. I wish to avoid Los Angeles. You acted wisely when you went home instead of going to Santa Barbara and you are perfectly right to keep away from the wealthy people as much as possible. After all they are in a different class and have different—ideals!

Always affectionately yours,

Carl

From Carl Eytel, letter to Edmund C. Jaeger, June 7, 1917

Palm Springs, June 7th, 1917
Mein Lieber Edmund [My Dear Edmund]:

…I do not know where you are now at this present moment so I send this letter to Riverside. I hope you will have a rich time at Laguna where you can study to your heart's content and also have the most beautiful scenery imaginable. Especially Arch beach and the entrance to Aliso Cañon where Chase and I camped for a week must be visited by you. How cool and refreshing it will be for you! Here it is very hot and the air is full of sand for several days so that one can not see the outlines of the Eastern mountains. But the season is still going on. People are buying lots and the town is growing. Mrs. Orr, the mother of Mrs. Coffman, is building a fine bungalow near the McManus orange orchard and several houses were built on the Brook's place which belongs to Miss Cornelia White (The Lady of the Nails). You know that Chase married one of the White sisters, Miss Isabella? Both of them are now back East to look over their eastern possessions, for Chase is now a wealthy man and has not to worry any more about book royalties, which drop down to zero. Thank Heavens that I never had the temptation to sell my soul and body for money in order to avoid hardship and starvation. And now I believe the time will come when I will have money enough to go back to Germany as soon as the war is over, for I do not like this country any more, which is sad to say, for I loved it and its people with all my heart. But I will see how things come out, for there is no use to make plans and stubbornly try to have your own way when God has decided otherwise.

It's fine that things come out well for you. Nice to get help from those wealthy friends of yours who can do it so easily and are able to remove the boulders which are on your trail and which you are not able to climb over or remove. We will keep a grateful heart for those rich people even if we do say bad things about them once in a while and if we do have no use for their automobiles? Well I was awful glad to have a ride in an automobile stage from Flagstaff to Tuba City [Arizona], a former Mormon settlement two miles west from Moencopi. But on my way back I missed the 'stage' at Tuba and walk 23 miles from there to the Little Colorado River. I started out from Tuba at 2 in the afternoon and came to the River next morning at 4. This included many stops on the road where I sketched and also a few hours rest in the night where I almost froze to death before the bright idea struck me to lay on top of a sheet of heavy paper which I happened to have in my knapsack and cover myself with another piece of the same paper.

What great experiences one does have out in the wilds and how rich he gets by those adventures. It surely is a great divine blessing far superior than if you should be blessed with the good luck offered to you in the marriage with Isabella, Cornelia, or Florestine [Florilla] White, money queens of the Colorado Desert! Don't it? We will have a good laugh about that when we meet again! He surely picked the homeliest specimen in the garden of female roses!

Well, good bye and good luck to you! And auf Wiedersehen!

Ever your friend,

Carl

⟞⟋⟍⟋⟍ From Carl Eytel, letter to Edmund C. Jaeger, no date; likely the early 1920s

Palm Springs, Sunday
My Dear Edmundus,

Now a letter to you. Time passes quickly and it seems a year since we saw each other and still it is not so very long ago. But in the mean time we both have had new experiences and even I can tell you about a trip which I made. It was a compulsory trip in a way, for Good Thursday night a bunch of female Russian Bolschenks took possession of friend Smith's cabin and made themselves to home. I suddenly remembered an invitation from a young man in Palm Cañon who wanted me to come and see him. Therefore I packed up and Friday morning asked Mr. O'Sullivan to drive me to Palm Cañon where I stayed overnight. On Saturday we, Mr. Malorey, and Mr. Stevens from Glendora, drove in the latter's Ford—a glass case affair—to Painted Cañon where we camped. Next day to Box Cañon and Shaver's Well and from there to Hidden Springs Cañon where we camped. I do not know if you were at Hidden Sp. Cañon. If not then you must make it a duty to your own self to see it. Monday evening we returned to Palm Springs. I started several paintings, two of the Salton Sea, one of the Hills of Mecca, one of the palms in Hidden Springs Cañon, and I expect to make good paintings out of them. The trip was a gem even if we had to drive through plenty of sand to Indio. But from that point on it was fine.

The days clear as crystal, the nights cool with fine stars. I feel the freedom of the Desert far more in the neighborhood of Mecca than in our part and the air seems to be more clear and transparent. Especially wonderful is the way those two great snowcapped sentinels [Mt. San Jacinto and San Gorgonio Peak] appear to your eye almost suddenly out of the heavenly blue, themselves ethereal blue phantoms rather than massive mountains, and the immense desert in the foreground more cruel and forbidding than in the neighborhood of Palm Springs, Indio, Coachella, makes it a wonderful, unforgettable experience....

On Good Friday a terrible accident happened in Palm S. Two of those wild riding girls went to Ta-quitch Cañon. On their way home while on the run they tried to pull each other from the horse, a gentle game of the cowboys! The stirrup broke on the saddle of one of the most dangerous horses ridden by the girl named Steward, who wanted to ride the horse against the warning of the owner of the stable. The horse dashed into a cactus bush and the girl was thrown and stepped on by the horse. Brought to Palm Springs, she died under the Doctor K.'s roof a few minutes later. Now the street seems very quiet, for this death put a damper on the girls' wild riding (at least for a while).

The days are getting pretty warm, close to 90° and soon there will be an exodus out of Palm Springs and only the regular resident town tarantulas and centipedes will be left....

Chase also had a very close call one night, even call it a visit from Death. He was closer to Death's door than any time before. The outward signs were on his face, and it was really miraculous that he came out of the Valley again to recover and get better gradually. I believe he will return to Pasadena within 10 days, as soon as he is able to travel safely. Strange that a man has to suffer so terribly between life and death.

G. Wharton James passed through P.S. yesterday and I saw him and was glad to meet him. He has no end of troubles with all kinds of worldly sorrows. Several books of his are now out of print, "The Wonders of the Colorado Desert" amongst them. It did not pay to print them. This is the fate of authors....

> With best wishes, always
> your sincere friend,
> Carl

Just What Was Needed: Edmund C. Jaeger

Somewhat surprisingly, although the desert was becoming ever more glittering in the public's mind during the early decades of the twentieth century, popular and authoritative books on the region's natural history were slow in coming. John C. Van Dyke's aesthetic soarings about the arid lands passed on whifty ruminations on coyotes, rattlesnakes, and greasewood, but they were horrors of misinformation. Honest J. Smeaton Chase offered reliable comments on the desert's plants, but they were more in the nature of addenda than central to the adventures of his pages. In short, the reader interested in a comprehensive introduction to the desert, covering its flora, fauna, geology, and the context of its climate, could find little succor in the bookstores.

Then, beginning in the 1920s, a young, former teacher in Palm Springs' one-room schoolhouse started coming out with just what was needed. Edmund C. Jaeger, who would go on to become an instructor of science at Riverside Junior College, began publishing a series on the natural history of the desert. The following excerpt from one of his best-known works is a bit dated, but, by comparison to the many subsequent handbooks catching the swing of the nation's growing fascination with deserts, Jaeger's remains outstanding. It is comprehensive in scope, reflecting the writer's own intimacy with the desert over years of enthusiastic exploration, and it takes us, as many a handbook does not, below the border into the Mexican portion of the Colorado Desert.

It is always tempting to form an image of a writer from his books. Jaeger's prose, although certainly agreeable, is somewhat staid, as befits his aim for accuracy. The man himself hardly was so. A person of conservative religious beliefs, Jaeger had his eccentricities. In the early days, tourists around Palm Springs stood shocked to see a naked man running about the sand dunes outside town. However, this and other of Jaeger's rumored predilections need not be explored here; what counts is that Jaeger, more than anyone else, gave accurate portraits of a fascinating landscape, inspiring the public to treasure a unique legacy and throw its support behind protecting our Southwestern heritage.

~~~ Edmund C. Jaeger,
from *The North American Deserts*

To the west of the Colorado River, mainly in southeastern California and northern Baja California, lies the Colorado Desert. Included in it are all of those areas which drain directly into the Colorado or into the Salton Sea, which from time to time in the past has had a direct connection to the river. Much of this desert lies below sea level, or just a little above it. The southern portion, south of the Salton Sea, in California, is called the Imperial Valley; like the Gulf's delta area south of the International Border, it has very deep and exceedingly rich alluvial soils which in recent years have been utilized more and more as agricultural lands, mainly for cotton and alfalfa growing and for truck farming. The portion of the Colorado Desert to the north of the Salton Sea, called the Coachella Valley, has equally rich soil, and today is the home of the California date industry. Most of the remainder of this region is sand and rock desert where the dominant plant cover consists of creosote bush (*Larrea divaricata*), burro bush (*Franseria dumosa*), and brittle bush (*Encelia farinosa*). Compared with the best of the arboreal or tree deserts of Sonora and southern Arizona, the Colorado Desert seems barren indeed.

Since to many the name "Colorado Desert" seems to be a poorly chosen one, it is well to point out that it was given because most of the area lies along the Colorado River and not because of any connection it has with the state of Colorado. This basin-like arid desert, euphoniously called "La Palma de la Mano de Díos" ("the hollow of God's hand") by the Mexicans, was named the Colorado Desert by William P. Blake in 1853, eight years before the state of Colorado was named.

In the broad sandy washes cutting the detrital slopes which border the steeply rising mountains, smoke trees (*Dalea spinosa*), palo verdes (*Cercidium floridum*), and desert willows (*Chilopsis linearis*), so prevalent to the eastward, are still found, but the widely traveled desert student certainly notices the absence of the large cacti and many of the shrubs which are so common in southern Arizona. The desert ironwood (*Olneya tesota*) is here, too; however, it is largely confined to the broad washes and gullies of the small, somewhat mountainous area between the Salton Sea and the Colorado River and southward along the Gulf of California.

So intimately is the history of the Colorado Desert linked with that of the lower Colorado River and the story of the Salton Sea, that a few statements concerning the geologic and recent history of the river and the sea are essential to a proper understanding of the region. Here there is indeed a close correlation between geology and biology.

The Salton Sink (also called the Salton Basin), wherein now lies the Salton Sea, is a depression some 273 feet below sea level at its lowest point and without a drainage outlet to the Gulf of California. It was formed by the gradual sinking of a 200-mile-long block of the earth's crust at a time when surrounding mountain ranges were slowly being elevated to the east and west. This "graben," as geologists term such a fault-depressed region, would now be nearly filled with water from the sea, at least as far north as Indio, if it were not for the natural fan-like "dam" or delta which the Colorado River built across its lower end where for long periods it discharged its tremendous load of silt into the upper end of the Gulf. Much of this material was derived from the Colorado Plateau far to the northeast, while the river was sculpturing the Grand Canyon. During heavy floods the river from time to time radically shifted its course across its low-lying delta and overflowed so that it sometimes emptied south into the Gulf and at other times northward into the below-sea-level Salton Sink or into another sink wherein now lies Laguna Salada. It created ephemeral shallow lakes in the sinks; these later evaporated, leaving the floor a dry flat until the next flooding.

Much more recently, but still many, many hundreds of years ago, the Colorado discharged into the Sink for a prolonged period, there to form a very large inland fresh-water sea with a depth of more than 300 feet. This sea was over 100 miles long and 35 miles across at its widest point. It extended from above the present town of Indio, California, to 17 miles south of the present U.S.-Mexican boundary. To this ancient body of water the geologists have given the name Lake LeConte (commemorating the able geologist J. N. LeConte, who early made studies of this sink); it has also been called Lake Cahuilla, a name given by William P. Blake, who was among the first to do extensive research on the origin and nature of the entire Salton Sea area. The name now most preferred is Lake LeConte. The sharply defined prehistoric beach lines and wave-cut terraces of this old fresh-water lake are still very evident, especially along the base of the spurs of the Santa Rosa Mountains at the northwest end of the present Salton Sea. Fine views of them may be had to the west as you drive from Indio toward El Centro.

A stop at Travertine Point, which was once an offshore island in Lake LeConte, is well worth while, for here can be seen at close range the old beach line and the strange, porous "travertine" (really a calcareous tufa formed by minute blue-green algae which encrusted the rocks that were under water at that remote time). In some places the coral-like "travertine" has been incised by some unknown prehistoric Indians as they made curious petroglyph designs. Many of these markings appear to have been partially obscured by later deposits of tufa, perhaps indicating that the people encamped along this shore as the encrustations were being precipitated. Near by, along other old beach lines, are some odd circular walls of tufa-covered rocks which have been called "fish traps." Today there is no agreement among anthropologists as to whether these crude walls were used as fish traps or as foundations for brush houses, as hunting blinds or as ceremonial sites.

The first of the two ancient Lake LeContes was probably an Inter-Glacial or Post-Glacial fresh-water body, but it is obviously younger than the Pluvial lake chains of the Great Basin and Mohave regions. Evidently it was in existence for a long time, perhaps several thousand years. This lake finally dried up after a southward shifting of the Colorado River's course; then followed a dry period of long duration. There is strong evidence of a second complete or high-level filling of Lake LeConte in recent times. Based on archaeological findings, this lake had a duration of about 450 years—from about A.D. 1000 to 1450 or 1500. That one or more high stages of the lake were accompanied by an abundant aquatic life, especially small fresh-water mollusks, is attested by the numerous fossil shells which remain to this day. Sometimes they occur in such numbers that in places the windblown sand surfaces are white with them. In allusion to these small shells, the valley northwest of the Salton Sea was named Coachella (a misspelling of the Spanish "conchilla," little shell).

Fossil evidence in the form of marine clams and snails seems to indicate that the area at present occupied by the Salton Sink was at least twice covered by the sea. The first sea invasion was before the Salton Basin existed. Recent studies seem to show that the last covering by the sea may have taken place between the two fresh-water stages of Lake LeConte just described. It is thought that the sea waters may have come in when very high tides from the Gulf of California entered the Sink through the low trough found at the western edge of the Colorado River delta. This invasion of tidal waters may have occurred when there was a temporary rise in the Gulf water level. This is a theory developed by Dr. Carl L. Hubbs of the Scripps Institution of Oceanography and Robert L. Miller of the University of Michigan. Both men have based their explanation on the latest findings.

After the waters of the last high-stage of Lake LeConte evaporated, the lowest part of the Salton Sink became but a salt-encrusted playa with only a small salt marsh in its center, kept moist by a few springs and by the occasional runoff of summer cloudbursts and winter-rain freshets. At the turn of the last century the rich alluvial soils of the basin, particularly those of the delta region, were recognized as valuable for agriculture and some of the Colorado River water was diverted onto them for irrigation. To obtain this water, an old dry arroyo was utilized and an opening made in the river bank. No adequate headgate was built—only an intake. For several years the system worked well and real estate boomed in what now became known as Imperial Valley. Later, to get additional much-needed water, a new intake was made below Yuma, in Mexico. That was the beginning of a devastating tragedy that no one at the time could envisage.

In 1905, the river, swollen by flood waters, suddenly began enlarging the intake of the canal system and in a matter of hours great volumes of water were pouring through the growing breach and coursing toward the bottom of Salton Basin. It seemed that nothing could be done to stop the wild inflow of the Colorado. Almost as if by magic, Lake LeConte was being re-created; but now it was to be called the Salton Sea. Dike after dike, each but a makeshift, was hurriedly constructed, only as quickly to be swept away by the raging river. At one time the breach was half a mile wide. Finally, in February 1907, after eighteen months of most desperate herculean struggle, the opening was closed by dumping in brush mats and vast amounts of rock brought in by the Southern Pacific Railroad. At a cost of over $2,000,000 the river had been brought under control and the Imperial Valley saved for future agricultural development.

The present Salton Sea (named after a now-submerged railway siding called Salton) is about 35 miles long and some 15 miles broad at its widest part. Its greatest depth is nearly 47 feet, but much of it is little more than waist deep. Because some old salt deposits on the east side were covered with the rising waters and much of the salt redissolved, and also because the sea has no outlet, it now slightly exceeds ocean water in salinity. Intake from rains and from waste irrigation water brought in by the All-American Canal have recently been exceeding the amount of water lost by evaporation.

At the southern end of the Salton Sea, near Niland, were once most interesting "mud pots" where hot waters, liquid mud, steam, and gases bubbled up constantly or at intervals through crater-like cones of fine silt and sand. All are now submerged by rising water. Similar hot-water vents are located at Volcano Lake on the flood plain of the Colorado delta about 25 miles south of Mexicali, in Baja, California. These two areas are thought to be located along the great San Andreas Rift or fault line, which parallels the Salton Sea on the east and extends from the Gulf northward through California to beyond San Francisco. Every few miles along the great earth fissure are springs or seeps, some of cold water and others of scalding-hot water (as at Desert Hot Springs, Hot Mineral Well, and Arrowhead Springs). Many of the desert's natural palm oases occur along this rift, where cool water seeps to the surface.

Between Yuma, Arizona, and the Imperial Valley of California lies a generally north-south series of the most extensive and highest sand dunes to be found on the entire Sonoran Desert. These are the Algodones (Spanish, "cotton") Dunes. They are about 5 miles in width but extend fully 50 miles, from below the Mexican border north along the Southern Pacific Railroad nearly to the town of Niland. The great side-branch of the All-American Canal, bringing irrigation water from the Imperial Dam northward to the lower Coachella Valley farmlands, cuts through, then skirts these magnificent dunes at their western edge. As you travel the highway across the dunes in going from El Centro to Yuma, you are on a wide, well-paved road, but in the early 1900s travelers precariously crossed this long, sandy stretch on a narrow, bumpy plank "roadbed" which had turnouts every quarter of a mile to permit passing. Even today sand-blasted, wrecked portions of this interesting plank road can be seen protruding here and there above the shifting dunes. (Incidentally, it may be mentioned that the Algodones Dunes have been the background for many Hollywood film epics with a Saharan locale.)

The pale yellow sands of the Algodones Dunes are of granitic origin. On their ever-changing surface, often exposed to desiccating heat and nearly daily blasts of wind, it is surprising to find any plants growing at all. However, there are several unique species that not only tenaciously survive but by dint of good luck actually seem to thrive under such adverse conditions. The most conspicuous of these is a sand grass (*Oryzopsis hymenoides*) and a large shrubby wild buckwheat (*Eriogonum deserticola*) which may reach a height of 5 feet and have a stem nearly 2 inches in diameter! This hardy plant has long vertical roots, sometimes over 12 feet long, which penetrate great depths to reach moisture trapped under the sand. Usually the upper portions of the roots, sometimes as much as half of them, are left prominently exposed when the capricious winds move the sand about. When, as sometimes happens, the plant finds it is in danger of being buried by the drifting sands, it slowly elongates its stems to keep above the surface. Certainly the most curious plant of the Algodones Dunes is the strange, rarely seen parasitic "sand food" (*Ammobroma sonorae*), which springs up after unusually wet winters. Its subterranean, succulent stem resembles a swollen felt-covered asparagus stalk, at the top of which appears on the surface of the sand a large thick button-shaped, sand-colored head, the top of which is thickly studded with small purplish flowers opening in successive circles. Roots, stems, and flower heads formerly were much prized as food by the local Cocopa, Papago, and Yuma Indians. The sand food may be seen also in favorable years on the sand hills of northwestern Sonora at the head of the Gulf of California. This plant attacks the roots of near-by host plants such as the sunflower (*Helianthus canus*), plaited leaf (*Coldenia*), croton (*Croton californica*), and the shrubby buckwheat previously mentioned.

Bordering the Imperial Valley far to the westward are the beautiful Laguna Mountains, a part of the Peninsular Range which stretches on southward into Baja, California. Hemmed in by these highlands on the west, by the Santa Rosa Mountains on the north and northeast, and by a boundary near the Salton Sea on the east, lies a large desert area of some 272,000 acres which has been set aside by the state of California as Anza-Borrego State Park. It contains several remote native palm oases and brilliantly colored badlands comprising a Californian "painted desert." Borrego State Park, of 188,760 acres, lies just about north of this. There is a privately owned area in the northern portion of this state park which has become a well-known winter resort. Most of Anza-Borrego State Park, like much of the adjacent desert, consists of a charming desert wasteland of plains and hills covered by ocotillo and creosote bush and containing the only known natural occurrence in California of the small-leafed elephant tree (*Bursera microphylla*). It includes very rich gypsum deposits and a calcite mine, in addition to thick black-banded beds of fossil marine organisms, especially oysters (*Ostrea lurida*). The Anza Desert State Park was named to commemorate the great Spanish explorer Juan Bautista de Anza, who traversed the western edge of this desert with his followers in 1775 while on their long and arduous overland journey to establish a settlement at San Francisco. Later the famed Butterfield stagecoaches followed this same route to Los Angeles.

Another desert state park has been established at the north end of the Salton Sea. This wonderfully scenic area, called Salton Sea State Park, takes in only a portion of the shore and beach. Adjacent are Box, Painted, and Hidden Springs canyons, where are some of the southwest's finest scenery and vertical-walled gorges. The Mecca Mud Hills in which these gorges are found are not of marine but fresh-water origin. They are composed, for the most part, of stratified non-fossil-bearing layers of Tertiary shales, sandstones, clays, and conglomerates, in many places brilliantly colored and banded, and nearly all tilted and twisted by the action of past uplifting forces. The only fossils known from the beds of the Mecca Mud Hills—other than various bivalve marine shells—are mostly those of mammals, such as horses and camels. Painted Canyon and Box Canyon, the most picturesque of the dozens of side canyons interfingering these hills, are accessible by a road. They are places well worth a visit in the cooler winter months.

At the far northwestern end of the Salton Sink, on the edge of the Coachella Valley, towers lofty San Jacinto Peak (10,832 feet), the north face of which is considered to have the greatest sheer drop of any mountain in the United States. It is the highest peak of the San Jacinto mountain range and forms the southern boundary of the San Gorgonio Pass. North of this pass, in the San Bernardino Mountains, rises massive San Gorgonio Peak, also called Grayback (11,502 feet).

In many of the steep-walled rocky canyons of the Colorado Desert's bordering ranges and in some of the shallow arroyos of the clay and sandstone hills east and north of the Salton Sea grow small, isolated, and often completely hidden groups of the beautiful robust-trunked desert fan palm (*Washingtonia filifera*). These same palms are also found in canyons along the east base of the San Pedro Mártir and Juárez mountains in adjacent Baja California; there they are often associated with blue palms of the genus *Erythea*. Since the desert fan palm is so largely confined to the Colorado Desert, it is often considered this desert's most distinctive indigenous large plant. The largest and most accessible of the fan palm oases are ensconced in the steep-walled granitic gorges on the east face of the San Jacinto Mountains and in the contorted canyons of metamorphic rock found in the contiguous Santa Rosa Range of California. Of these, Palm Canyon and Andreas Canyon, about 6 miles south of the city of Palm Springs, are reached by good roads. In Palm Canyon it is estimated that about 4,000 wild palms are growing, many of the trees probably well over a hundred years old. A few sizable palm groups occur on the north side of the Coachella Valley in the Indio Mud Hills; those at Thousand Palms and Willis Palms can be easily visited. Other well-known palm groups are in the Borrego State Park area southwest of the Salton Sea. Fire is the great enemy of a palm oasis, and although the flames will not actually kill the trees, they will forever remove the beautiful fawn-colored "leaf skirts" that normally clothe the palm trunk from head to foot. In groups of palms untouched by fire the leaf-skirted trunks form dense "jungles," and it is always a pleasure to crawl or walk in and out among them.

At Palm Springs is located the Palm Springs Desert Museum, devoted exclusively to the interpretation of desert surroundings. Its programs and other educational offerings include field trips, illustrated lectures, motion picture showings, and exhibits of living animals. The displays in the main gallery are frequently changed, so a visit at any time to this active institution is a stimulating experience.

Between Indio in the Coachella Valley and Blythe on the California side of the Colorado River, a highway passes eastward through a very scenic intermountain trough. Some 24 miles east of Indio a side road leads northward through Cottonwood Springs, the Pinto Basin, and other parts of the Joshua Tree National Monument [now Park]. To the left of the main highway are a series of picturesque ranges: the colorful Eagle Mountains where large deposits of iron ore are mined for the Kaiser Steel Mills at Fontana, the serrated Coxcomb Mountains, and the sharply rising Palen and McCoy mountains. To the right of this road are the very rocky and photogenic Orocopia and Chuckawalla mountains.

In both the Coachella and Imperial valleys of the Colorado Desert, cotton, winter vegetables, grapes, and citrus fruits are extensively cultivated. One of the most important crops, however, is the date, and thousands of acres are devoted to its culture. One may see well-kept date gardens and may visit the packing houses and attractively kept roadside markets where many varieties of choice dates can be purchased. It may be said parenthetically that the date palm (*Phoenix dactilifera*) is not native, but was introduced from North Africa and Arabia at the turn of the century. Here it has thrived as well as in its original habitat.

From the village of Palm Desert extends a highly scenic road called the Palms-to-Pines Highway. It passes westward up into and across the pinyon-clad Santa Rosa Mountains to the high pine forests of the San Jacinto Range. A trip over this gently winding highway gives the traveler an opportunity to study the gradual zonation of plants from desert lowland (Lower Sonoran Life Zone) through the piñon-juniper country (Upper Sonoran), to the zone of Ponderosa yellow pines (Transition). A short climb from Idyllwild, a resort village among the pines, will lead you on up into the even higher Boreal Life Zone. There are very few places so easily accessible where all of these life zones can be seen in such a short lateral distance. The trip is especially rewarding because of the spectacular panoramic view it affords of much of the Salton Sink. There too is always the chance of glimpsing a wild desert bighorn sheep (*Ovis cremnobates*), several small but rigidly protected bands of which live in a state game refuge traversed by this road.

South of the Chuckawalla Mountains is a large triangular area bounded on the southwest by the Chocolate Mountains and on the east by the Colorado River. Its broad plains are drained by numerous branch washes of the Milpitas Wash, also called the Arroyo Seca (Spanish, *seca,* "dry"). Prior to the occupation of this beautiful area by the United States Navy in 1941, both the large-eared burro deer (*Odocoileus hemionus eremicus*) and a few pronghorn antelope (*Antilocapra americana*) were known to roam there.

The only known native specimens of the sahurao [saguaro] cactus in California are found in a few of the low hills at the far eastern end of the Little Chuckawalla Mountains, also near the potholes along the Colorado River, and on the east side of the Whipple Mountains a short distance above Parker Dam.

A little-used road on the north side of the Coachella Valley, called the Aqueduct or Dillon Road, parallels the great San Andreas Rift or "earthquake fault." Near it are several thermal springs and hot wells. The road was originally made during the construction of the Metropolitan Aqueduct which brings drinking water through open canals, tunnels, and conduits from the Colorado River at Parker Dam to Los Angeles and several other southern California areas.

The northeastern part of Baja, California, along the Gulf of California as far south as Bahía de Los Angeles, lies within the rain shadow of the Sierra Juárez and the Sierra San Pedro Mártir, and is but a southern extension of the Colorado Desert of California. This Mexican Colorado Desert can best be studied by traveling from Mexicali south 125 miles to the small village of San Felipe, noted for its shrimp and big-game fishing. Along the first 50 miles of road is a low-lying delta area of rich agricultural land where Mexican farmers grow cotton, sugar beets, corn, and alfalfa. The quaint but often extremely crude huts and houses of these tillers of the soil are interesting. One is impressed by the wide use made of ocotillo stems in the walls and roofs of the simple dwellings, and in the erection of fences and corals.

At El Mayor the road passes along the Río Hardy, really backwater from the Colorado River. On the west are the conspicuous Cocopa Mountains, around the southern end of which flood waters and occasionally even tidal waters from the Colorado River have flowed northward into a major below-sea-level lake basin similar to the Salton Sink and, like it, cut off from the Gulf of California by the massive delta of the river. It is called Laguna Salada or Laguna Maquata. Ordinarily this inland lake basin is dry, but records indicate that between 1884 and 1929 a lake occupied the basin at least six times. Great numbers of fish, mostly mullet (*Mugil cephalus*), dwelt in the lake after each filling. Each time the laguna dried up, it is said, coyotes came in numbers to feast upon the carcasses of the dead and dying fish.

After leaving the end of the Cocopa Mountains, the highway passes southward over great barren mud flats whitened with dried crusts and crystals of salt. Near by to the southeast is a dazzling white salt flat (*salina*) some 20 miles long. The highly and richly colored volcanic mountains immediately to the west are the Sierra Pinta ("painted mountains").

The traveler now enters a dry and lonely desert, luxuriant with scattered ironwood and palo verde trees, and great ocotillo-covered plains made golden in spring by the numerous flowers of the low shrubby brittle bush (*Encelia farinose*) and other composites. Now beginning to make their appearance on sand hummocks are scattered colonies of senita cactus (*Cereus thurberi*), a species sparingly represented in the United States by only about fifty native plants, all in Organ Pipe Cactus National Monument. A peculiar tree with dark green leaves and a short, fleshy gray-barked trunk also appears. This is one of the copals (*Elaphrium macdougalii*), locally known as elephant tree. When not too closely scrutinized, it appears, because of the dark tan or purple-red bark of its numerous side limbs and branchlets, somewhat like a squat-crowned, thickly branched apple tree. This elephant tree loses its leaves in late spring, very rapidly regaining them after summer or winter rains.

The sandy bottomed, dry watercourses abound in small shrubs, and after seasons of good rains there is a luxuriant but ephemeral growth of annual plants often overspread with brilliantly colored flowers. The desert plants grow right down to the flats and bluffs overlooking the Gulf, and here often have somewhat larger leaves and more rankly growing stems than plants growing elsewhere on the near-by desert. Many of the sand dunes along the roadsides are covered with short-statured, half-buried mesquite trees, the curious senita cactus, and a sand burr (*Cenchrus palmeri*), which has very spiny green burrs that change to a purple-brown on drying. The spines of the burrs are almost as sharp and stiff as the thorns of a cactus, and may make walking over the dunes very uncomfortable. In the disturbed soil on the shoulders of the road occur numerous plants of the large white-flowered prickly poppy (*Argemone hispida*), apricot mallow (*Sphaeralcea ambigua*), Spanish needle (*Palafoxia linearis*), several varieties of evening primroses (*Oenothera*), sand verbena (*Abronia villosa*), and long slender-stemmed spiderling (*Boerhaavia* sp.).

The 88-mile stretch of sandy, rock-strewn, lowland, coastal desert between El Mayor on the Río Hardy and San Felipe is known as El Desierto de Los Chinos ("Desert of the Chinese"). In August of 1902 an ill-fated party of forty-two Orientals and their guides started on foot what proved to be a long disastrous trek between San Felipe and Mexicali. All but eight perished in agonizing deaths due to heat, thirst, and exhaustion. They were poorly informed, ill shod, and badly prepared in every way for such a hazardous journey. The water holes they sought were never found and most of the ill-starred party fell down to die before the journey was half over.

On the east side of the high Sierra Juárez and the Sierra San Pedro Mártir, which border this desert region on the west, are several large scenic canyons with springs or perennial streams of water. In some of their lower boulder-choked reaches are many unusual shrubs and picturesque groups of desert fan palms (*Washingtonia filifera*) and blue palms (*Erythea armata*). Here, the author has recently discovered two new land snails. In the arid valley along the mountain bases there occur fine specimens of the massive cardon (*Pachycereus pringlei*), the largest tree cactus that is found more plentifully farther south on the Vizcaino Desert. Some of the washes contain fine "forests" of large copals, little-leaf palo verde, and ironwood, offering pleasant camp sites.

Summer travel (May through October) in this part of our desert is to be discouraged. The days then are often exceedingly warm (day temperatures of from 110° F. to 115° F. are frequent), and sometimes when storms are moving up along the Gulf the humidity is uncomfortably high. Such weather makes one miserable indeed, especially if the nights are hot, and even the most spectacular scenery cannot be appreciated. Plan your trip here in the clear, warm days of late autumn, winter, or spring.

The season of rains for the Colorado Desert begins about the last week in December. The incoming clouds are brought in by strong westerly or southwesterly winds which frequently kick up sand and dust. However, as a rule the winds soon die down after rain begins to fall. The worst and most persistent winds are those of the late spring season. These generally occur when heavy fogs are prevalent in the cismontane valleys along the Pacific Coast. Summer tropical storms, some of them of considerable intensity, at times move up along the Gulf into the southern California deserts, leaving behind varying amounts of moisture.

The Colorado Desert possesses an unusual fauna of notable variety and specialized form. One of its commonest smaller animals is the widely distributed antelope ground squirrel (*Ammospermophilus leucurus*), often locally called desert chipmunk because it has stripes. These white bands end at the shoulder instead of continuing on to the end of the nose as in true chipmunks. The "antelope" part of its common name is given in reference to the white tail, which is carried curved up over the back when running. It is twitched nervously when the animal is excited. This friendly little "ammo" is one of the few American ground squirrels that remain active all winter.

Other mammals include several species of wood or pack rats (*Neotoma*), the bright-eyed small round-tailed ground squirrel (*Citellus tereticaudus*), dainty pocket mice of several kinds (*Perognathus*), nimble white-footed mice (*Peromyscus*), the spotted skunk (*Spilogale arizonae*), the fleet-footed jack rabbit or desert hare (*Lepus californicus deserticola*), the desert coyote (*Canis ochropus estor*), the bobcat (*Lynx eremicus*), the small big-eared desert kit fox (*Vulpes macrotis*), the ringtail "cat" or cacomistle (*Bassariscus astutus*), and many kinds of bats.

Representative birds of this desert include the roadrunner (*Geococcyx californianus*), LeConte thrasher (*Toxostoma lecontei*), Salton Sea song sparrow (*Melospiza melodia saltonis*), phainopepla (*Phainopepla nitens*), Say phoebe (*Sayornis saya*), Gambel or desert quail (*Lophortyx gambeli*), white-rumped shrike or butcher bird (*Lanius excubitoroides*), verdin (*Auriparus flaviceps*), plumbeous gnatcatcher (*Polioptila plumbea*), cactus wren (*Heleodytes brunneicapilllus couesi*), and rock wren (*Salpinctes obsoletus*).

The roadrunner is certainly the bird clown of the desert. He may not look it to those who only glimpse him dashing across the highway ahead of their car or running for a moment at breakneck speed along the road before gliding gracefully off into the brush. But if he can be watched about some desert settler's home, where he has become more or less a backyard pet, he will be seen to be a most ludicrous, sportive, and knowing bird. This prankster loves to worry the cat, play with the dog, and get acquainted with all the other farmyard pets. Even in the wild he enjoys jumping about in topsy-turvy manner or running in circles just for the fun of it. Although he eats wild fruits and berries, most of his food is of animal origin. Cleverly he stalks and pounces upon hapless lizards, small snakes, or large insects such as cicadas or grasshoppers. If hungry enough he may attack and kill a rattlesnake by piercing its brain. The favorite haunts of the roadrunner are brush-covered areas where he can find good feeding grounds and ready shelter from avian foes such as hawks. He is most plentiful in shrubby regions along the Colorado and Gila rivers and in somewhat similar situations in Mexico in Chihuahua, Sonora, and Baja California.

The phainopepla, one of the silky flycatchers, is the only small black bird of the open desert; the male can be readily identified at a distance because of his contrasting color, the white patches on the underside of the wing, and the easily seen blue-jay-like headcrest. He is particularly a bird of the mesquite and cat's-claw thickets where mistletoe infestation is heavy. Often he feeds almost entirely upon mistletoe berries. Because only the thin berry pulp is digested, the seeds pass on through the bird unharmed and if dropped on a favorable site, as on a young tender-barked twig, they may germinate and start a new plant. There is here shown a most interesting animal-plant relationship. The phainopepla is largely dependent on the mistletoe for food, and the plant in turn relies on the bird for dispersal.

On the Colorado Desert the most commonly seen reptiles include the desert iguana or crested lizard (*Dipsosaurus dorsalis*), gridiron-tailed or zebra-tailed lizard (*Callisaurus draconoides*), leopard lizard (*Crotaphytus wisliseni*), collared lizard (*Crotaphytus collaris baileyi*), ocellated sand lizard (*Uma notata*), desert brown-shouldered lizard (*Uta stansburyana elegans*), flat-tailed horned "toad" or lizard (*Phyrnosoma m'callii*), the chuckawalla (*Sauromalus obesus*), sidewinder or horned rattler (*Crotalus cerastes*), desert diamond-back rattlesnake (*Crotalus atrox*), speckled rattler (*Crotalus mitchelli*), desert or rosy boa (*Lichanura rosefusca*), spotted night snake (*Hypsiglena ochrorhynchus*), leaf-nosed snake (*Phyllorhynchus*), glossy or faded snake (*Arizona elegans*), red racer (*Coluber flagellum*), desert king or milk snake (*Lampropeltis getulus*), and the desert gopher or bull snake (*Pituophis catenifer*). The desert tortoise (*Gopherus agassizi*) is seldom seen in the low portions of the Salton Sink, but may be occasionally found in and to the east of the Mecca Mudhills and in the Orocopia and Chuckawalla mountains. Desert snakes are most active during the warm summer nights, from May through September. They seldom venture abroad during the heat of the day since even ten minutes of full summer sun may be sufficient to kill them. At the approach of winter all snakes, lizards (except the small Stansbury uta), and tortoises go beneath the sand or into rock crevices, or dig special burrows where they hibernate for a brief period.

Of the many desert lizards, certainly one of the most amazing is the almost sand-white gridiron-tailed or zebra-tailed lizard, so named because of the dark scorched-appearing bands on the tail. It is the prize runner of all its kind, darting across the sand like a silver streak, at an almost unbelievable speed. So agile and quick is it that it is hardly possible to run one down. When in flight this lizard, like the desert iguana and collared lizard, actually elevates itself on its hind legs. The long tail is curved up as a balancer and the fore limbs are held close to the body. The lizard now appears for all the world like a miniature bipedal dinosaur, speeding lightly over the ground surface.

The beautifully patterned fringe-footed uma or sand lizard is the most perfectly adjusted of all lizards for living in a sandy habitat. The hind feet have very long slender toes, each of which is equipped with a row of elongated scales that overlap with those of the next toe to form a sort of webbed or paddle foot. When pursued the lizard often dives headlong into the sand and literally swims out of sight within a matter of seconds. To facilitate its easy entry into the sands, nature has provided it with a head flattened somewhat like a shovel. For protection the eyelids have thickened scales about their edges and the nostrils have valves to keep out sand particles.

The waters of the northernmost portion of the Gulf of California, adjacent to the Mexican portion of the Colorado Desert, are considerably cooler than those of the subtropical southern portion and support a fauna which in many respects is quite different from that to the south. The warmer southern waters act as a barrier, in much the same way that a mountain range might, and several invertebrate species trapped and isolated in the northern portion of the Gulf are found nowhere else. Peculiarly some of these, particularly some of the spiny lobsters and fishes, are very similar to or identical with those found in the Pacific Ocean on the opposite side of the peninsula. This is thought to indicate that at one time the waters of the lower Gulf were cooler and made possible free passage between the upper Gulf and the Pacific Ocean.

Very recently fossil remains of about 45 different prehistoric land animals have been found in the Anza-Borrego desert area, south of the Salton Sea. The region, once covered by the waters of the Gulf of California, later (perhaps some 500,000 years ago) became a grass-and-forest-covered land supporting a wide assortment of grass-, herb-, and tree-feeding animals such as the rare medium-sized ground sloth (*Megalonyx*), a large horse, a giant 16-foot long-limbed camel, a tapir, two types of deer, antelope, pocket gophers, and land tortoises, remains of all of which have been excavated. Bones of a giant condor-like vulture with wing spread of fully 17 feet were among the exciting discoveries.

Two Wealthy Feminists from Cleveland: A Great Hole Full of Blue Mist

The desert was a hard sell. It was one thing to read about the glories of this new Wonderland in the popular books of Van Dyke and James. That was as fascinating as entering the world of a lavish fairy tale or following the intricacies of a fantastic love story. On the other hand, it was quite something else to get up and go to the desert. That took some doing.

Today, with our "adventure travel tours" we take pride in seeing the most remote places possible, whether Antarctica or Nepal, the more remote and unusual the better for conversations at backyard barbecues. In the early years of the twentieth century, this was not the case. For those who could afford vacations, favor was very strong for lounging about, playing croquet in the green and civilized resorts of the nearby Berkshires or the Catskills; but go to the desert? One would have to be addled for such a choice. If some eccentric uncle had visions of striking it rich out there in the sands or developing an agricultural empire, that was admissible, if a bit oddball, but in the long run at least understandable. Yet to travel to the desert simply for the pleasure of it, a region generating visions of skeletons ringing dried-up waterholes, that seemed lunatic. Furthermore, travel was expensive, and the desert was not an easy place to get to. First, one had to take the train, spending days crossing the continent. Secondly, one arrived in alluring places such as Los Angeles or San Diego. Their gracious hotels overlooking the balmy Pacific Ocean and their winding, flower-lined walks—these were siren songs. Why forego any of that? Nonetheless, for those few people determined to actually follow Van Dyke and James and strike out beyond comfort into the barren lands over the coastal mountains, prospects were not good. Desert roads were linear sand traps, to be considered with circumspection, especially when one was advising two middle-aged women from Cleveland off on an obvious lark. Why, they didn't seem to have their senses completely about them. Brows furrowed. People were still being found out there mummified in their broken-down automobiles.

Sometimes it takes the headstrong and slightly irrational to break new trails. Weary from their political campaigning for women's rights and more dyed-in-the-wool than most in their romantic fantasies, Edna Brush Perkins and Charlotte Hannahs Jordan (the one the daughter of an inventor whose company eventually became part of General Electric, the other the wife of a famous automobile manufacturer) decided to let their hair down and throw their fates to the winds. They wanted to go to the wildest and most dangerous place possible; the desert would be just the right tonic.

We meet them at the beginning of their adventure, when, topping the pleasant green mountains beyond San Diego, the two Easterners peer down somewhat shocked into an impossible thing, a vast abyss full of blue mist stretching out to the far horizon. It was just the thing to jolt the matrons out of their urban ennui and rake their bodies with the grand, new frisson they desired.

—*mm*— Edna Brush Perkins,
from *The White Heart of Mojave: An Adventure with the Outdoors of the Desert*

In our ... mood we hated the coast and were guilty of speeding along the fine macadam between Los Angeles and San Diego in our eagerness to leave it. We turned due east from the green little city on the shores of its beautiful harbor and headed for the desert. Our unsatisfactory interview at the Automobile Club had led us to believe that the Imperial Valley, irrigated or not, was a wild and lonely place, the desert itself, for it seemed to be surrounded by difficulties.

The road from San Diego proved to be good, presenting no hindrances not easily surmounted, and as we drove along it we told each other what we thought about the Automobile Club. Gradually the character of the country changed. A little of the prickly, spiky desert vegetation with which we were to become so familiar appeared. The round hills gave way to piles of bare, colored rock, the soil became a gravelly sand on which scrub oak and manzanita grew. The houses became fewer. In one place we had to detour and found deep, soft sand, nothing to the sand of a real desert road, but we did not know that then. The change was subtle, yet we felt it. The country took on the harshness that had repelled us from the train windows. Being alone in it was at first a little dreadful.

After a day or so of leisurely driving we came suddenly to the edge of the valley. The ground fell before us, cut into rough canyons and foothills, two thousand feet to a blue depth. It was like a great hole full of blue mist, surrounded by red and chocolate-colored mountains. Nothing was clear down there though the mountains were sharply defined and had indigo shadows on them. The valley was a pure, light blue, of the quality of the sky, as though the sky reached down into it. We lingered a long time eating our lunch on a jagged rock, trying to pierce the blue veils and see the Salton Sea, a big salt lake which we knew was there with the tracks of the Southern Pacific beside it, the sand dunes we had heard of, and the town of El Centro where we were to spend the night. We could see nothing of them, only a phantasy of changing color, an unreality.

We found the whole desert full of drama, but the Imperial Valley is perhaps the most dramatic spot of all, except Death Valley, that other deep hole below sea-level which is so much more remote and so utterly lonely. The great basin of the Imperial Valley was once a part of the ocean until the gradual silting up of its narrow opening separated it from the Gulf of California. The bottom of the valley then became an inland sea which slowly evaporated under the hot sun, leaving as it receded a thick deposit of salt on the sand. At last the valley was dry, a deep glistening bowl between chocolate-colored mountains, a white desolation undisturbed by man or beast, covered with silence. For ages it lay thus while morning and evening painted the hills.

Then the railroad came with its thread of life, connecting Yuma with San Bernardino and Los Angeles. Soon a salt-works was built in what had once been the bottom of the ocean, and later an irrigation system for the southern end of the valley from the Colorado River which flows just east of the Chocolate Mountains. The white desolation was made to bloom and, in spite of the intense heat of summer, has become one of the richest farming districts of California. But the drama is still going on. A few years ago the untamed Colorado River that had fought its way through the Grand Canyon and come two hundred miles across the desert turned wild and flooded into the Imperial Valley. It was shut out again, but it left the new Salton Sea in the old ocean bed. Its yellow waves now break near the irrigated area; it drowned the salt works. The Salton Sea is slowly vanishing as its predecessor did; in a little while the valley will again be dry and white and glistening.

The road descended before us in jigjags to the blue depth. It was a good road but narrow in places, dropping sheer at the edge, and steep. Very carefully we drove down, emerging at last through a narrow, rough canyon onto the sandy floor of the valley. A macadam road led like a shining band through the sagebrush. This evidence of civilization was strange in the surrounding wilderness, for as yet we could see no sign of life in the valley. The sand came up to the edge of the road and was blown into dunes between us and the new sea. There was nothing but sunshine and sagebrush and flowers. The flowers amazed us, for why should they grow there? There was a yellow kind that outshone our perennial garden coreopsis, and numberless little flowers pressed close to the sand with spread-out velvet, or shining, or crinkled blue or frosted leaves. We had to get out of the car to see them, and whenever we got out we felt the heat blaze around us. We were below sea-level and even in February it was very hot. The light was almost blinding, and a silver heat-shimmer swam between us and the mountain walls. The mountains seemed to be of many colors which changed as the afternoon advanced. The sun set in a more vivid purple and gold than we had ever seen.

We lingered so long looking at the strange plants and flowers that twilight found us still alone with the desert. Only the white macadam band promised any end to it. Realizing that night was coming and we had an unknown number of miles before us we stepped on the accelerator with more energy than wisdom. The result was a loud explosion of one of the brand-new rear tires. We found the tire so hot that we had to wait for it to cool before we could change it, and the road hot to touch though the sun had been down for some time. We called ourselves all manner of names for being such fools as to try to drive fast on that sizzling surface. It was the first practical lesson about getting along on the desert.

Soon after that we came to an irrigation ditch. Instantly everything was changed and we were in a farming country. El Centro is a hustling town with a modern four-story hotel. We wished it were not four stories when we learned that part of it had recently been shaken down by an earthquake, and especially when we experienced three small shocks during that night. The earthquakes themselves did not seem surprising, they were a fitting part of the weird experiences of the day. We felt as though we had been very near to the elemental forces of nature; we had been with the bare earth and volcanic rocks and strange plants that flourish in dryness, and felt the unmitigated beat of the sun. It was like seeing the great drama of nature unveiled, fierce and beautiful.

We stayed several days in the Imperial Valley, visiting the Salton Sea, figuring out the beach lines of that other more ancient sea, and walking among the sand dunes. We found that we always went away from the farms into the desert. She was calling us loudly enough now. We heard her and were determined to find more of her. When we tried to go on, however, we met with the same universal discouragement. In El Centro they said that the road out through Yuma to the desert east of the Chocolate Mountains was very bad, and the road up the Valley through Palm Springs and Banning no road at all. Besides, there was no water anywhere. Later we found out that none of these things were exactly true, but it probably seemed the best advice to give two lone women with no experience of desert roads. Our appearance must have been against us. Certainly it was no lack of persistence, for we interviewed everybody, hotel managers, ranchers, druggists and garage men. They all looked us over and gave the same advice.

A Tiny Figure Wavering in the Blue Mists

In one way of looking at it, Edna Brush Perkins was predictable. The foray of Anza was predictable and the boosterism of James, too. These were products of historical and cultural forces. Given the need to provision California missions lying far from the supply bases in Mexico, someone, inevitably, would try to blaze an overland route to them; a nation that seems to commercialize everything, including nature, almost by ordination produced a James; and such as erumpent Perkins was almost a mathematical result of a burgeoning women's movement combined with ambitious romanticism and the prosperity that made her adventure possible. That is not to take anything away from the personal courage and talent of such people; it is, however, to consider them as growing from their contexts.

Had the excited ladies from Cleveland peered closely into the blue mists of the desert abyss that so stirred them, they might have seen a tiny figure leading his horse, the two trudging across the ancient sea bed far below where the tourists had parked their car. For those who believe that the best of art arises from individual genius in spite of, rather than because of, the social matrix, J. Smeaton Chase should be a paragon. And even those who don't hold such beliefs might well consider him a traveler of unique dimensions.

A son in a prosperous London publishing family that had fallen on hard times, Chase grew up in an orphanage, hardly a propitious beginning for those Dickensian conditions. Somehow, likely driven by his failing health, as a young man he made his way to the United States and the providential climate of Southern California. There, after much striving, he managed to establish himself as a well-known travel writer, exploring Yosemite and, in a grand, lone adventure, riding his horse the length of the then-wild California coast. Such was the happy fortune of Chase, to blend his art with a successful economic tack on life.

When it came to the desert, however, other than turning out another income producer, he was an outlier. Others came to the desert with predetermined agendas, whether to hype up a Wonderland in the making or to find the thrills, as indeed they did, that they knew already were waiting for them out there. Chase came with no such burning foresight eagerly fulfilled. A lover of fog and greenery, he didn't even particularly like the arid lands; and when he was out in the middle of them, floundering around, lost, out of water, he often wondered what on earth he was doing in such a hideous place. Rather, unlike the host of contemporary desert writers, Chase came to the desert out of curiosity, simply to see what was out there in that rumored land, to become as intimate with it as a man who was fascinated by all landscapes possibly could; in short, as far as is humanly possible, to appreciate the desert for what it was, in terms to the I-Thou relationship later articulated by Martin Buber.

And yet Chase failed. Despite his journalistic ideals, he was human; he was high-strung and a man of near preternatural abilities to see and describe. For that, he never was able to achieve the objectivity he desired. He suffered too much; he became too excited, despite his aversion to cracked rock and foregrounds stretching to horizons of sand, by the surreal flickerings all around him. All to our benefit, for the result, in contrast to the sometimes cloyingly sweet syllabubs produced by the enthusiasts, is a work of unprecedented emotional range, accuracy, and human depth in desert literature as Chase, sometimes hallucinating from exertion and dehydration, tries to make sense of a phantasmagoric land that, as reality wavers before him, sometimes seems bent on killing him.

~~~ J. Smeaton Chase,
from *California Desert Trails*

THE FLOOD

Some miles to the south [of Palm Springs] is Andreas Cañon, another of the gateways to the same mountain [San Jacinto]. It also is named after an Indian, old Captain Andreas, the remains of whose adobe hut and orchard of vines and figs are yet in evidence. Here the following winter I camped for nearly three months, gratifying aboriginal instincts by a return to cave life. The cavern which served for dining-room, study, and kitchen had been the home of Indians, and was adorned with their picture-writings, while a sort of upper story was quite a museum of age-dimmed records in red and black. One upright stone was worn into grooves like knuckles, where arrow-shafts had been smoothed; another showed evidence of having been used for polishing the obsidian points. The great table-like rock where I kept a store of hay for my horse Kaweah (Mesquit and I had had a difference and parted) was bored in a dozen places with circular holes where acorn and mesquit meal had been ground by generations of diligent squaws, whose deer-horn awls and ornaments of shell and clay I occasionally unearthed: as I did also bones in remarkable numbers and of questionable shapes.

Of Andreas, now long gathered to his fathers, the word goes that he was given to the distilling of *aguardiente* from his grapes, breaking thereby the law of the land. However, considering that the art had been learned from the whites, that he had no voice in making the law, and that the land in question had been taken from him and his people, there seems not much logic in blaming him. Peace to your ashes, Andreas! I can certify that your fig trees still do bud, and yield better fruit perhaps than some of us.

The same striking conjunction of desert and coast vegetation rules here as in Chino Cañon. Down to the very neck, a bare hundred yards from where open desert comes in view, trees grow in full verdure, curtained in wild-grape vines that make an arbor of summer green or autumn chrome and sienna over the darkling pools of the creek. At the point where they cease they are met by a colony of palms, and these give place to the low-toned herbage of the desert. The cañon is notable for a fine rank of "palisade" cliffs, which with their massive sculpturing and dark Egyptian hue make a wonderful foil for the beauty of the palms. Some of these stand statue-like in vertical alcoves of the wall: others bend in tropic grace above crystalline pools, or spring in rocket-like curve from thickets of mesquit or arrowweed.

One cluster, arranged in the form of a great hall, especially took my fancy. The palms that compose it have kept all their dead foliage, which, hanging in straw-yellow masses about the stems, gives them impressive girth and solidity. While wind is stirring the fronded capitals, these massive pillars, standing in unbroken stillness, seem like the immemorial columns of Babylon. My nights in that strange place, worked up into mystery by glimmer of star or trickle of wandering moonbeam through the tracery of the roof, were the sort of experience one loves to repeat in memory.

In a narrow gateway of the upper cañon stands a single stately palm, framed by tall cliffs of Egyptian red. Its solitariness, spiry grace, and statuesque pose give it special individuality, and sentimentally I allowed myself to name it "La Reina del Cañon" [The Queen of the Canyon].

Evenings by the camp-fire in the cave were enlivened by visitors, kangaroo-mice, skunks, and tarantulas, who adopted me without reserve into the ancient order of cave-dwellers. The mice were charming companions, eating beans and hardtack with me off our common plate, and only occasionally needing an admonitory rap with the spoon. By day, quail were frequent callers, aligning themselves on a shelving rock overhead to criticize my housekeeping; and once a lynx halted bashfully when ten yards from the breakfast-table. Bighorn tracks were often fresh on the cactus mesa beyond the creek, and my regular morning alarum was the practising of chromatic scales by a cañon-wren midway up the cliff.

Andreas Cañon had become endeared to me by these and other social ties when, about noon one Saturday, a gentle but persistent rain began—one of the occasions one recognizes as meant for the cooking of beans. I charged my biggest pot and passed the afternoon in holding the fire at that scientific minimum that the "free-holy" justly demands and wondrously repays. The rain continued, taking on the industrious look that Californians know and love as forecasting a successful season in real estate. At intervals I brought in fuel, storing it in dry crannies of the cave.

Kaweah, protected by his heavy blanket, was tied close to the creek, under a tree against which I had built his manger. Darkness came early, and the rain increased to a heavy downpour. I ate supper in dusk, fed and watered the horse, covered the hay with a tarpaulin, and turned into the blankets on my camp-cot to smoke a pipe. This proved more than usually cheering. A tent with sousing rain were revealed as the ideal conditions for the combustion of Virginia Long-Cut. This discovery I had opportunity to confirm in the days that ensued.

Before turning in finally I lighted the lantern and took a look at the creek. It had risen a few inches, as was natural in a cañon stream, but the tent was six or eight feet above it and a rod back from the bank. Nothing to worry about, so I went to bed, and, lulled by the roar of rain on the canvas, was soon fast asleep.

This placidity was ill-judged. Some suffocating object, something heavy and wet and cold, came down and embraced me with what I felt to be undue familiarity. For a few moments I was puzzled, then realized—

the tent: it had sagged with weight of water and the pegs had pulled from the softened ground. I noticed, too, that the sound of rushing water was oddly close. Pushing away the wet canvas I put out a foot. Instead of the expected boot it encountered a cold swirl of water that came half to the knee. Next my groping hand took note of the abnormal position of the tent-pole, which leaned almost horizontal under the ruin of the canvas. I saw what had happened: the creek was over its banks, had undermined the pole and brought down the tent, and was making a clean breach through my quarters.

My thoughts flew to Kaweah. He was some twenty-five yards downstream from me and on lower ground. Struggling under the water-logged canvas I hurriedly got into my soaking clothes and somehow got clear of the tent. It was pitch-dark, raining like fury, and the water was now knee-high and running like a sluice. I stumbled down to Kaweah, who neighed shrilly when he saw me. He had taken the highest spot his rope allowed him, but the water was almost to his belly, and we were both in some danger of being swept away. Cutting the rope I scrambled with him up the bank and tied him on high ground near the cave.

Then for an hour I slopped to and fro rescuing what remained of my effects and storing them in dry corners of the cave. Not a few articles had been carried away, but most were caught under the collapsed tent, which itself was anchored by a rock against which it had stranded. It was wet work, but warming, and I soon worked up a first-rate Turkish bath.

The next need was fire. By now the cave was a poor refuge, though it might have looked enjoyable to a naiad. Rain dripped everywhere from the shelving rocks that formed at best a nominal roof, and cascades ran picturesquely down the walls. The floor was a mere bog. Only a space about three feet square was free from overhead drip, and on this islet I built a tiny fire over which I crouched in partial shelter. I supposed it was near daybreak, but on looking at my watch found it was eleven o'clock.

I cherished that fire as few things are cherished on this planet. When gusts blew the rain in upon it, I covered it with my hat. When it sulked and sputtered because the bog encroached, I fed it with splinters from my tripod. When the wind scattered the cupful of embers, I scraped them up reverently like a Parsee. At last I got a good blaze, made a billy of coffee, and settled to the night's work of drying myself, blankets, gun, camera, and "et cæteras."

The storm maintained a headlong deluge which did not moderate for a moment. The creek had risen higher, and was making wild uproar as huge boulders began to come down from the upper cañon, thundering and bumping along like barrels tumbling down a stairway. With the boulders went the trees. The one to which Kaweah had been tied (a full-grown sycamore) had disappeared soon after I moved him. Only by a few minutes had he escaped going with it. Now I watched tree after tree succumb. First their tops, which showed dimly against the sky, would begin to shiver as the water tore away the earth like a terrier at a rat-hole: then as roots broke from their grip the victim stooped lower and lower, until water and granite between them gave the *coup-de-grâce*, and the unlucky alder or sycamore toppled over and was whirled off to make camp-fires for fortunate prospectors.

Daylight came, and with it the end of my fuel. By now the cave was worthless: water poured in steady streams from roof and walls, and the floor had become a pool. Among my salvaged traps was a little three-by-six-foot tent of light waterproof stuff which I carry on winter horseback trips. This I pitched on the highest spot available, first laying a thick stratum of arrowweed over the sodden ground. Inside I spread half a bale of dry hay: then crept in and sat tight.

This was Sunday. It passed; also Monday, Tuesday, and Wednesday, and not for a moment did the storm hold off. I read, smoked, ate, slept, and dashed out when necessary to attend to Kaweah or drive the tent-stakes deeper into the spongy earth. When I awoke on Thursday a yellow glow was brightening my tentlet. It was the sun, shining in the old, whole-hearted, California way, and I hurried out to renew acquaintance. Looking up the cañon there was little that I recognized. The place where the other tent had stood could be known by a scrap of canvas projecting above a new creek-bed of dazzling, freshly scoured granite, while Kaweah's former quarters were submerged in mid-stream.

In the afternoon came Pablo, Marcos, and Miguel, to round up their remaining cattle and mourn the six or eight head that had vanished in the storm together with all their possibilities of *pesos*, *carne*, and *cuero* [money, meat, and leather]. Finding me in the act of replenishing the bean-pot they expressed slight Indian surprise, and mentioned that, certain of my belongings having been picked up some miles away where the flood had carried them, it had been supposed that I was drowned.

THE BADLANDS

Two hours brought us to the edge of the badlands, in the form of a deep, abrupt *barranca*, the first of dozens through which we must thread our way. In we dived: and, indeed, to plunge into one of these mazes is much like diving into unknown water: when, where, or whether one will get out is somewhat a matter of chance. In and out, up and down, we went for hours, scrambling up and sliddering down. Now and then we left the horses and climbed out to get our bearings afresh. It was not reassuring to see that Wellson was often at fault, though it was natural, since he was gauging landmarks from an unfamiliar side.

We reached at length a rim from which we looked out over a still more intricate piece of country. With a sweep of the hand my companion remarked, "There's the worst stretch of country I know, and I know 'most all the bad layouts from Idaho down. More men have got lost in that mess of stuff than any other place I ever saw, and most of 'em are there yet. Miner's Hell I call it, easy to get in and the devil to get out. Well, I know where we are, anyway. I wasn't sure before, but now there'll be monuments, if we can find 'em, so I reckon we'll get through."

It was a remarkable sight. Imagine a cauldron of molten rock, miles wide, thrown by earthquake shock into the complexity of a choppy sea and then struck immovable. Looking down on it one would say that not a stick or leaf of herbage was there, still less any animal life in that sterility of vermilion, ochre, and gray. Life there is of both kinds, but so scant that it is merely the scientific minimum, almost more theory than fact.

Our eyes needed to be on the alert every moment to get the benefit of the monuments. They were sometimes a hundred yards, sometimes half a mile apart, and such casual affairs that without a sort of instinct one would not know them. However, with one or two mistakes we worked our way through and found ourselves in the main cañon. The name of Split Mountain fairly describes its appearance. The spectacular part of the defile begins some distance from the mouth, but already high walls shut us in, and made a narrow corridor with level floor of white sand in which a few bits of brush huddled close to the cliffs for shelter from the blasting sun.

Before getting far into the cañon we came to the place that gave our only chance of water. On a boulder was dimly written in English and Spanish, "Water 100 feet West. Dig": with an arrow marking the direction. Pacing off the distance we looked for a likely spot and went to work. The first hole giving no encouragement, we tried another, then a third: but after half an hour of thirsty work we concluded that it was hopeless, and ceased. Earlier in the year we might have had success: now the water level had sunk out of reach. Traces of others' attempts could be seen, and I hoped that none of them stood for the last struggle of some fellow mortal....

We picked our way round the shoulder of Fish Creek Mountain, an imposing mass that even in half darkness showed a metallic look, very noticeable by daylight. I expect to hear some day of fortunes coming out of that mountain, which has hardly been touched by prospectors, on account of the difficulty of taking in sufficient water for a stay long enough for effective work.

Wellson was making for a "dry camp" of his on the way to which we should pass an old mining shaft in which a little liquid was sometimes to be found. This, though quite impossible for human beings, Wellson had known his animals to drink when hard pushed.

It was long after dark when we reached the hole. We hauled up a bucket of the stuff, the horses crowding round for first chance. The stench was atrocious, and it was all I could do to avoid being violently sick. One after another the animals did their best to drink, putting their noses to it thirstily time after time, but it was too foul and they would not take it. We drew bucket after bucket in hope of getting something a degree less disgusting. At last one of Wellson's horses reluctantly drank a little, rolling back her lips after each mouthful to get rid of the filthy taste and odor. Her mate, and my Kaweah, who is unusually scrupulous, could not bring themselves to touch it, though their eagerness was pitiful.

A MOONLIT TREK

I sat down and figured things over. We were now clear of the Chuck-wallas. To the south was a ridge of hills that, as I reckoned, shut me off from sight of the Salton Sea. Ahead a wide valley opened, running due west for many miles. If I could make southwest across country I ought to come out into the Dos Palmas road; but it was nearly dark, the country was a labyrinth of *barrancas*—the worst of all country to get lost in—the last traces of any trail had been left behind hours ago, and the spectre of thirst was keeping me ever closer company. Even if I could find Corn Springs again my problem would not be finally solved. On the whole, the open valley ahead was the best prospect. It led in the Cottonwood Springs direction and ought to bring me into the road by which, two months before, I had come from Dale. We would go ahead and see what happened.

We had not eaten for twelve hours, for I had been too much preoccupied to think of food. Kaweah had not drunk either, but I relied on the coolness of the night to refresh him. I gave him the last feed of barley, ate a scratch meal myself, and with an encouraging word to my anxious companion we started on.

Daylight had gone but the moon was well up and afforded aid and comfort. Except for the discomfort of doubt I could have reveled in the charm of the scene. The uncouth Chuckwallas rose dark behind and to my right. Moonlight whitened here and there the angle of some buttress, touching with charm of fancy the leagues of shadowy mountain. Our shadows marched before us, mingling with filmy pattern of creosote or skeleton of cactus or ocotillo. To the left the horizon line was a procession of dusky shapes, shifting and vanishing like monsters seen in a nightmare.

We had gone for a few miles in a sort of dogged muddle, when wagon tracks appeared without warning, crosswise of our line of march. Whither they might lead in either direction I had no idea, but they came as a vast relief. I made a rapid guess and chose the right-hand track. Another mile and we ran into an unmistakable road and were heading westerly into the long valley. It was now only a question of Kaweah's holding out. He was certainly very tired and necessarily very thirsty, while by my reckoning we were about twenty-five miles from water, whether we reached it at Cottonwood Springs or Shafer's Well. But the coolness of the night would help us out, and Kaweah, blessings on his tough little carcass, is pure Indian and would go till he dropped. As for myself, though I was muscle-weary to the limit (for I had been on foot all day) I felt I could travel forever in that refreshing temperature, and I still had a quart or so of water.

All night we toiled along. Played out as Kaweah was, whenever I stopped him he was anxious to go on, though with dragging step and muzzle almost touching his knees. I tried to buck him up with promises of the bully times we would have the coming winter—We'll chuck this everlasting clutter of saddle-bags, blankets, and canteens, and just knock about and enjoy ourselves, eh, pony boy? And it was clear how all in he was when he failed to respond to my fraternal slap with humorous show of ill-temper such as flattened ears or playful pretence of a bite. Stars rose, stars set: the moon overtook, passed us, and sailed ahead as if rallying us on our despicable pace. I was drowsy, but well content so long as the track kept on westward, for I knew it must bring us into some road that ran down to Mecca. So I whistled, dozed, and plodded on, cheering my plucky little nag, and counting off the miles by the hours we traveled. Rabbits played about in the road, careless of our approach until we almost kicked them away.

The Ansel Adams of the Desert:
Stephen H. Willard

Inevitably, the Colorado Desert as a unique place in the process of discovery and the dramatic setting of Palm Springs attracted its share of photographers along with writers and painters. Among them were Fred P. Clatworthy, William W. Lockwood, and J. Smeaton Chase, whose workmanlike images illustrated his own books.

Photographers, as with writers and painters, are a dime a dozen; all a person need do is claim the status to put on that mantle. Hence, economics can be cruel in winnowing them out, not often according to their lasting artistic merit. It's always a little surprising, then, as well as gratifying, when someone of Stephen H. Willard's talents manages to make a go of it, although not without a great deal of initiative. The young photographer sold postcards, illustrated articles, and scrambled about the country giving lectures informing the public about a landscape that was being revealed to him through his own art.

To compare Stephen H. Willard to Ansel Adams is not mere hyperbole. As fascinating as the desert is, often any adequately made image bears its own interest by virtue of its subject if for nothing else. As Christine Giles of the Palm Springs Art Museum observes, Willard's sense of composition and use of sharp contrasts in shadow and light in recording the desert immediately call to mind a similar sensitivity Adams successfully employed when revealing far different landscapes. Emerging out of such features is something far less definable, that touch of the alchemical both men possessed conveying an innate sense of profundity through their images.

We are fortunate that the Palm Springs Art Museum has become a repository of Willard's extensive materials. It also might be noted that Willard's charming Palm

Springs home, built in the Mediterranean style, although not open to the public, may be seen on the grounds of the Moorten Botanical Garden, a mile or so south of downtown.

~~~ **Christine Giles,**
from "Stephen H. Willard: Photography Collection and Archive"

In 1999, Dr. Beatrice Willard donated her father's life's work to the Palm Springs Art Museum. This generous gift of over 16,000 items includes original glass and film negatives, vintage photographs, hand-colored lantern slides, photo-paintings, postcards, stereographs, cameras, lenses and other photographic equipment, and personal papers and memorabilia including maps, correspondence, and publications.

Over a period of nearly 60 years, Willard produced thousands of photographs documenting areas of the West few Americans had seen or visited. The collection contains images of deserts, valleys, and mountains focusing on California, Arizona, New Mexico, and Northern Mexico. He also photographed important historical sites and activities, including mining operations, Native American villages, cities, and towns. In the early 1920s, Willard began applying oil paint to the surface of select photographs to create photo-paintings. He sold his photo-paintings and photographs to visitors and tourists, and his images were reproduced in maps, brochures, and periodicals. Most importantly his photographs helped convince President Franklin D. Roosevelt to establish the Joshua Tree National Monument in 1936, now a National Park. Willard also promoted the preservation of other natural lands including Death Valley. Yet, in spite of his record of achievements, Willard's legacy remains largely unknown, and his name has been omitted from photography, art, and history books. It is the goal of the Palm Springs Desert Museum to preserve Willard's legacy and reintroduce his photography to a national and international audience through exhibitions, publications, the internet, and other programs.

Born in Illinois, Stephen Hallet Willard (1894–1966) grew up in Corona, California. Willard's interest in landscape photography began at a very early age. Given his love of landscape, the diversity of Southern California provided Willard with mountains, seacoasts, lakes, and vast desert scenes to hone his photographic skills. Between 1908 and 1912 he began to experiment with a variety of photographic techniques and papers, organizing his efforts into an album now part of the collection. During this period, Willard began taking photography camping trips into nearby Angeles National Forest. By the time he graduated from Corona High School in 1912, he had developed the skills needed for a career in photography.

Around 1914, Willard began to travel regularly to the deserts around Palm Springs and in a 1916 magazine article entitled "The Land of the Purple Shadow," he described his love of the area:

> In Southern California, east and south from the Pass of San Gorgonio, in the great, purple shadow of Mt. San Jacinto, there lives a wonderland of desert and mountain, canyon and mesa. It is surpassed by no desert land for subtle charm and fascination....

From this point on, desert landscape photography would become Willard's passion.

Willard's desert trips were interrupted in 1918 when he enlisted in the army as a photographer and served in the 319th Engineer Battalion, 8th Division (A.E.F.) in France during WW I. He photographed the camp and soldiers as well as the landscape and people of France. Many of these images, now preserved in the collection, were printed as postcards and sold to the troops. After he was honorably discharged in the summer of 1919 he returned to Southern California.

In 1921, Willard married Beatrice Armstrong. After a year of traveling and photographing the deserts throughout the South, they settled permanently in Palm Springs and opened a studio and gallery. To escape the summer heat, they opened a second studio in Mammoth. This pattern of living in the desert in the winter and the Sierras in the summer became Willard's lifestyle. Discouraged by the increasing development and population growth in the Coachella Valley, in 1947 the Willards moved to Owens Valley. Stephen H. Willard died there in 1966.

Willard regarded photography as a fine art and himself as an artist. The desert offered the tonal vocabulary he sought for his black and white photographs: sharp contrasts of light, expansive uninterrupted horizons, folded mountain ranges, layered ridge lines, and long shadows created by the morning and afternoon sun. Enduring harsh conditions, he often spent days traveling by burro or car to remote desert locations. Once he found his subject, he might wait for hours for the correct light and conditions to capture the image he wanted. Willard described his experience and the quality he sought for his images:

The desert, above all subjects in nature, contains, for me, some elements of spiritual quality which are not to be captured by a casual trip along paved highways where traffic passes every few minutes. The spirit of the subject is best felt miles away from any habitation or work of man, where the desert lives "silent, hot, and fierce."

Willard considered himself a realist working in the style of "straight photography." His approach to landscape photography can be compared to his better known contemporaries such as Ansel Adams and Edward Weston. Willard's choice of subjects, composition, and use of sharp contrasts combine to make his images not only valuable artistic masterpieces but also provide a historic record of the desert and mountain environments.

The Excitements of Celluloid:
The Camel's Nose

Devoted as they were to the creation of art and the love of nature, the gentle writers, photographers, and naturalists of Palm Springs could get a little bored with the routine. Every day a cheery sun swung over once again with staid predictability. And the charms of their village, with its vine-covered cottages and drowsy pepper trees overhanging the streets, for all the heartfelt quaintness, lacked an enticing irregularity. Surely, there were the assignations and minor scandals of any village, but they, too, became old, lacking a grand dimension to stir the soul.

All the more welcome, then, when the moviemakers came to town. With their cowboys, Arabs, and legionnaires, and their daring deeds as the cameras churned, they injected at least the temporary excitements of another, faster world. These made a few ebullient days to give the locals pause, to put down their pens and brushes and enjoy the wonders unfolding before them. Then the exotic figures packed up and left, disappearing as quickly as a bewildering but beautiful mirage. Hence, this scene—a bit slapstick perhaps, but also fairly representative of the circumstances of moviemaking in the desert—by William C. deMille, an accomplished movie director in his own right and the elder brother of the more famous Cecil B.

For their part, the movie people found Palm Springs, rude as it was, a great boon. The weather was almost always fine for shooting, the village was just over the mountains from Hollywood and fairly accessible by railroad, and with the dramatic variety of its settings, of mountains, palm canyons, desert, and rushing creeks, a little fudging with the camera could turn the place into Egypt, Turkey, South America, or just about any locale a script might call for.

After the flurry of wrathy Bedouins charging en masse down the dunes and Indians whooping after speeding stagecoaches, feeling a little blessed from the excitements the amused Palm Springers returned to their cottages to continue their more serious pursuits, knowing with a pleasurable anticipation that the moviemakers would be back to stir them once again. What the villagers didn't think about, however, was how much the Hollywood types would come to like Palm Springs and how long they'd come to stay, their money and anathematic styles rudely sweeping aside the mild ways of the contemplative villagers.

‒‒‒‒ William C. deMille,
from *Hollywood Saga*

I remember the desert's heat in August. By some strange decree of fate, which we never could understand nor, apparently, avoid, it always seemed to be the case that water-stuff had to be done in the colder months, while desert-stuff invariably occurred in the hottest part of summer.

In this particular August I was shooting "The Heir to the Hoorah," and Tom Meighan was my leading man. Our headquarters were at Palm Springs, under the shadow of Mount Jacinto [*sic*] in the Mojave Desert. This was in the days when Palm Springs had not yet been adopted by the movie colony as a resort. The town was only a cluster of weather-beaten dwellings, served by a typical, Western country store; a desert settlement in an Indian reservation. If you walked a few hundred yards from the little oasis of the village, you were in the trackless waste of the desert itself, with all its mysterious sense of loneliness, its mirages, its deceiving distances and its cruel grandeur.

At the foot of Palm Canyon, where we were working, the temperature was 130° and the camera crew had to keep wet cloths over the film cases to cool them by evaporation. There was no ice within fifty miles. If you wanted a drink of water you took it warm and noticed that it was strongly "on the alkaline side."

Tom, playing our hero, was supposed to be lost in the desert. His canteen empty, he is dying of thirst as he reaches the water-hole only to find it dried up. He has his moment of despair and then, half-crazed and delirious, he sees a beautiful mirage across the shimmering sand and forces himself to struggle on until he disappears from view over an outcropping ledge. It was really quite an effective scene, with miles of desolation as a background and no sign of human habitation visible.

The heat was so killing that I had not let Tom play up in rehearsal; just walked him through it to get camera composition and position and also to be sure that the route he traversed was fairly clear of rattlesnakes, scorpions, centipedes and other items which might have taken an actor out of the proper mood. The boys had made a lovely dried water-hole surrounded by various skulls and bones brought all the way from Hollywood.

"All right, Tom," I said to him finally, "we're all ready to go; do your stuff and don't stop acting until you go over that rocky ledge. I want to see your figure get smaller and smaller until it represents the insignificance of man opposed to the desert's silent power."

"Okay," said Tom. "Let's go."

I started the camera and Tom threw himself into his part. This was one time when he didn't have to pretend to feel the heat and we didn't have to fake the sweat on his face. His acting was so sincere that when he staggered away from the water-hole and started after the imaginary mirage he left the route we had planned and followed his artistic imagination.

"Look out, Charlie," I said to the cameraman, "he's off the trail; can you keep him in?"

"Sure," said Charlie. "He can't get away. He looks loco all right—fine stuff."

Tom reached the ledge, though not at the chosen spot. Being a good actor he knew that the farther he got away from the camera the broader his gestures had to be. He knew, also, that the ledge was his exit, and paused on the edge to do a superb piece of acting à la Monte Cristo. Then he disappeared from sight and as I gave the order to "cut," a wild yell came over the air from Tom's general direction. An expert might have analyzed that cry as being composed of pain, rage, surprise, disgust and appeal.

"Come on, boys," I called, and we dropped everything and rushed to see what had happened. As we reached the ledge and looked over, we saw. Tom, carried away by his art, had not looked before he leaped. He had landed, in a sitting posture, upon a bed of spiny cactus. He was keeping motionless but not quiet.

I could appreciate his lack of desire to move: I knew that kind of cactus. Its two-inch needles would go through shoe leather, and I had even used them in my phonograph to produce a softer tone than could be got from steel.

They did not, however, produce a softer tone from Tom. His language was listened to with respect and just a little awe by myself and the boys; we realized that up to now we had led sheltered lives; that all the profanity we knew was so pitifully inadequate as to be useless.

"Are you hurt, Tom?" I asked thoughtlessly.

I cannot even translate his reply, but from it I gathered that he was most uncomfortable; that he was feeling all the tortures of the damned, but that that was child's play to what he felt if he stirred. He suggested that I cease standing there like some Biblical example of an ass and do something about it; also that time was an element which was becoming increasingly valuable to him, if not to me. He even criticized my direction but, under the circumstances, I forbore to remind him that he and not I had chosen this particular spot for his exit.

I could think of only one way to rescue him: he had to be lifted bodily from his seat of pain and carried to a less penetrating resting place. We set about it and four of us grasped him, at the price of getting a few spines in our own legs.

"Gently, boys, go easy," I warned, and added to the sufferer, "This is going to hurt a little, Tom; those needles will come out of the plant easier than they will out of you."

Using short, primitive words Tom urged immediate action and postponement of discussion and analysis.

"Okay, boys, all together," I said, and we lifted.

"Owooo—oo!" said Tom.

As I had predicted, the needles tore out at their roots, which left Tom portable and voluble but not at all philosophical. With much care we bore him from the cactus and laid him, for obvious reasons, face down on the desert floor. We removed his nether garments, an act which, in itself, turned out to be something of a major operation, and started the long process of extracting the spines, one by one, using mechanic's pliers as forceps. We made an interesting group, although not ideal for screen purposes, and I wondered how many times this same desert had seen similar bands of pioneers aiding a wounded comrade. But the picture was not quite perfect in heroic atmosphere, for Tom, brave though he was, saw no reason to be stoical and the removal of each barbed arrow was marked by a sharp yelp.

Later, after the film was finished, I never saw that particular sequence without feeling an irrepressible desire to giggle. How fortunate for us, whose business it is to create illusion, that the audience cannot see what happens in the course of production. Incidents behind the scenes are usually interesting, but the picture left in the mind is not always romantic, which, I suppose, is one reason why every company employs a highly paid and brilliantly imaginative publicity department to aid the public in weaving magic webs of fancy about its stars. They must not be thought of as common clay, these charming shadows who take us out of our workaday world into a more exciting life. It is the will of the people that these be gods and not mortals—or, as one of them naïvely confided to me, "It is the voice of the *vox populi.*"

25

The Excitements of Celluloid:
The Camel Victorious

In light of the preceding, the following is self-explanatory.

⁓ California: A Guide to the Golden State

Palm Springs, (430 alt., pop. subject to seasonal changes), one of the newest playgrounds of rich America, has been successively the domain of Cahuilla Indians, a stagecoach stop, and a desert home for the convalescent and tubercular. Today this ultrasmart winter resort for movie stars and for people who like and can afford to live where and as movie stars live, gleams as brightly as a new toy village. Its buildings are uniformly of California pseudo-Spanish architecture: the white, lemon, or buff-colored dwellings, entered by doors painted bright red, blue, or yellow, are surmounted by red tile roofs and enclosed by wooden fences, bordered by rows of pink and white oleanders or the green feathery plumage of tamarisk trees. Here are branches of the most expensive New York and Los Angeles shops; golf courses and hotels that range from the palatial to the modestly magnificent; private and public schools and no lack of masseurs and masseuses; dude cowhands for atmosphere and branch brokerage offices for the bigger businessmen.

First known as Agua Caliente (hot water)—so named by De Anza in 1774 because of its hot springs—the settlement dates from 1876, when the Southern Pacific first laid down its tracks through Coachella Valley. Until

1913 Palm Springs remained a sleepy little hamlet with a single store and a roadside inn on a poor desert road. A nearby gold mine, the Virginia Dale, offered the only attraction to people in search of a living, and the warm dry climate (average noontime temperature, 81°; average evening temperature, 45°) made it an excellent but little known health resort. Then Hollywood, early in the 1930s, discovered the climatic and topographical charm of the little village resting on a shelf of the San Jacinto Mountain base at the edge of the desert. A new highway was cut through, Los Angeles and New York promoters got to work, and the modern town sprang up almost with the speed of a movie set.

Here one finds the desert safely pushed to the borders of a transplanted section of Hollywood Blvd. Guests sprint about town on bicycles, sip cocktails, play table tennis, explore the nearby desert on horseback, or, relaxing in some hotel garden, enjoy the lengthening shadow of the San Jacinto and the quiet of the land stretching out to the eastern hills. After dark they visit the night clubs, casinos, and movies.

The town's Sulphur Springs lie just east of the business district on the Agua Caliente Reservation; here the Indians who own the property maintain a bathhouse on the spot where their forefathers camped for hundreds of years. The commercial competition of the Indians has aroused the bitter antagonism of the townspeople.

Each year La Fiesta de los Monos (the feast of the images) is held on the reservation—now in a somewhat corrupt form owing to the presence of prosperous strangers who want quaint entertainment. The ancient Cahuilla rite is designed to aid the spirit in departing from this earth after death. When the number of deaths in a family reaches eight, the survivors gather to dance, wail, and chant. They make effigies of the deceased on wooden frames five feet high; dressing, painting, and decorating them is an elaborate ceremony lasting several days, during which the family is obliged to entertain a great crowd of tribal visitors. When the images have been completed, the tribe has an all-night dance; money is distributed among the guests. At dawn, when Lucero, the morning star, reaches a certain height, the images are burned in a pit, and their released spirits depart to the upper regions.

Directly west of Palm Springs is Tachevan (dry rock) Canyon; a short walk leads to a mountain stream trickling among brightly painted rocks—an ideal picnic site.

Right 0.5 m. from Palm Springs on a county road to the Palm Springs Airport.

North of Palm Springs small white stucco and plaster buildings, housing the offices of Los Angeles realtors and promoters, border State 111 more frequently than the date palms. Mesquite-covered desert land stretches northwest to the brown foothills of the Little San Bernardino Mountains.

After God ... Gen. George S. Patton!

Well, not really. Feisty as he was, as far as we know, "Old Blood and Guts" did not possess Divine powers. However, symbolically he did.

When we stand on a peak overlooking the great sweeps before us without any evidence of human meddling, let alone signs of human habitation, the desert seems a land of freedom, a realm far beyond the cranky neighbors, choked freeways, and other irritating features of civilization we must daily endure, a place where we could at last, if we chose, live our lives as we pleased.

That is a pleasant illusion. In fact, next in line to the forces of nature, the largest influence on the desert is the government in all its guises, federal, state, and local. It is the government that decides where freeways go, provides the research fueling agricultural development, and, yes, even on the desert, dictates building codes to escaping individuals hammering away at their desert hideaways. Going further back in history, it was the government that funded such early explorations as geologist William P. Blake's reconnaissance of the desert, then paid for the publication of his tome; and the government, too, that, through encouraging legislation, subsidized the railroads now crisscrossing the desert. And, lest we forget as we revel in our freedom, it is the government that administers most of the preserves where we hike with the levitating feeling that we're the first to lay eyes on a pristine landscape.

As to bellicose aspects of government, most military installations now lie north of the Colorado Desert, in the Mojave Desert, where the nighttime traveler sometimes sees the dense sky shimmer into an aurora borealis of exploding ordnance. Yet during World War II the Colorado Desert was overrun with thousands of tanks, Jeeps, and half-tracks sending their plumes high into the pristine desert sky. This was because of events thousands of miles away. In 1942, Rommel was driving east across North Africa, threatening to crush the British and seize the Suez Canal. The British drove him west again out into the desert, but in an accordion warfare, as soon as the overextended British ran out of steam, Rommel was back, hammering away at the defenses of the lifeline Canal with his tanks.

Obviously, if the British, their resources nearly depleted, were to be rescued, the Americans would have to do it. Just as obviously, the United States had no experience in this kind of warfare. The Americans, however, learned fast. A near maniac for excellence, realist Patton carved out a huge territory in southeastern California, western Arizona, and southern Nevada, and began readying his troops with maneuvers that in a few months, in a marvel of rugged training, would toughen them to rout the well-seasoned Germans out of North Africa.

It would be pleasant to think that we could live without governments, and indeed without wars, that we could build our desert shack in any whimsical way we pleased, but the reality is that we live in a world of complex institutions, one hopes for the better, not for the worse. After decades, Gen. Patton's tank tracks still crisscross the Colorado Desert as irrefutable evidence of that.

~~~ John S. Lynch, John W. Kennedy, and Robert L. Wooley, from *Patton's Desert Training Center*

One of the original units to be transferred to the DTC [Desert Training Center] was the 773rd Tank Destroyer Battalion commanded by Lieutenant Colonel F. G. Spiess. It had previously taken part in the Louisiana and North Carolina maneuvers and was said to have traveled some 9,500 miles through seven states over a period of four months, but the men were to find a new experience at Camp Young where they arrived shortly after April 5, 1942. Their official history relates that, "Camp Young was the world's largest Army Post and the greatest training maneuver area in U.S. military history. Eighteen thousand square miles of nothing, in a desert designed for Hell." One soldier who had endured it reported that clothes, equipment such as water bags, radios, vehicles, armored vehicles of all types and weapons were to be severely tested in this desert area. "Water in the Lister bags sometimes reached 90 degrees. After you have been inside the tanks for a while, water even at 90 degrees seemed cool. The tank destroyers were even hotter because they had the open top turrets. Sometimes the heat registered at 152 degrees. Inspection of tools and equipment was made early in the mornings or late in the evening as any equipment or tools laid out on tarps by the individual vehicles, in the desert sun, could not be picked up as they would burn the hands."

Not all of the recollections of those who spent time on the desert were unpleasant. Another member of the 773rd Tank Destroyer Battalion recorded that "My greatest experience for the desert was observing the beauties of nature, both on the desert and also the nearby mountains. My worst experience was being stranded for two days in Pahlen Dry Lake in a disabled half track with four crewmen during which time we had one can of sardines, one can of corn, and one and one-half canteens of water."

Before the first mass maneuver, and to add to initial confusion, an epidemic of yellow jaundice (hepatitis) swept the camps in July. This filled all of the hospitals in the California area. Convalescence of the patients was slow and this further delayed training. As we now know this was due to the contamination of the yellow fever vaccine given to the troops with a then undiscovered virus which caused hepatitis and jaundice. The yellow fever vaccine had been stabilized with human blood serum. The serum had been derived from volunteer medical students. This blood had been drawn from at least one student who had suffered from hepatitis previously. Thus, this widespread Army epidemic of hepatitis was iatrogenic in origin and it was devastating. Hundreds who received the yellow fever vaccine were thus inadvertently inoculated with another disease, hepatitis.

All accounts related that, as the first commanding general, Patton certainly stamped his brand on the training center. The hill from which he could observe a wide area was called "The King's Throne." It was a lone elevation between the Crocopia and the Chuckwalla Mountains and separated them both. The General used to sit or stand up there scrutinizing critically the line of march of tanks and motorized units below him. Detecting a mistake or way to improve, he would shout instructions into his radio. Something ought to be said about Patton's radio. The official Army history of the Desert Training Center simply states the above but Porter B. Williamson in *Patton's Principles* gives a detailed and delightful account of Patton's communication system. This is how he describes the situation of the I Armored Corps Headquarters: "Our headquarters was approximately sixty miles east of Indio, California. Radio reception in our tents was poor due to the long distance between our portable radios and the broadcasting stations in Palm Springs and Los Angeles. General Patton's first concern was always the welfare of the troops, so he purchased radio broadcasting equipment. The initial investment was his own money! Our Signal Corps troops installed the radio broadcasting equipment. The station broadcast only news and music. It was a quick method of communication with the troops. General Patton wanted to talk to the troops as often as possible. At a staff meeting he said, 'This new station could save several weeks of training. We can reach the troops, every one of them, as often as we need. In an emergency, we could reach every man in seconds.'"

Williamson continued, "Our desert radio broadcasting station had one unusual feature. There was a microphone in General Patton's office and a second microphone by his bed in his tent. Day and night General Patton would cut off all broadcasting and announce a special message or order from his personal mike. When the music would click off we knew we would hear, 'This is General Patton.' He would use it to commend the special efforts by the troops. He would announce, 'Found a damn good soldier today!' He would continue giving the name of the man and the organization. This officer encouraged every man and officer to give his best effort at all times. Often his harsh words for an officer would provoke laughter from others. For example, one time General Patton ordered, 'Col. Blank, you are removed from command! If you know what is good for you, you will stay away from me for a week.'"

The Commanding General was "uncompromising." Firstly, he was not easy on his men. When they did not drill they policed. He was a driver and a disciplinarian. Secondly, he was uncompromising with himself as well. He demanded that his men appear in uniform. Despite the heat and sand he himself wore his uniform in a military manner. He did not live in Indio but in a tent at Camp Young. In fact, one of the first things he did when he reported to the desert area was empty out the hotel at Indio. Only one officer was left behind and it was said that he was sick and could not be moved. In the third place, he wanted housekeeping arrangements to be minimal and tactical and technical instruction to be at the maximum.

It was initially planned that there would be a maneuver of troops in the area on July 15, but due to the logistics snarl, and the late arrival of troops, it was postponed until October 18. Gen. Patton prepared for the first DTC maneuvers but he was not to command them. He was relieved and his I Armored Corps was needed for action in North Africa. As one reviews various facets of the development of this maneuver area, it seems almost incredible that within a period of six to eight months, in spite of the fact that it was never fully operable under Patton, he left his lasting imprint. His technique of training continued until the maneuver area was closed.

The Desert Training Center was a war baby and it was a thorn to the spirit with its isolation, evasive dust and extreme shifts in temperature. Men had to be acclimated. The 3rd Armored Division suffered many casualties from heat prostration. Other units did too, but there is very little in the official reports on this subject. The surgeon under General Patton warned the command that danger lurked in reaching for an object on the ground unless you were sure that a rattlesnake wasn't coiled around it. He advised that liquids be drunk slowly and in small amounts, but with an eventual increased intake over a 24 hour period and to avoid overexposure in the sun. Three 10-grain salt tablets were to be taken daily.

Problems with the civilian population in the area were not particularly unique. These camps which sprang up all over the zone of interior in the States created a great deal of stress on adjacent communities, many of which were small. There was a flood of wives and families trying to follow their loved ones as they trained, discovering that housing, food, the whole bit was very difficult. The official history relates that "the situation in Indio was deplorable."

Initially the train transportation was snarled and deficient, which delayed proper distribution of food, water and other supplies; however, in time this was corrected. Water supplies were increased after wells were completed. Generally rations were the modified "B" ration with fresh milk and frozen beef added at a later date. The latter must have been the exception, for the majority of those interviewed recall that two of the camps on the Arizona side were forbidden to have ice for long periods and they were not permitted fresh fruit or vegetables. The beer ration, when available, was served warm.

Equipment was in very short supply during the major portion of the maneuver area activation. The 5th Armored Division, which had been activated a year earlier, still lacked 40 percent of its equipment at the time it maneuvered in the desert. Service units were in very short supply and all vehicles were used to their limits without proper maintenance. The original concept was for units not to bring new equipment, other than personal, into the maneuver area. Instead an outgoing division was to leave its trucks, tanks, signal equipment and all of that type of field materiel properly serviced so as to be used by an incoming division. Major General

George Ruhlen, now retired, remembers, "the 4th Armored Division's unit issue of tanks, trucks, and the like being in horrible condition and it was in even worse shape when the 4th Armored Division left Camp Ibis. The idea of leaving equipment for the following unit at least relieved the strain on the supply and rail services."

The Desert Training Center severely taxed civilians as well as the military. It doesn't make much difference if one is talking about Indio, Yuma, Blythe or the larger towns such as Phoenix, the civilians learned that when the troops were on leave, especially weekends, the civilians were not going to get into restaurants, movie theaters, trains and busses. The increased demand sometimes deprived the local civilian population of certain foods. In Yuma, after the 6th Armored Division spent a weekend, eggs and beef were in very short supply.

Desert Magazine and Marshal South:
Living like Indians

It's a running debate among desert aficionados: Does the desert attract eccentrics, or does some mystical quality turn normal people into oddballs once they get there? Related to this, perhaps psychologists can explain why the general public avidly believes fantastic tales about the desert which people would blush to entertain about other landscapes.

First from El Centro, near the Mexican border, then from Palm Desert just east of Palm Springs, beginning in 1937 *Desert Magazine* projected a eupeptic image of the desert as an effervescent elixir for body and soul. The desert, so it was portrayed in the popular monthly, was a vast Disneyland where artists happily painted and weekend hobbyists might gleefully pick up semiprecious stones.

It was good entertainment if one read a bit cautiously, and the articles leading readers to the out-of-the-way discoveries of ghost towns and long-ignored historic sites were quite valuable.

But where is the line between providing pleasure, if sometimes zipped up for effect, and outright lies designed to sell magazines?

For years the monthly's most popular feature was a series by a man who claimed to be living "like an Indian" on a mountaintop, harvesting the abundance of wild food nature provided in that nearly rainless land, while in constant communication with the Great Spirit.

We chuckle now at that, at how our grandparents, yearning to believe a romantic tale, were so easily duped, yet may conclude that little harm was done for the magazine's profitable hoodwinking. Perhaps. Yet fantasies can have their pernicious effects if they delude us in harmful ways. Marshal South and family did, indeed, live on an isolated mountaintop, but beyond that he was a fraud, for his food came from town, as the heap of rusting tin cans behind the ruins of his house testifies to this day. Perhaps worse, in fact he was not the warmhearted lover of all creatures he pretended to be but a violent control freak. His wife finally left him, claiming that he threatened to kill her for refusing to go to South America to start a sex colony.

Marshal South's pages offer a cozening dream, a warm bath of wish fulfillment. However, his writing also illustrates the dangers, as seen in Diana Lindsay's happy study of the man, of glibly clinging to what we, sometimes desperately, want to believe. After all, we might better show respect for nature by appreciating the desert for what it is, rather than twisting it to serve our childish fantasies.

Marshal South,
from "Desert Refuge"

Yes, we wish it would rain. But there is health in heat and in sunshine, notwithstanding the discomfort which is inseparable from desert midsummer. The dry heat of the desert is charged with benefits for the human body. Humanity gets far too little of the sun—that is, civilized humanity. The unspoiled savage was, and is, different. But civilized man has turned his face to the darkness, in more ways than one. You may read articles and listen to discourses which seek to prove that sunlight should be taken in cautious doses, that too much of it is a positive danger. All of which sounds very official. But the exponents of these theories make a very poor showing in actual health. About ninety per cent of the people I know are afraid of the sun, afraid to expose their skins to it, saying that they will burn. Which they do. But most of them are sick in some way or another....

It was said by one of the ancient philosophers that "The proper study of mankind is man." But I think that this advice should be amplified to include the whole of animate creation. For certainly man may learn a great deal by intelligently studying his "younger brothers" of fur and feather and all their many classes of relatives. Not studying them in the sense of knowing their Latin names or their exact measurements. But by seeing the world—their world—as far as possible, through their eyes. In this way much may be learned of their "human" reactions to various situations. Also the varying degrees of intelligence possessed by not only different classes of creatures, but by different individuals of the same class. Study of this sort will do much to rid man of the exalted mythology of greatness which he has woven about himself. The Indian, before his liberties and his soul were destroyed by his ignorant white conquerors, knew much of this lore. To him the creatures of the desert and of the forest were not just "animals." They were younger brothers, about whom a vast store of knowledge and understanding were accumulated. Something that today is thrust aside by those who stampede along in the mad scramble for the baubles of "civilization." The Indian knew better. But then the Indian was part of the natural picture. And he had the advantage of being unhampered by books. Books are all very well in their place. But they are a menace if overdone.

But the Book of Nature—the same one that the Indian studied so successfully—still is available free to all. And the Desert Edition of it, whose pages we on Ghost Mountain ruffle through every day by the aid of wind and sunshine, always provides interesting items and food for thought.

There was, for instance, the chapter written by our pair of flycatchers and the brown racer snake. A chapter of tragedy. But one nevertheless which contained many side lights on bird and snake intelligence.

This pair of flycatchers nested very late this year. They were a long time deciding on their nest box. Also they took their time about building. Finally the job was complete and the eggs laid. The female took up the task of hatching them. A few hot days passed. Frequently in the afternoons she would come and sit in the nest box opening, cooling off.

It was one of these hot afternoons that a wild outcry arose from the children. Rider had seen a long "something" hanging out of the nest box—a shape at which the frantic bird, hovering near the entrance, was wildly pecking. "There's something in the flycatcher house" was the wild shout that brought Tanya and me running.

It was the young brown racer snake who has spent all his life around Yaquitepec. He is now about 30 inches long and full of misguided humor. His lithe tail hung out of the nest box, which is situated in the summit of a gnarled juniper tree. And as I came rushing up and grabbed him, he withdrew a startled head and a mouth full of nest feathers. He looked innocently astonished.

The poor flycatcher was swooping and fluttering around in frantic terror. So tumbling his snakeship unceremoniously on his head among the branches—from which he hastily scooted—I wrenched open the nest box door and felt in the deep little nest pocket. There were still two eggs left. We secured the door of the box again and went quickly away to give the terrified bird a chance to return. The snake, we felt, having had some un-gentle handling and a scare, would not be likely to return.

It took the flycatcher a long time to calm herself. We would have wor-ried about the eggs chilling had it not been such warm weather. She hov-ered around and around the nest and peered at it from vantage points on the branches for so long that we grew tired of watching and went about our work. And then we heard again a frantic twittering and crying. And again we dashed out.

It was the snake again. He hung half out of the box as before. This time I was really angry. Without ceremony I yanked him forth and sent him whirling out over the mescals and rubber bushes. I distinctly remem-ber how stiffly he went round and round in the air. Just like a stiff stick. And, luckily for him, he landed in a springy rubberbush a considerable distance away. Rider, racing to the spot, advised that he was making off across country at top speed.

He had managed to get another egg. That left a solitary one. We de-cided to move the nest box. We sawed it from its wooden pole support and remounted it atop a long length of steel pipe, which we set up in a crack of some great boulders some ten feet from its original treetop site. We feared that this was the end of the flycatchers' homemaking. It didn't seem possi-ble that they would ever come back after this. And they didn't.

But the snake did. Incredible as it may seem that slim brown piece of rascality came back for the third time, looking for the last egg. Shortly after we had finished the job of establishing the nest box upon its steel pole I discovered him sprawled out along the branches in the juniper tree. He was looking at the severed end of the nest box pole in a puzzled sort of way. He conveyed the impression of one who, having imbibed too freely, is "seeing things"—or, in this case, *not* seeing them.

I shook my finger at him and gave him a wrathful lecture. But you can't get really angry with a racer snake. They are so full of humor. He just looked at me with his peculiarly expressive eyes. He seemed to wink. Then he slid swiftly away.

"Why didn't you kill him?" a friend asked us later. He couldn't un-derstand why we hadn't swatted the robber. But things aren't managed that way at Yaquitepec. We do not shed the blood of our brothers—it is only the ignorant who resort to killing as a solution to problems. Gaining thereby not a solution but an intensification of the trouble. The command "Thou shalt not kill" is a very real plank of our religion. There was a time once on Ghost mountain, when—through ignorance and a fear for what baby footsteps might blunder into—we backslid on our convictions as far as rattlesnakes were concerned. But we have repented of our failure and our error. And the rattlers now rest, with all our other brothers, under the seal of peace. For we have seen what this upsetting of the balance of nature does, even in the short period when we were guilty of it. For the squirrels and the packrats of Yaquitepec have increased alarmingly. And the native vegetation suffers. He who is wise will leave the balance alone.

28

Pegleg Smith:
A Legend Found—Then Lost Again

The great strikes of gold and silver in Southern California occurred elsewhere than on the Colorado Desert, mainly to the north, on its sister desert, the Mojave. All the better, perhaps, for the rumors of great bonanzas still awaiting discovery on the Colorado Desert persist down to this day. In this sense, perhaps the most delectable of fortunes, as with so many other things in our lives, are not those that we actually grasp but, like some Holy Grail, lie always ahead, the lure itself becoming its own richest treasure for the imagination.

— **John D. Mitchell,**
   from "Black Nuggets in the Valley of Phantom Buttes"

John Mitchell believes that the Pegleg Smith lost buttes of the black nuggets are located near the point where the eastern ends of the Chuckawalla and Chocolate mountains converge, on the north side of Salton Sea. John is sure they are there because he once found the place and brought away three of the black nuggets. But he did not know until many years later that the manganese-coated stones he picked up were gold. Here is a new version of the legendary Pegleg gold strike.

The lost Pegleg Smith gold mine with its piles of black gold nuggets is one of the celebrated traditions of the great Southwest. Much time and money have been spent and many lives lost in the quest for this fabulously rich gold deposit believed to be located in the heart of the great California desert—the Sahara of America.

For more than a century prospectors and adventurers from every part of the civilized world have searched these waste lands for some trace of the "Lost Valley of the Phantom Buttes" from whence came the many black gold nuggets brought out of the desert by the Indians and the few white men who were willing to gamble their lives against those twin demons of the desert—heat and thirst.

Pegleg Smith, early day trapper, found the deposit while on his way across the desert to the Spanish settlements on the Pacific Coast in the year 1829 to market a cargo of furs. But he was never able to return to it.

Thomas L. Smith was born in 1801 in Garrard County, Kentucky, the son of Christopher Smith, an Irish immigrant who fought in the Indian wars of the Northwest under St. Clair. After varied experiences on the Mississippi River, Smith, at the age of 23, joined a caravan of 80 wagons and 150 men bound for Santa Fe, New Mexico, to trade with the Indians. The caravan fought its way across the great plains then swarming with buffalo and hostile Indians, scaled the Rockies and wound down through the sunset canyons and out onto one of God's most beautiful stages—the great Southwest. Smith took along several mule loads of goods for his own use in trading with the Indians.

Shortly after arrival in Santa Fe, young Smith joined another large party bound for the Snake and Utah Indian territory. Later this party split up into smaller companies and Smith and his men returned to the Grand River country in Colorado where they became involved with the Indians and Smith was shot in the leg while trying to bring in the body of a dead companion. The heavy arrow shattered the bone of his left leg just above the ankle. Smith borrowed a butcher knife from the camp cook and completed the job. After the wound had been bandaged he was placed on a litter between two mules and carried 150 miles to a Snake Indian village where the squaws nursed him back to health. When the stub leg had healed sufficiently to enable him to get around Smith fashioned himself a wooden leg from an ash tree. Henceforth he was known to his companions and the Indians as Pegleg.

Here amid snowcapped peaks, tumbling waterfalls, quiet lakes and swift running streams the little party hunted wild game, trapped beaver and lived the life of sturdy pioneers. Pegleg and his companions trapped the tributaries of the Virgin and the Colorado down to the junction of the Gila, arriving there in 1829.

Here, on the site of what later became the town of Yuma, Smith and another trapper named LaRue were entrusted with the task of taking a mule train of pelts to the Spanish settlements on the Pacific coast. Ahead of these men lay one of the most arid deserts in the American Southwest—the great Salton Sink.

It was into this no man's land that Pegleg and LaRue plunged with 15 or 20 pack animals loaded with furs and kegs of water. After floundering through the soft sand for days and making dry camps at night, it became increasingly apparent they would never be able to get out of the desert with their heavy loads of furs and the small amount of water they had left. It was decided to cache half of the furs in the sand dunes.

Late one evening Smith and LaRue camped at the base of the Chocolate Mountains near three small black buttes. To get his bearings and if possible locate some green spot where water might be found Smith climbed to the top of the highest butte. On his way down his attention was attracted by some black pebbles that lay scattered over the sides and around the base of the butte. Picking up several of them he found they were very heavy and put some of them in his pocket. Finally they found their way out through a pass to the northwest and at the foot of a green mountain they found cottonwood trees and a good supply of spring water.

Upon their arrival in the Spanish settlements on the coast Smith was told that the black pebbles were solid gold which in some unknown manner had been coated over by nature with a thin film of manganese. After they had marketed their first load of furs they returned to the desert and brought out the balance and with the proceeds of the combined sales they proceeded to go on a spree that lasted several weeks. After they had been ordered out of the settlement by the Spanish officials they rounded up a herd of horses and mules and headed for the Bear River country to the north.

In 1848, just before the stampede of the Argonauts, Pegleg was back again in the desert searching for the three black buttes where years before he had picked up the black nuggets. Finally he gave up the search and returned to San Francisco where he died in 1866.

During the 85 years which have intervened since the death of Pegleg Smith the story of his fabulous discovery—with many variations—has become a legend of the desert country. It became impossible to attribute to one man all the experiences told about Pegleg Smith, so a second Pegleg Smith has been conceived. Many of the old prospectors who have spent years looking for the black nuggets firmly believe there were two Peglegs— and that both of them actually found the lost butte of the gold nuggets.

There is still another legend bearing on the Pegleg discovery. The story is that in the middle of the last century a white man was guided to the gold by Indians, and he reported the three buttes were part of the rim of a great volcanic crater, and that he was almost overcome with gas fumes welling up from its floor. However, he and his Indian companion were able to bring out about 50 pounds of the black-coated metal, and eventually received $65,000 for their treasure.

My own connection with this strange adventure dates back about 25 years to the little town of Parker, Arizona, on the Colorado river. Some of the older inhabitants of the place had been telling me about a large meteor that had streaked through the night sky only a few years before, and that the vacuum or suction created by it was so great that it had picked up empty oil barrels on the platform at the depot in the little town of Vidal, California, just across the river and pulled them down the track for several thousand feet.

A great explosion was heard a few seconds later and it was believed to have struck a mountain a few miles south of Parker.

I was in the vicinity examining guano deposits at the time and decided to look for the meteorite. Later at Niland, California, I was informed by Mexicans that the meteorite had fallen northwest of that place and about 15 miles south of Corn Springs. I returned to Blythe, California, and purchased a mule from a contractor who had the contract to grade the approaches to the Colorado River bridge. After purchasing a saddle, saddle bags and some provisions it became noised around town that I was headed for the Corn Springs country and was told by some of the bootleggers that I had better stay away from Corn Springs as it was headquarters for a tough bootlegger who would shoot on sight.

Next day I headed down the road through Palo Verde Valley and made a dry camp the first night. The following morning I turned west along the old Bradshaw stage road and that night reached Chuckawalla well. I had just hobbled the mule and started supper on my little campfire when a young Mojave Indian and his wife came into camp. He was mounted on an Indian pony and the girl was walking by his side carrying a small sack of jerky and pinole. They seemed grateful for the opportunity to share my evening meal and rest by the campfire. Like most Indians they were uncommunicative and I did not press them for an answer as to where they were headed. Next morning after breakfast the woman filled the two-gallon canteen, hung it over the horn of the saddle and the man again mounted the horse and prepared to depart. I asked him why his wife did not ride and he replied, "Oh, she ain't got no horse." I watched them with some apprehension as they passed over the horizon and out of sight. It was the last time I ever saw them.

After prospecting for two days in the vicinity of the desert waterhole without finding any signs of the meteorite I decided to head west to the road that runs from Mecca to Blythe. I left the next morning after an early breakfast, rode hard until about 5:00 o'clock in the afternoon. My water supply had dwindled to about one half gallon and the mule was showing signs of weariness. I had reached the eastern end of a long ridge or hogback.

Both the mule and myself were tired and thirsty and while the blackened rocks and scorched earth in the immediate vicinity did not offer much hope, I felt that there must be water some place in the hills and sat down on a large rock to figure things out.

Presently I saw doves and other birds flying rapidly toward the south. I knew that birds flying rapidly in a straight line was a likely sign of water in that direction. I started to follow them and in a short time saw them break their flight in mid-air and drop down toward a break in the dark colored rocks. Further investigation disclosed a narrow crevice about seven or eight feet wide and 50 or 60 feet long. A dolorite dike cut across the west end forming a natural tank in the hard bedrock, full of clear water. There was no broken pottery or any other signs in the vicinity that would indicate the tank was known to Indian or white man.

Not caring to disturb the birds that had unknowingly led me to their water supply, I made camp a short distance away.

After an early breakfast next morning, I filled my canteen, watered the mule and headed up the long ridge toward the western horizon. About 5:00 o'clock that afternoon I reached the summit and then suddenly the top of a small black butte appeared and as I rode forward two smaller ones, one on each side, appeared. All were setting in a small valley or crater-like depression which was partly filled with white sand.

A brisk wind was blowing from the desert and a great yellow cloud came rolling up from the southeast. I knew that we were in for a sand storm and hurriedly led the mule down into the crater and tied him to the limb of a dead ironwood tree that stood near a wall of rock. Hardly had I tied him and removed the saddle and bags of provisions and stored them under a shelving rock before the storm was upon us with all its force.

Sheets of fine sand poured over the edge of the crater like water over a waterfall. The swirling winds swept the bottom of the crater clean in places and piled the sand high in others. Not until about 4:00 o'clock in the morning did the wind cease to blow, and at daybreak I climbed out of the crater and cooked my breakfast.

Then, climbing the highest butte I found it literally covered with black pebbles, nuggets of brown hematite, and small boulders of white silica, all worn smooth. I picked up three of the stones and put them in my pocket. Later I gathered two small bags of them for I wanted to have them assayed.

I continued my search for the meteoric crater and at 3:00 o'clock the next afternoon found it. A 300-pound meteorite was partially buried in the gravel near the pit where the main mass had struck. I broke off a piece of it, and headed north through the Chuckawalla Mountains toward the old Gruendyke well which I knew lay somewhere northwest of Corn Springs. The going was hard, and to spare the animal I finally cached the two bags of rocks from the crater, planning to return for them later.

Late in the day I reached the Blythe-Mecca road and came upon a small covered wagon where a tall grey-haired man was cooking his supper of beans. He invited me to have a plate of them, with dutch oven biscuits. He said his name was John Anderson and he was trapping coyote and fox.

Twenty years later I met John Anderson in the Hell Canyon country north of Prescott. He was very old, but he recalled our meeting in the Chuckawalla valley.

"Were you looking for the Lost Pegleg mine?" he asked.

I told him I had been out searching for a lost meteorite. This conversation recalled the three black stones I had picked up on that trip. Searching through my trunk later in the evening I found one of them. With a light tap of the hammer I broke off the black crust, and there was the loveliest gold nugget I have ever seen.

And now at the age of 68 years I am on my way back to the Colorado desert. If I do not succeed in finding the "Lost Valley Of The Phantom Buttes," I may at least find the $12,000 or $13,000 in black gold nuggets that I cached in the Chuckawalla Mountains.

As I recall the black gold deposit, it is another of those rare chimneys that have always produced so much gold. I saw one from which a fortune in gold nuggets was taken. The Black Gold Crater seems to be another chimney the top of which has been broken down by erosion, scattering the black gold nuggets, pieces of iron and small pebbles of white silica over the sides of the butte and around its base. Some chemical process in nature turned the nuggets black by coating them over with a film of manganese—Desert Varnish, the old-timers call it.

With modern transportation I believe that one could make hurried trips in and out of the desert and bring out a large amount of gold from this deposit. Provided however, that they can locate the lost valley.

Most of the prospectors who have been looking for the Lost Pegleg have been searching too far south and have been following the lines of least resistance. It is located in the higher and more difficult part of the mountains and can be found only by taking to the higher ridges and rough places and then only by accident as it cannot be seen until almost upon it. The buttes appear suddenly and cannot be seen from any direction until almost upon the edge of the crater.

Sands That Blossom into Viking Ships

It's seemingly unpredictable, and for that all the more intriguing, but some years the desert erupts into living masses of yellows and lavenders raving to the horizon and beyond. The spring flowering, much anticipated by locals and tourists alike, occurs when the winter rains have come at just the right time to match just the right temperatures of March and April. Then tiny seeds that may have lain dormant for years burst into an unbelievable surprise before us.

Metaphorically, it takes not water but the imagination to show the strange fecundity of desert sands. It may be impossible to measure, but one can suggest that the most barren lands produce the most bizarre stories. It's as if the mind simply won't accept a lack of mental flora and must have its way, creating the most fantastic tales, the richest tapestries, whether about Pegleg Smith or by Marshal South, out of the least promising material.

I have never stopped short on a hike to see the prow of a Viking ship sailing high above out of a canyon wall, and really don't expect I ever will, but I have heard tales of such things adamantly declaimed in the hops-laden, clammy coolness of desert bars when just the right bonhomie prevailed; and I'm glad that I have, for the brightness of such flowering likely far surpasses seeing the real, or unreal, thing.

And shame on you doubters, for once again we encounter, this time more palpably before us than ever, Ives' beloved but wayward *Explorer* long after the lieutenant with the middle name of Christmas had passed into the great oneiric beyond, perhaps continuing to dream of his old friend along with whatever it is he continues to dream.

~~~ **Choral Pepper,**
   from "Ships That Pass in Desert Sands"

Most Desert dwellers are familiar with an old Indian legend about an ancient vessel that came floating like a great bird with white wings into the Coachella Valley basin now filled by the Salton Sea. Chronicles of 17th Century Spanish pearlers, accounts of grizzled prospectors, evidence uncovered by an early Imperial Valley farmer and even a contemporary weekend camper have reinforced the possibility that the Indian legend may have been based on fact.

But first, how could it have happened? How could an ancient vessel, be it a Viking galley, Spanish pearler or pirate raider, lie buried in the sands of the Colorado Desert of Southern California? Did the legend arise from a drugged dream produced by native hallucinogens? A misty mirage? A cover for a jewel thief? A hoax?

Were it not for fossil evidence of ancient seas and the fact that the Colorado River ran amok in 1906 to create the Salton Sea and prove once and for all that seas can appear overnight, the old Indian legend would sound less plausible. Countless transitions from sandpit to sea appear to have occurred in the past. Some scholars contend that the Gulf of California once extended as far north as Banning and as far west as the present Yuha desert, where vast petrified oyster-shell beds intrigue desert wanderers today. Others claim that these seas were fresh water ones caused by the Colorado River cutting new troughs into the below-sea-level Salton Sink. Tiny fresh water shells left from an ancient Lake Cahuilla (no relation to the present lake of that name) and primitive Indian fish traps along the base of the Santa Rosa Mountains testify to this. Probably both theories are right, the water invasions occurring at different epochs.

A song recorded in the 1920s by an anthropologist studying the Seri Indians on Tiburon Island in the Gulf of California refers to another mysterious ship. This once-murderous tribe preserved its history through songs passed on for generations. The story line of one tells of the "Came From Afar Man" who arrived in a huge boat containing men with yellow hair and a woman with red hair. The strangers remained on the island for many days while the men hunted with arrows and spears. One man, their chief, remained behind with the woman. After the hunters returned with their game, the boat departed the land of the Seris and was never seen again. Could it have been caught between freak tides where the Colorado

River met Gulf waters, and then been shunted through a rampaging canal into a temporary sea flooding the Colorado Desert?

In the late 1960s, I interviewed Myrtle Botts, a librarian from the picturesque old mining town of Julian in San Diego County. An amateur botanist, Myrtle was one of the founders of the popular wildflower show that attracts throngs of visitors to Julian each year. On a weekend camping trip in 1933 to search for new species of desert wildflowers, the Botts family camped in the vicinity of Agua Caliente Springs. While Myrtle prepared dinner, a semi-literate prospector arrived to replenish his water supply. The Botts invited him to join them, hoping he could enlighten them about remote areas where they might find uncommon desert flora.

Instead, mellowed by the scent of a savory stew bubbling over the campfire, the garrulous old prospector told them of a strange ship he had seen sticking out of a canyon wall a few days earlier.

Unbelieving, but still curious, the Botts traveled on the following day "yonder up the canyon" as directed by the prospector. When they could force their old Ford no further, they set up camp and then hiked along the floor of a narrow defile until the grade became so steep and rough they had to rest.

Myrtle saw it first. Jutting out of the canyon wall over their heads was the forward portion of a large and very ancient vessel. A curved step swept up from its prow. Along both sides of the vessel were clearly discernible circular marks in the wood, possibly left by shields which had been attached to the vessel. Near the bow on one side of the ship were four deep furrows in the wood. The craft was high enough to hide its interior from the Botts' view, and the side of the canyon was too steep for them to scale.

Taking note of all landmarks, the Botts hiked back to their car. Almost the moment they emerged from the canyon, they were thrown to the ground. As they clutched the earth in panic, they watched their camp shaking itself to pieces. When the accompanying rumble finally ceased, they gathered up their scattered belongings and raced back to Julian.

The earthquake had been a severe one, causing extensive damage all the way to the coast. But, as in the case of most natural disasters, it was soon forgotten. Not forgotten by the Botts, however, was the strange ship in the desert.

A preliminary search in her library confirmed Myrtle Botts' impression that the vessel most nearly resembled an old Viking ship. Knowing that most people would doubt her sanity if she told the story, she decided to return to the site and photograph the craft to support her disclosure.

The Botts again set forth to camp in the desert, equipped this time with a camera. Once again they hiked up the steep canyon, but when they reached the spot where previously they paused to rest, their passage was blocked. Tons of unstable earth from the mountainside had fallen into the canyon, shaken loose by the heavy trembler. There was no sign of the ship. Discouraged as they were, the Botts had to be grateful that they had escaped the catastrophe. Along with the ship, they would have been buried alive.

Was this the ancient vessel in the song of the Series, the ship carrying Vikings into uncharted waters in a strange land? Santiago Socia might agree. He was a Mexican with a quick temper who had fled from the law in Los Angeles and escaped to the border town of Tecate. There, while awaiting the arrival of his wife, Petra, who was to follow him, he heard about an *olla* filled with gold buried about forty kilometers northeast of Tecate, above the border. Santiago waited for Petra to arrive, then set forth alone to capture the treasure, chancing the trip across the border. He returned a few weeks later with no *olla* filled with gold, but bearing a souvenir disc made of metal which Petra ever after used for a griddle to heat her tortillas.

Santiago's story, which became well-known around Tecate, described an ancient ship projecting from a canyon wall in a remote area of the desert northeast of Tecate. The bow of the ship was curved and carved, like the long neck of a bird. A series of large, round metal plates were attached to the side of the ship. Santiago often displayed Petra's griddle to prove his story, but since no treasure appeared to be connected with the ship, his listeners speculated over its origin, but didn't bother to visit it.

Was this the Viking ship seen by the Botts?

Of lost pearl ships that purportedly ran aground in the desert, the most likely legend concerns an expedition led by Captain Juan de Iturbe.

In 1615, Iturbe departed San Blas with three ships assigned to a pearling mission off La Paz. Six months later, with his ships laden with pearls, he prepared to return to San Blas. Within an hour after his departure, the ships were attacked by the Dutch corsair, Joris van Spielbergen, who promptly captured one of the ships and removed its cargo of pearls. Iturbe dispatched the other ship to warn the overdue Manila galleon of the corsair's presence, then fled in his own ship to the north. The corsair elected to chase Iturbe, knowing that eventually he would trap him at the head of the Gulf.

However, when Iturbe reached the end of the Gulf, he found that it narrowed into a wide channel. He sailed into it on the tide and, to his amazement, found himself on another large sea.

Charts at that time showed clearly that Baja California was a peninsula and not an island, but there wasn't a naval officer alive who didn't secretly cherish the idea that previous explorers were mistaken and the legendary Strait of Anian actually existed to provide passage from the Gulf to the Pacific Ocean.

Convinced that he had found it, Iturbe sailed north and then around the mountains to the west. At approximately 34 degrees latitude, which is the present site of the Salton Sea, he found his passage blocked. Other than a river entering the sea, there was nothing but desert sand, foothills and distant mountains.

Disappointed, he turned south, but the wide channel through which he had entered from the Gulf was now nothing more than a small stream, barely large enough to permit passage for a longboat. He turned back toward the north. By then the river that fed the inland sea had vanished. He was landlocked. When the ship ultimately ran aground, Iturbe abandoned it with its valuable cargo of pearls, hiked back to the Gulf, and with his crew eventually made his way back to Mexico.

Another chronicler of desert lore, explorer-writer Harold Weight, tells of a firsthand interview with an old-timer who had found remnants of a lost ship. These pieces were discovered in 1907 on a ranch in Imperial Valley where one Elmer Carver, then a boy of seventeen, worked for a farmer named Nels Jacobson. The farmer had gone to Los Angeles on a business trip and had hired young Carver to guard Mrs. Jacobson and keep an eye on the ranch. During this interlude, the lady revealed the truth about some hog pens that had aroused the boy's curiosity. Made of planks two to three inches thick, eighteen inches wide and up to thirty feet long, they were fastened by iron bolts through holes bored into the planks, rather than nailed together as was customary. Carter couldn't imagine why such fine timber would have been hauled into the valley, nor why it would be used for hog pens.

Mrs. Jacobson then explained that the planks had come from an old boat that lay partially buried in a hill behind the house. When Carver investigated, he found additional immense timbers, along with ribs of the boat, still in the sand. As far as he could tell, no iron had been used in the boat's construction and the timbers were so hard they appeared to be petrified.

As he gained Mrs. Jacobson's confidence, she further confided that an iron chest filled with jewels had been buried inside the boat. One of the jewels she displayed, a red ruby, was worth more than all of the other jewels together, she believed. Among the other jewels were emeralds and a golden crucifix set with sapphires. The real reason for Jacobson's trip, Carver learned, was to consult with a lawyer and a pawnbroker who were conspiring with the Jacobsons to sell the jewels.

When Jacobson returned to his ranch the following week, he had no further need for Carver, who left the area and never saw him again.

In his research, Weight discovered an historical account about early valley settlers. One item referred to Nels Jacobson, "a well-known Imperial rancher who had come to Imperial with $4,000 and had left seven years later with $137,350."

Perhaps this gentleman farmer was the only one to have profited by a ship that passed in the desert.

Not all buried ships have remained unidentified, however. In 1940 Randall Henderson, founder of *Desert Magazine*, made a trek to the delta between the Colorado River and the Gulf of California to investigate reports of a rusting hulk partly buried in the silt of a channel long abandoned by the fickle waters of the Colorado. Although little more than ribs remained, there was enough evidence to definitely identify it as the *Explorer*, a 56-foot stern-wheel steamer built by the U.S. War Department in 1860 to accommodate a Colorado River exploration conducted by Lt. Joseph C. Ives of the U.S. Topographic Engineers. The *Explorer* was knocked down in eight sections and shipped by boat to the Isthmus of Panama, thence overland to the Pacific, again by boat to San Francisco, and finally to the mud flats at the mouth of the Colorado River where it was reassembled.

It was the reconnaissance by this ship to the present site of Hoover Dam that first proved the Colorado River navigable. After the expedition, the *Explorer* was sold to Yuma rivermen and used to haul wood until it broke from its moorings one day, floated downstream and disappeared. Seventy-nine years later it was found by an aged Cocopah Indian, whose report initiated Henderson's trek.

And so they lie, some found and some still missing, elusive testimony to a romantic history, those mysterious ships that passed in desert sands.

30

The Death of Chuckawalla Bill

As the accident of geography dictates, the flight from Phoenix to Palm Springs is a straight shot due west. Also, as the accident of technology has it, the little, twin-engine puddle jumper flies at about 10,000 feet. That's just about right, close enough to the arid landscape below to maintain intimacy but high enough to get in the sweep of things. Down there is a minimalist study of one brown range after another, cleft with meaningful shadows in the bright sun, moving along one after another as if in a progression toward some distant and always elusive meaning during this dream in flight. Yet the abstract painter knows what he's doing. The eye suddenly starts at an acrylic-green strip right down the center of the canvas. Beyond the reality of art is the everyday reality. That radical band is the reason for being of a few little towns on the eastern edge of the Colorado Desert beside the river that gives the area its name. They're grubby places whose citizens, surrounded by cotton and alfalfa fields, smell of fertilizer and transcend their lot mainly during sex and the exhilaration of Friday night basketball games. Good places for the setting of existential novels showing the futility of lives that the residents mercifully don't recognize.

One of the farming hamlets, Palo Verde, is where Chuckawalla Bill spent his last years. He lived in a tent off in the arrowweed with his old, mop-browed dog. Existentialism, however, may be the affliction of the overly intellectualized and the etiolated, not of the high-school junior or senior who after the Big Game is chaired through the town. At the end of his days, Bill was happy enough to live out there at the edge of town by the irrigation ditch stirring his very unsanitary pot of chili. Old desert rats don't poison their lives into misery with introspection.

That world-famous wanderer Colin Fletcher got a book out of Bill is something of a marvel. True, Chuckawalla Bill has an intriguing name; he once lived in a cave, and, a slightly scurrilous man, he once went by a puzzling variety of names and consorted with a variety of down-at-the-heels women. Yet he wasn't all that remarkable. He spent much of his time as a prospector halfheartedly wandering the Colorado Desert but finding little worth note except the riches of just being out there moving around.

That's not much on which to build a book. Some people will judge the work a literary failure, the story of a simple old coot whose interest, if any, is due far more to the strange obsession of the writer piecing a mundane life together rendered through writing talent than to any innate value in the subject. Just as good a case, and I think a better one, can be made that no life is insignificant if keenly explored and revealed, and that the writer sometimes reaches a supreme accomplishment, his talents at full glow, when taking on the least promising subjects, those that force him to bring to bear genuine artistic sympathy where pyrotechnics are lacking.

Whatever the case, Colin Fletcher has done us a huge cultural favor by presenting a Wordsworthian figure who, if not trailing clouds of glory, nevertheless tells us a good deal about the richness of a common way of living just recently passed into the history of the Colorado Desert.

⎯⎯⎯ Colin Fletcher,
from *The Man from the Cave*

I went back to the place Bill had lived with the Parsons, north of Palo Verde. Progress had begun to catch up with that quiet corner.

On the site of the old bar stood a modern house. Its owner vaguely remembered that when he bought the place there was a kind of old chicken shack out back, and he showed me where it had stood. From an arbor of gnarled and ancient tamarisks you looked out across plowed fields to distant mountains. In Bill's time, the land beyond the arbor had still been unplowed, was still natural, and the moment I saw the place I understood why he had been happy to live there.

"When I came," said the new owner, "it was a hell of a mess back here. Inches deep in tamarisk needles, so that your feet sank into it like it was a carpet. There was none of this landscaping then." He swung an arm. Its sweep encompassed a level and lifeless patch of gravel, a concrete barbecuing block and three or four red reflector lights nailed to tamarisk boles. "You can't believe what a difference the landscaping made."

"Oh, I think I can," I said.

Finally, I went to see Charlie Herrington.

"You'll like Charlie," the Parsons had assured me. "Bill liked him better than anyone else down there in Palo Verde."

Charlie had moved to Palo Verde in 1946 and two years later had built the village's second beer joint, a hundred yards down the road from Al Workman's. Now retired, he lived in a trailer camp, a dozen miles downriver.

From the start it was obvious that although he had known Bill for only four years, he had been genuinely fond of him.

"Oh, he was one nice man, old Chuckawalla Bill. He'd come over to my beer joint every day and stay about an hour and drink maybe three beers and then go home. Oh, he could drink beer, that man, but he didn't get drunk too often and if he did it was just a-singing. Mind you, he'd get in a fight, too. Wouldn't take nothing from nobody. Give old Dick Parsons a black eye once—and he was on into his seventies then, and maybe more. But he was gentle, too, Bill was. He didn't like you to kill nothing. Not like these people who come in now there's a paved road and drive around the desert in their Hondas and four-wheel drives killing everything that walks or crawls or flies. Call themselves varmint hunters! Huh! They don't leave the animals no place to go. But old Bill, he wasn't like that at all.

"I can see him walking down the street now with that little goatee of his, wearing nothing but a pair of shorts and a pair of shoes—tennis shoes or just a pair of slippers. No shirt. Never wore a shirt in summer. He always walked real straight, too, with his chest sticking out like this." Charlie demonstrated. "The hair on his chest had all turned white, but hell, that man, he'd walk better than I could. Yeah, I can see him now…. Hell, I think I've got a photo somewhere of him and Lonny Lannerman a-standing outside of my beer joint."

"You have?"

"Sure," said Charlie.

He brought an album stacked with loose snapshots and began sifting. "Jesus Christ, he's dead … and he's dead … and she's dead, too…. That guy was ninety-four when he fell in a ditch and drowned himself.…Christ, they're all dead…. That guy hung himself with a piece of wire…. Yeah, here's that photo. There's old Bill in the middle with the stick, a-sucking at his old pipe. Must have been wintertime for him to be wearing all those clothes. That's Lonny Lannerman on the left. He's been dead these ten years. Cancer. And, hell, that's me on the right. Must have took it right after I built my place. Forty-nine, probably."

The faces in the snapshot were all shadow, mere daubs of black. But the middle figure, leaning on a stick, was somehow consistent with what I would have expected in the last year of Bill's life: shoulders still thrown back; yet a stance more relaxed and unposed than the other two had managed.

"Hell, that takes me back," said Charlie. He smiled, back down the years. "Old Bill, he'd sometimes come along when I went down the river, plugging for bass. He didn't fish, but he'd go a-swimming naked in the river and then fool around with my old dog, Jacob. That dog, he was crazy about old Chuckawalla Bill. One time, Bill had fallen down and cut his hand and it wouldn't heal. And that dog, every morning he'd go out there and lick Bill's hand. And he kept licking it until, by God, it healed up and you couldn't even never tell. Yes, you're right, old Bill had a dog too. I'd forgotten that. Old mixed-up dog with hair hanging down over his eyes. Always there a-sitting beside Bill when you went up to see him."

Sometime in early 1949, Bill had moved out of the cabin he rented, up along the lagoon, and pitched his tent just outside the village.

"I used to go up there to his camp a lot and bullshit about the places he'd been and the women he'd lived with. We'd talk about Pennsylvania, too, because I was born about sixty miles south of Pittsburgh, where he came from. And sometimes four or five of us guys would go up—Lonny Lannerman and George Cox and Little Red and Pete—and we'd take a couple of six-packs of beer and just chew the fat and maybe play three-handed cutthroat pinochle, fifteen cents a game. Old Bill, he'd get so mad he'd jump up and down. But half an hour later he'd forgotten it all...

"A nice little camp, Bill had, out there in the arrowweed. Nothing fancy, you know. Just a piece of canvas over it for shade—though there was a big cottonwood for shade, too. Hell, you don't need no roof in this country. But when it rained, old Bill, he could lie on his bed there—a couple of two-by-fours and some blankets—just lie right there and watch it rain. Come to think of it, maybe he had a little tent, too. But he didn't sleep in it very often, so far as I remember. He had a bucket with a rope on it and when he wanted water he'd just throw it in the irrigation ditch and then let the water stand for a while for the mud to settle. He always had a pot o' coffee set back there on his stove, and all he had to do was throw another stick of wood on it and it was boiling. A nice little stove it was. But I remember he had some rusty old stovepipe on it that was full of holes and the smoke bothered him, and one day I went into town and bought him three lengths of stovepipe and we drove a length of half-inch pipe in the ground and wired the new pipe to it and then he had a real good stove. And old Bill, he liked to cook. You'd walk along the ditch bank and hear him down there a-singing. A-singing and a-cooking.

"He was a good cook, too. And he liked to eat. But hell, he didn't never get fat. Usually he had a pot of something stewing there on the stove, like chili and beans. Yessir, he really liked chili. In summer, sometimes, when it got to be a hundred and ten or a hundred and twelve, his beans would be sitting there in the sun a-bubbling all by themselves."

I asked where the camp had been.

"Just west of town, in old river bottom," said Charlie. "Right on the county line, beside an irrigation ditch. There used to be an old mill there, and a lake where it was all flooded, over on Joe Clark's ranch."

"Wait a minute. That sounds like the place Dick Parsons told me about. Bill said it was the first place he camped in Palo Verde."

"That's right," said Charlie. "He told me about that. Said it was the same place he'd pitched his tent the first time he came here. Old Bill, he didn't give a shit if he died. But he didn't want to owe nobody nothing. 'I don't want to die until I get my check and pay everybody,' he used to say. And he wanted to die in Palo Verde. 'I love this desert and this country,' he told me once. 'And I want to die right here.'"

Charlie grinned. "Me, too. I don't never want to live nowhere but right here till I die.... Yessir, old Bill said that that camp of his was where he wanted to end up. He would have done, too, if they hadn't carted him off to Sawtelle. But he went down real fast, that last year. Just getting old, I guess. Toward the end, he got pretty cranky."

"Yes," I said. "I was talking to Mrs. Mills, who was postmistress then. She only knew him for about a year, and all she could remember was a cranky old man who was kind of frail and would boom his cane on the floor of the post office if he didn't get prompt service, no matter how many people were there before him—as if he figured he'd been around long enough to be privileged."

Charlie smiled.

"Mrs. Mills was still the postmistress," I said, "when I passed through in 1958, on a walk up California, and picked up my first mail here."

But Charlie was still smiling back into his own past. "Yeah, old Bill got cranky all right, there at the end. But don't let that fool you. He was just a nice old guy. One real nice man...."

"Those last few days, I think he just laid there. Maybe he got up on his feet, but he didn't leave the tent. And I doubt if he ate anything very much. He just laid on the goddam ground, in the tent. Almost died here."

The last day, Charlie Herrington had been away. But Al Workman remembered.

"I went up there when Harry West hauled him away to Sawtelle Hospital. Harry West was our deputy sheriff then. Old Bill, he was in bad shape. They pretty well had to carry him into the pickup. And that camp! Oh, it was…I don't know how in the world he ever lived there like he did. That tent, it wasn't as high as the ceiling in this trailer of mine. And he cooked outside. It was a mess, I tell you."

I came to the highway, stopped beside my car and turned and looked back across the freshly bulldozed soil toward the corner by the levee.

During those last days in his last camp under the big cottonwood tree, out there among the arrowweed and mesquite, Bill had known that his life was drawing to a close. In a sense, of course, he had known it for a long time. That was why he had moved back. That was why he had given the shotgun and his Spanish-American War medallion to his old friend John DeLaGarza when he turned up as if by accident. But toward the end Bill must have known that the light was failing fast.

It was not difficult to see how things had gone.

For a while he continued to cook meals. But the shadows kept drawing in. Eventually he stopped bothering about food. Old Fellow sat beside his bed, eyes mournful, and occasionally licked his hand.

For a long time, Bill just lay there.

Out of the shadows emerged memories that were no longer mere memories. He lay in his enormous, tiny bed and heard another load come clanking down No. 2 Incline, then swoosh out with a sound that began as a roar but softened to a whisper as the coal covered the floor of the wagon. He crouched among Braddock greenery, in a magical, pulsating universe of firefly dances, and dreamed of Indians and the young George Washington, on that very ground. He sat in the little frame house in Twin Lakes, Colorado, listening to the prospecting stories of his Uncle Anton.…

So there at the very end, when he was off his last legs and just plain running down in the way most of us will likely approach the gate that is the sure terminus for all things born—when he was no longer alive in any warm and human sense—he generated the densest written chronicle of his threescore years and fifteen.

Anthony William Simmons was admitted to the General Medical and Surgical Hospital, Veterans Administration Center, Los Angeles 25, California, on November 2, 1949. On admission he had forty-two dollars in his possession. He gave his age as eighty-one, his religion as Catholic, his marital status as divorced. He said among other things that he had no children and no known living relatives, was retired and had lived in California for fifty-five years. He designated Patricia and Harold Swafford, friends, of Palo Verde, California, to receive all his property in case of death. According to Charlie Herrington, the Swaffords at that time ran what is now the Sleepy Burro Café; but they had long ago left Palo Verde and no one had heard of them since.

Bill was brought to the hospital by "a friend," Harry West, Jr., Deputy Sheriff, also of Palo Verde, "because he was unable to care for himself."

The initial diagnosis was "gastritis and emphysema of lungs.... Hypertension.... Heart disease with failure."

During the first weeks he must have rallied a little.

"After they hauled him off to the hospital," Charlie Harrington told me, "I knew he'd want to come back. And sure enough, he wrote to my wife, Dorothy, and said he was feeling much better and wanted to come back. He didn't want to die in that damned hospital. But I hadn't got a car good enough to drive to L.A. and none of the other guys would go get him. I felt real bad about that. Always have done. 'Cause old Bill, he wanted to die right here in Palo Verde.... He wrote Dorothy about some effects he wanted, too, and we went up to his camp and got a folder with a bunch of damned old letters and junk in it. Didn't amount to nothing...."

Other things were happening, too, around Bill's last camp. "After they took Bill away," Al Workman told me, "that old dog of his just left the tent and never come back. Went half a mile north up the ditch and laid down there. And a few days later, Lonny Lannerman went up along the ditch and found the old dog a-laying there. He wasn't dead, just laying right out there. And Lonny shot him.... No, that dog never come back to the tent, not after they took Bill away."

31

Murder in Fru-Fru Land

Ever since the Hollywood crowd with its party nonchalance elbowed the bewildered locals aside and took over the village in the 1930s, Palm Springs has been a huge attraction and a huge target. We like glitter, but we also like to mock it, and thereby ease our own foolishness. Think of Palm Springs in this way, as a huge, pink, white-fringed pillow, shaped like a heart. It's adored by a pretentious and narcissistic lot with more money than is good for them but lacking any depth of taste. Such folks have overwhelmed Palm Springs in recent decades. Whatever we may think of Chuckawalla Bill, living on the outskirts of a desert nowheresville, there's a genuine quality to the man who sat in his tent and talked to his dog. Not so Palm Springs, land of gold Mercedes and gilded bathrooms with lilac wallpaper imported from France. It's hard to miss that mark with barbs of ridicule.

Certainly, Raymond Chandler's shafts go in delightfully but deep with the thinly veiled *Poodle Springs*. It offers a unique combination of tough-guy whodunit as wisecracking detective Philip Marlowe takes us through the seamy underworld beneath the puffery visitors adore from the windows of their tour buses. We also enjoy a riotous, flint-edged exposé of just how cheapened human beings can become when they live in self-absorption and tinny make-believe. Sadly, it's an accurate portrait of what much of modern Palm Springs is today. Added to that is another unique feature of the book. The famed Raymond Chandler died before finishing his crime thriller; building on the four chapters left behind, mystery writer Robert B. Parker, much on the uptake, managed the literary coup of expanding the good beginning into a seamless novel. Below, the stinging first chapter, almost preternatural in its contemporary comment.

～ Raymond Chandler and Robert B. Parker,
from *Poodle Springs*

Linda stopped the Fleetwood convertible in front of the house without turning into the driveway. She leaned back and looked at the house and then looked at me.

"It's a new section of the Springs, darling. I rented the house for the season. It's a bit on the chi-chi side, but so is Poodle Springs."

"The pool is too small," I said. "And no springboard."

"I've permission from the owner to put one in. I hope you will like the house, darling. There are only two bedrooms, but the master bedroom has a Hollywood bed that looks as big as a tennis court."

"That's nice. If we don't get together, we can be distant."

"The bathroom is out of this world—out of any world. The adjoining dressing room has ankle-deep pink carpeting, wall to wall. It has every kind of cosmetic you ever heard of on three plate-glass shelves. The toilet—if you'll excuse my being earthy—is all alone in an annex with a door and the toilet cover has a large rose on it in *relief*. And every room in the house looks out on a patio or the pool."

"I can hardly wait to take three or four baths. And then go to bed."

"It's only eleven o'clock in the morning," she said demurely.

"I'll wait until eleven-thirty."

"Darling, at Acapulco—"

"Acapulco was fine. But we only had the cosmetics you brought with you and the bed was just a bed, not a pasture, and other people were allowed to dunk in the swimming pool and the bathroom didn't have any carpet at all."

"Darling, you *can* be a bastard. Let's go in. I'm paying twelve hundred dollars a month for this dive. I want you to like it."

"I'll love it. Twelve hundred a month is more than I make being a detective. It'll be the first time I've been kept. Can I wear a sarong and paint my little toenails?"

"Damn you, Marlowe, it's not my fault that I'm rich. And if I have the damn money I'm going to spend it. And if you are around some of it is bound to rub off on you. You'll just have to put up with that."

"Yes, darling." I kissed her. "I'll get a pet monkey and after a while you won't be able to tell us apart."

"You can't have a monkey in Poodle Springs. You have to have a poodle. I have a beauty coming. Black as coal and very talented. He's had piano lessons. Perhaps he can play the Hammond organ in the house."

"We got a Hammond organ? Now that's something I've always dreamed of doing without."

"Shut up! I'm beginning to think I should have married the Comte de Vaugirard. He was rather sweet, except that he used perfume."

"Can I take the poodle to work? I could have a small electric organ, one of the babies you can play if you have an ear like a corn-beef sandwich. The poodle could play it while the clients lie to me. What's the poodle's name?"

"Inky."

"A big brain worked on that one."

"Don't be nasty or I won't—you know."

"Oh, yes you will. You can hardly wait."

She backed the Fleetwood and turned it into the driveway. "Never mind the garage door. Augustino will put the car away, but you don't really have to in this dry desert climate."

"Oh yeah, the house boy, butler, cook and comforter of sad hearts. Nice kid. I like him. But there's something wrong here. We can't get along on just one Fleetwood. I have to have one to drive to the office."

"Goddam you! I'll get my white whip out if you're not polite. It has steel inserts in the lash."

"The typical American wife," I said and went around the car to help her out. She fell into my arms. She smelled divine. I kissed her again. A man turning off a sprinkler in front of the next house grinned and waved.

"That's Mister Tomlinson," she said between my teeth. "He's a broker."

"Broker, stoker, what do I care?" I went on kissing her.

We had been married just three weeks and four days.

Consequences: The Sea of Poisons

Smack in the middle of the parched Colorado Desert is a huge anomaly—a sea thirty-five miles long and fifteen miles wide. It's full of poisons. You wouldn't want to eat fish from it for fear of glowing in the dark and breeding weird children with ears growing out of their elbows.

The rhetorical and moral potential here is tremendous. In terms of the last chapter, one could easily wax self-righteous and deliver a thundersome sermon on the stinking cesspool as our civilization's punishment, the Hand of the Lord smiting the sinners of Sodom and Gomorrah, the profligate, tinsel-bedecked communities of the Colorado Desert, for their excesses. You violate nature, and nature kicks back. There's an appealing neatness in the view and a certain amount of truth.

The Salton Sea is a poisonous sump in the middle of the desert because of salts and toxins in the irrigation runoff draining into the low-lying area from the agricultural miracle of the Imperial Valley miles to the south. With that, our self-righteous storm might continue, but the moral argument behind it breaks down. However one might feel about the violations of nature, the Salton Sea is a chemical cocktail because of physics, the drainage pattern of the land, not because of right or wrong. The environment is a balloon. When you poke it in one place, it bulges in another. If you want cheap vegetables in your supermarket, you're going to pay for them, sometimes in unexpected ways.

For that, the bubbling witch's brew of the Salton Sea is a modern exemplum and a warning. For thousands of years, humans have been hugely successful at manipulating nature to the species' advantage. Now we're doing it at such an accelerated rate that in our blissful speed we're blind to the consequences that, however ignored, remain festering in our midst. An opposite temptation is to say that we need to go back to more primitive, more "natural," ways of doing things. That also has tremendous appeal, the childish appeal of a simple answer. The desert Indians who practiced agriculture certainly didn't have problems with selenium, but their numbers remained small because they never were successful enough to manipulate their environment and escape the disasters of drought and flood that periodically decimated their numbers. They never enjoyed our success of garnering huge bounties of food produced by a handful of people while the rest of the population, gilded as the lily, danced in prosperous abandon.

It could be that we, too, are on our own fateful course, but so arrayed and dazzled that we don't recognize what's coming. The question, however, is moot. Given the size of our population and the complex ways that support it, the course is set; no wishful thinking, no return to cutting weeds with stone hoes, will save us. Our society either will fail or figure things out in workable ways. With a certain incongruity, that challenge is most blatantly presented to us in a land both of extreme scarcity and extreme abundance.

William deBuys,
from *Salt Dreams: Land and Water in Low-Down California*

In low places consequences collect, and Clark Bloom, the grizzled manager of the Salton Sea National Wildlife Refuge, has collected a lot of them.

As Bloom explains, perhaps for the thousandth time, the fundamental problem of the Salton Sea, being lowest of the low, is that it cannot pass along its troubles to someone or someplace farther downstream. The greater part of the American West stands above it and discharges a fair portion of its waters into it. Without an outlet to the ocean, the Salton Sea must stew in its own juices. Because infiltration to the underlying geology is negligible, only vapor leaves the sea's tepid precincts. Everything else—salts, minerals, pesticides, organic compounds, toxins—stays behind, and the resulting witches' brew, in recent years, has proved lethal for a substantial portion of the wild creatures unfortunate enough to depend upon it.

Bloom, on this early March morning, is in his office giving yet another interview. The day outside is warming toward a high in the mid-nineties—mild by local standards. The sky is windless and cloudless and the unruffled sea, reflecting the emptiness above it, presents an image of peacefulness, or at least of torpor. Elsewhere, water may symbolize restlessness, but at the Salton Sea it more often stands for inertia. Nothing moves in the seascape, not the statuesque cormorants in the dead, flooded trees at shoreline, not the glassy, somewhat oily surface of the water, not the flat hazy horizon. The fierce weight of downpouring heat and light seems to hold everything immobile.

It is good to be indoors, away from the sun, and Bloom's cool office, like so many hot-country buildings, is almost windowless. Its concrete-block walls give a cave-like, protective feel, somewhat like a bunker, which, under the circumstances, is an appropriate analog for the headquarters of the Salton Sea National Wildlife Refuge. "It's not like I am managing a refuge now," says Bloom. "It's more like a battlefield." His voice is gravelly, his tone resigned. It is not hard to hear the inflection of fatigue and discouragement in what he says. Bloom, whose pressed uniform, trim moustache, and close-cropped hair give him a slightly military air, is a veteran of nearly three decades with the U.S. Fish and Wildlife Service. He has had abundant experience in the management of budgets, visitors, and habitat and in the operation of wildlife refuges that function essentially as migratory bird farms. Before coming to the Salton Sea refuge in 1992, he had almost always been able to set his own and his staff's day-to-day work priorities according to goals and plans that he had helped determine. Not at Salton Sea, where circumstances far beyond his control hold sway. "What we do here," he explains, "goes by what's dying and how fast it's dying."

The dying began a few months before Bloom came to the refuge. On December 16, 1991, as the full moon approached, a refuge equipment operator working east of the Alamo River delta reported seeing a group of eared grebes that appeared sick. Given the sea's huge population of wintering birds, especially grebes, a handful of dying birds was hardly unusual. Nevertheless, refuge staff collected several carcasses and sent them to the National Wildlife Health Research Center in Madison, Wisconsin, for necropsy. They expected the lab to determine that the birds had died of avian cholera, a common affliction of large, crowded populations. To everyone's surprise, the report came back with no finding of bacterial or viral infection. In fact, the lab failed to identify any cause of death.

A month later, in the third week of January 1992, refuge managers discovered nearly two hundred dead and dying grebes on the barnacle beach west of the refuge headquarters. Some of the birds were partly decomposed, but others, still alive, sought shelter among the few rocks and larger shore-line flotsam in order to escape the herring gulls that preyed upon them. The grebes appeared unable to dodge or flee as the gulls stalked among them, attacking with thick bills, hammering at the grebes' heads as they would at a mussel until the skulls of the smaller birds split open. The gulls feasted on the warm brains. The living grebes appeared too dazed and dis-oriented to resist. Nor did they resist the refuge workers who picked them up and wrung their necks as a farmer might kill a chicken. Eight more specimens were sent to the Madison lab, and again, a suite of tests proved inconclusive. Soon, however, the moon began to wane, and repeated pa-trols of the refuge shoreline turned up only three more dead grebes. The crisis, whatever it was, appeared to have passed.

Then came the third week of February. Waves of thousands of dead grebes began to wash ashore, and not just at the refuge. Phones rang inces-santly as birders called in with accounts of strange grebe behavior and res-idents of Salton City reported large numbers of carcasses windrowed on their beach....

But as tens of thousands of grebes fell victim to the mysterious plague of the Salton Sea, they left the lake's familiar waters for the unwelcoming and inhospitable beaches, where they lolled and staggered. They preened constantly, as though their skin were irritated or they could no longer pro-duce the oils that prevented their feathers from waterlogging and drowning them. They arrived on land like aliens on a hostile planet, and they yielded to the voracious gulls as hopelessly and passively as sheep at a shearing. Radke and his colleagues watched them gulp freshwater, as though in a losing battle against dehydration. With every wave and gust of wind, more carcasses washed in.

Refuge personnel collected specimen birds by the dozens, both live and dead, sick and healthy. They also collected samples of the pile worms and other invertebrates on which the stricken grebes had been feeding. They sent the carcasses to Madison wildlife lab and the invertebrates to Patuxent National Wildlife Refuge in Maryland. A team of biologists from the U.S. Fish and Wildlife Service and California Department of Fish and Game assembled at the refuge. They were acutely aware that a mass mor-tality of wild, aquatic birds constituted a rare event and that such a die-off in the vicinity of a national wildlife refuge, with resources and research-ers available to record the outbreak, was rarer still. They felt the weight of a considerable responsibility, and the weight only grew heavier as the laboratories failed to answer their questions.

Consistent with earlier tests, the results of necropsies continued to rule out avian cholera and botulism as primary causes of the grebe die-off. Cholera, however, proved to have killed most of the relatively small number of other birds, mainly ruddy ducks, whose carcasses were collected along with the grebes. Lest a secondary cholera epidemic or another infectious disease break out, the refuge organized a large-scale carcass cleanup, which continued through March and most of April, during which time the die-off mercifully abated. Ultimately, volunteers and agency personnel picked up some 46,040 dead birds from forty miles of shoreline.

Extrapolating those results to the rest of the sea, and factoring in data from supplemental aerial and shoreline surveys, researchers concluded that approximately 150,000 eared grebes had perished. This colossal toll, one of the largest recorded bird die-offs in North American history, represented nearly 8 percent of the estimated continental population of the species. Additionally, about 5,500 shorebirds, gulls, ducks, and other species died of avian cholera. Fortunately, a larger outbreak failed to materialize.

The laboratory results continued to trickle in. Try as they might, researchers found no evidence that the grebes had died of bacterial or viral infection. Indeed, no cause of death could be determined at all, yet the necropsies still yielded plenty of chilling data. Compared with samples collected years before the die-off, the livers of the grebes showed elevated levels of selenium, mercury, DDE (a derivative of the pesticide DDT), and chromium. Average selenium values in both grebes and pile worms appeared to have doubled in three years, and all grebe liver samples showed selenium concentrations higher than the known threshold for adverse health impacts. For a long time, biologists had been monitoring the concentration of selenium in the ecosystems of the Salton Sea, and for just as long they had been expecting a dire manifestation of its toxicity. Now, although proof of such a manifestation seemed close at hand, the levels of selenium and other contaminants in the grebe carcasses, though dangerously high, were insufficient to have caused death. Indeed, none of the contaminants, acting alone appeared to have triggered mortality among the grebes. Still, no one familiar with the contaminants' potential for toxicity could avoid the conclusion that they might have compromised the grebes' immune systems and made them vulnerable to the mysterious agent that ultimately killed them.

A further conclusion was also obvious. The Salton Sea was tainted and sick, and it posed considerable danger to the wildlife that innocently depended on it. The danger seemed no less grave for being only partly understood. Contrary to their hopes, few observers expected that the worst was over....

Since time immemorial, the soils of Imperial Valley have collected salts. Through all the prehistoric comings and goings of Lake Cahuilla, through every inland flood of the river and every application of irrigation water, they have retained what evaporation and flowing water could not carry away. As a result the valley's agricultural soils tend to be two to five times more saline than the water used to irrigate them. Farmers must therefore flush these soils regularly—usually during the hot summer season when fields are sometimes fallowed—to drive salts below the root zones of their crops. Toward this end they use about 15 percent more water than their crops actually need for biological growth. And the crops they grow are thirsty ones: an acre of alfalfa, one of the principal crops of the valley, requires about six acre-feet of water. This water would accumulate underground and gradually waterlog the fields of the valley, pushing salts back up into the root zone, were it not for drainpipes buried under virtually every field. These pipes collect wastewater, together with large amounts of salts, and deliver it to the canals that ultimately empty into the Salton Sea.

The result of all this flushing and draining, this fight against the salty buildup that doomed the civilizations of Mesopotamia and other ancient lands, is to deliver water to the Salton Sea that is three times as salty as the "sweet" Colorado River water that teases life from Imperial Valley fields. Four million tons of salt—three tons in every acre-foot of inflow—enter the Salton Sea each year. Without water to do the work of transportation, one would need forty thousand railcars to move such a quantity of salt.

Salt and water enter the sea, but only water vapor leaves. Inexorably, salinity increases. The threat this poses to aquatic life has long been understood. In 1961 a state-sponsored study of the ecology of the sea forecast destruction of the existing food chain by 1980 or 1990. The days of gloom actually arrived later than predicted because of the huge dilutive inflows of the 1970s and 1980s, but the study was essentially on target.

By 1985 the salinity of the sea had passed 40,000 ppm, and a decade later, as it approached 45,000 ppm, it had entered the fateful zone in which the reproduction of its coveted fishery began to falter. Adult fish appeared able to endure the caustic waters, which were now a quarter again as salty as the Pacific, but their eggs and fry survived less frequently. Fishing declined. The halcyon days of endless "luck" and thick corvine filets receded into memory. People searched for someone to blame. Without fishing, there would be no recreation. Without recreation, there would be no resurgence of land values and no revival of depressed communities by the water's edge....

If biologists had possessed the capacity to "round up the usual suspects," they would have quickly arrested selenium, a naturally occurring mineral that the waters of the Colorado have collected from vast areas of the West and concentrated in the sediments of the Salton Sea. Of all the substances on earth necessary for life and health, none is subject to narrower tolerances. An essential nutrient, selenium becomes toxic to humans when ingestion rises by just a few ten-thousandths of a gram per day. A healthy male, for instance, needs about 0.000076 grams daily, but that male will become unhealthy—suffering decline of the immune and nervous systems, plus a host of skin, digestive, and motor disorders—if his daily intake rises to 0.0005 grams. These small amounts grow still smaller for the very young and very old. Given a choice between consuming equal amounts of arsenic and selenium, one should not hesitate to take the arsenic, for selenium is five times more poisonous.

Selenium is ubiquitous in the American West, for it is a common constituent of the marine shale formations that overlie thousands of square miles from Montana to New Mexico. Although mineral selenium is not readily soluble, in the process of weathering it oxidizes into water-soluble selenate. Additionally, certain plants are well adapted to seleniferous soils and can extract mineral selenium from deep within their root zones, recombining it in organic compounds which they build into their tissues. As the plants grow, shed leaves and blossoms, and ultimately die, they deposit a halo of selenate on the ground around them. Rainwater and snowmelt dissolve these compounds and carry them away. Wherever western rivers end in an evaporative sump, the water's freight of selenium, like its salt, stays behind, relentlessly increasing.

Prior to the die-offs at the Salton Sea, an outbreak of avian birth defects at Kesterson National Wildlife Refuge in California's central valley had alerted the world to selenium's unhappy relationship to irrigation agriculture. Kesterson, like the Salton Sea, was a sump for drain waters, and in the early summer of 1983 biologists became aware that Kesterson's ponds and reedy marshes had grown unnaturally silent. Investigation revealed the cause. In nest after nest, they found dead chicks with stumps where legs or wings should have been, external stomachs, bulging brains, eyes missing, corkscrewed beaks, all manner of deformity. Nearly all species present were affected: gadwalls, mallards, teal, stilts, avocets, and killdeer. Hardest hit were the embryos of the lowly coot and, as at Salton Sea, the eared grebe, of which 64 percent suffered death or deformity.

The Preserved Lands:
Ecstasy and Agony

Sometimes we poison land, sometimes we preserve it.

People who feel that connecting with wild nature and with the ancient peoples who lived in it will link them to an authenticity far more profound and satisfying than anything found in our modern lives often turn to the desert. And with good reason. I could take you on a stroll of just a few minutes up the mountainside beyond the bustle and boutiques of fashionable downtown Palm Springs to sheltered overhangs littered with potsherds and chips from the making of arrowheads. From there, only twenty feet or so above the desert floor, if one can squint out the clutter of golf courses and shopping malls in the middle ground below, lies at least an illusion of blue-tinged desert mountains stretching in all directions to the horizons beyond, fertile ground for the heart's wild desires.

Possibly, there is some hope. Despite the huge influx of population into the Colorado Desert over the last few decades, a common roadmap will show huge chunks of the area, millions of acres, set aside, inviolate, one hopes, for all time to come.

It would be pleasant to think that these preserves, most of them under the stewardship of various state and federal agencies, came about by the idealism of citizens who, inspired by desert writers, next rose up to demand that those special features endearing the desert to us be honored by placing nature beyond the development that has ravaged much of America. Yes, that's part of the story. Yet, as desert wanderer Lawrence Hogue shows, the process hardly was that simple and the result not nearly the perfection we'd wish. Parks and preserves, as holds true of so much of our public lives, were the result of conflicting and often not-at-all idealistic forces.

Some politicians feared creation of parks because they would mean the removal of lands from the tax base, while others, hardly less greedy, favored the preserves because they envisioned that parks would mean tourist dollars tumbling in to public and private coffers. Parks, then, as Mr. Hogue points out, often embody the very contradictions of warring factions of society. In what may be a more realistic than cynical view, beauty may be a happy accident, the product of what falls between the grates, of what's left over after rivals have had their way. Yet whatever the case, as we sling on our packs and head up the trail toward a palm oasis deep in a canyon, and additionally excited by the possibility of seeing a bighorn sheep looking down on us from the crags above, we can give thanks for the blessings of these preserves, however they came about.

mmm **Lawrence Hogue,**
from *All the Wild and Lonely Places: Journeys in a Desert Landscape*

The best place to experience the sublime, Chase and his predecessors claimed, was in the desert. John Van Dyke was the first to make that claim; *The Desert*, which he published in 1901, is widely credited as the book that turned the popular conception of deserts on its head, influencing later generations of desert writers right down to iconoclast and money-wrencher Edward Abbey. Van Dyke, an art critic first and desert traveler second, wrote, "In sublimity—the superlative degree of beauty— what land can equal the desert with its wide plains, its grim mountains, and its expanding canopy of sky!"

For Van Dyke, life's highest calling was the appreciation of beauty, and beauty found its highest expression in nature, especially the desert; therefore, the desert should be left in its natural state. Van Dyke's chapter titled "The Bottom of the Bowl" provides the best picture we have of the floor of the Salton Trough before it was inundated. His descriptions of the way the desert light played on the sand dunes or created the water mirage are wonders of detail and clarity. Alarmed at the effect irrigation would have on these qualities of light, Van Dyke made one of the first calls for desert preservation, warning that "the deserts should never be reclaimed."

There were almost no people in Van Dyke's desert—no Indians, no railwaymen, no cowboys, no farmers—and he liked it that way. But George Wharton James, the second of Chase's predecessors, put people squarely in the foreground of *The Wonders of the Colorado Desert*. When James published his 536-page tome in 1906, some of what Van Dyke had foreseen had already come to pass: the newly named Imperial Valley had been irrigated and converted to farmland, and the Salton Trough was slowly filling with the floodwaters of the Colorado River. But surprisingly—considering that he celebrated the same qualities Van Dyke found in the desert—James was remarkably sanguine regarding those changes. If Van Dyke was an impressionist, then James was a social realist, showing farmers and engineers confidently taming the desert, with just a glimpse of pristine landscape visible in the background. In his attempts to blend preservation with boosterism, James came off as a mixture of John Muir and Floyd Dominy, that inveterate dam builder and foe of the Sierra Club. James concluded his book with the weak lament that "it would be a tremendous pity to reclaim all the desert. We need it for other and better things than growing melons and corn."

The viewpoint of Mary Austin, the third of these seminal desert writers, lies somewhere between these two extremes. Her desert is more like an Asian landscape, with tiny human figures occupying the middle ground. Published in 1903, *The Land of Little Rain* was not immediately popular in the United States, and it has never received as much credit as *The Desert* for changing our views of arid landscapes. But Austin's work was based on a longer and deeper experience with the region and its people. She had lived near the Mojave Desert since 1891 and was able to draw on a decade's worth of observing desert plants, animals, weather, and geography and of visiting with prospectors, ranchers, and Paiute Indians. She included those people throughout *Land of Little Rain*, asking how they affected the desert and, most of all, how the desert affected them. Austin was a bioregionalist before her time, and her work has something thoroughly modern about it. She seems to have had as great an influence as Van Dyke on later writers such as Edward Abbey, from expectations of what deserts have to offer right down to certain phrases. In his own book, Chase expressed doubt about whether any writer could ever capture the essence of the desert, but to my way of thinking, among this first generation of desert writers, Mary Austin came closest.

Austin focused on the Mojave Desert and the nearby Sierra Nevada and Tehachapi Mountains. This leaves to Chase the distinction of being the best writer to focus on the Anza-Borrego region, blending an accurate eye for detail, an engaging sense of humor, and just enough purple-prosed celebration to let the reader feel his fascination. Although historians have cast doubt on whether Van Dyke really made his famously rugged journeys across the Southwest, Chase's description of his own trip is too accurate to have been fabricated. Whereas Van Dyke insisted on finding beauty and James insisted on finding "wonders," Chase was not afraid to admit that there is ugliness, dreariness, and even boredom in the desert.

Together, Van Dyke, James, and Austin had helped to change people's ideas about deserts. When Chase came along, he wrote that "a few people are just beginning to catch the idea" that the desert is a place of beauty, and he hoped that more would do so. By 1920, when he called for the creation of a desert park, the idea did not seem ludicrous, as it might have just twenty years earlier.

Today, I find good reason to be thankful for Van Dyke's and Chase's calls for preservation and the state park that eventually resulted. After a brief visit to Seventeen Palms—where Chase noted that the water gave his tea "a dirty gray curdle and a flavor like bilge"—I head home. On the way, I stop at an isolated mesa on the park's western edge. It is covered with desert pavement, a mosaic of rocks and pebbles created by wind and water eroding the sand in between. Soon I strike a trail, a slightly smoother, foot-wide track in the already even surface. Nearby, another trail runs parallel to this one, but it makes several S-shaped curves and doesn't seem to lead anywhere. A few feet away, a similar shape parallels the first.

I've seen aerial photographs of ancient ground figures, types of rock art known as intaglios or geoglyphs, and I wonder whether this might be one. Someone has left a single metal stake in the ground nearby as if to mark this as a significant spot. If this is a geoglyph, it was most likely left by the San Dieguito people, who inhabited the region long before either the Kumeyaay or the Cahuilla.

Farther on, I come to patterns of larger rocks in the trail. At first, I think they must be modern, but they are deeply imbedded, so they can't have been placed recently. One is an arrow pointing in the direction I'm heading. The other is a vaguely circular shape. Together, the figures look something like the Shoshone "water marks" Mary Austin described in *Land of Little Rain*.

An ancient trail, a possible intaglio, and a possible water sign—I've hiked for a decade in this desert just to come across something like this, something I didn't expect, something not on the map or in the guidebook. I'm filled with wonder and respect for the people who left these traces and for the depths of time they represent. As a kind of offering, I add a rock to one of the ducks that marks the trail.

I'm glad these figures are in the state park and not on BLM [Bureau of Land Management] land. In the BLM-controlled Yuha Desert, south of Anza-Borrego, dirt bikers deliberately carved "doughnuts" over two other intaglios, virtually destroying them. With the BLM's loose rules and loose enforcement, it would be just a matter of time before off-roaders headed this way. Even if they had no malicious intent—and most of them probably don't—they might not notice these faint tracings before the damage was done.

Chase made one of the first and strongest calls for preserving the desert, advocating the establishment of a national park centered on the lush palm canyons near Palm Springs. In *California Desert Trails*, he wrote, "Scenically the place is more than remarkable; it is strictly unique for this country, as well as strangely beautiful: while for its botanical rarity alone it should be preserved in the public interest." It's strange that he wanted to preserve these oases rather than the more austere regions that so captured his imagination; perhaps he was just guessing about what would draw tourists and support for a park. Palm Springs was the wrong place, though, partly because land prices there were already too high but mainly because the major canyons were owned by the Cahuilla.

Chase had the right idea, though, even if he chose the wrong spot. In 1927, when the newly formed State Park Commission began surveying lands for a state park system, members of the San Diego Society of Natural History lobbied for a desert park that would include the palm canyons near the Borrego Valley. The first proposal called for a park in the range of 150,000 to 300,000 acres, but the vision was soon expanded to a million-acre park connecting Borrego Valley and the Cuyamaca and San Jacinto Mountains and possibly extending all the way to the Salton Sea. Proponents pointed to many of the same desert qualities Van Dyke and Chase had extolled. The director of the park commission, Frederick Law Olmsted Jr., a prominent landscape architect and the son of the designer of New York's Central Park, wrote in his report, "Certain desert areas have a distinctive and subtle charm, in part dependent on spaciousness, solitude, and escape from the evidence of human control and manipulation of the earth." He could have been quoting Van Dyke or Chase.

The first lands for what would become Anza-Borrego Desert State Park were turned over to the state in 1932, but it would take another fifteen years for the park to reach roughly its present shape. During that time, the dream of a million-acre park would vanish as the desert became a battleground between those who wanted to develop every available inch of land and those who wanted to preserve it for its scenic or botanical value. In *Our Historic Desert*, published in 1973, Diana Lindsay explored the machinations of county supervisors who saw the desert as a "tax base" and of boomers who bought land in or near the prospective park territory, hoping to either sell it for a high price or develop resorts near the park. She showed that the resulting compromises and delays in the state's land acquisition forced major changes in the size and shape of the park.

The result is a crazy-quilt patchwork of boundaries defining the park and the many private inholdings still within it. The biggest of those inholdings is Borrego Springs, a thirty-five-square-mile chunk right in the middle of the park's northern section. Borrego Springs encompasses orange and grapefruit groves, luxury golf and tennis resorts, and a town of 3,000 people (double that in winter). All of that development relies on local groundwater, and as the town of Borrego Springs and the surrounding farms grew, the spring for which the town was named went dry. Today, farmers are moving into the area because, unlike the Colorado River water used to irrigate the Coachella and Imperial Valleys, the water here is free for the price of drilling and pumping. That pumping threatens even downstream oases such as San Sebastian Marsh.

In other places, private land or holdings of the federal government create strange gaps in the contour of the park's boundary. The Table Mountain area, for instance, is a block of BLM land surrounded on three sides by Anza-Borrego; it was withheld when other federal lands were transferred to the park because of potential mineral sources such as the Mica Gem Mine. And until 1998, the biologically rich Sentenac Ciénega, an obvious gateway to the park, was privately owned and heavily grazed.

Ideally, the park would have been based on some natural boundary, such as a watershed or even a natural vista; instead, it was based on the whims of land speculators and those opposed to removing land from the tax base. The park expresses the contradictions in society's views of nature and the way it should be treated. It expressly protects "cultural features" such as these geoglyphs, but it fails to protect other cultural features, such as Indian land management practices, many of which would conflict with preservation of the park in its "natural state."

Yet every time I tread on BLM land, I am thankful for the park and the efforts of Van Dyke, Chase, Olmsted, and the San Diego Society of Natural History. The park effectively made a reality of Van Dyke's vision of the desert as a place devoid of people, but that was probably the only vision that would have protected it. In the Colorado Desert as a whole, on the other hand, it is George Wharton James' vision, not Van Dyke's or Austin's or Chase's, that has come to pass. Some desert areas are given over totally to human endeavors, while others are reserved for what we call pure nature. Areas managed as wilderness, where it is illegal to remove even a rock, sit next to off-road vehicle areas where it seems the purpose is to destroy every living thing. And these border on the fields of the Imperial Valley, where the desert has ceased to exist at all, having been replaced by another type of habitat. James wasn't successful in reconciling these competing demands, and neither are we today.

34

Bighorn Sheep

Our synecdochical turn of mind, that urge to let a part stand for a whole, is wonderfully handy. We see a drawing of a giant saguaro cactus, and immediately the whole American Southwest, with Indians in warbonnets dancing on mountaintops, leaps before us. Or the image of a camel and sand dunes appears, and at once we conjure the entire Sahara Desert, with caravans plodding along and maybe flute music quavering mysteriously out of a moonlit oasis at midnight. This emblematic thinking is a great convenience, releasing us of the heavy burden of defining the details of the thing itself before we can even begin talking about it. The bent, however, also is a gross oversimplification. Whatever their representative impact, saguaro cactuses cover only a fraction of America's deserts; and, furthermore, whatever their chromatic aspects of our vision and of the travel brochures encouraging them, although Indians do, indeed, dance on some of the region's mesas, they do so on very special occasions, as profound and intricate rites of their religion, and, despite the colorful appeal, they do not wear warbonnets, which are not part of their traditional culture. As to the camel, does it have one hump or two? And the Sahara is a far more complex and varied place than the comforting image of the long-legged ruminant conveys, in fact a place where the camel, whatever the romance surrounding it, is rapidly giving way to modern ways of transportation.

Nonetheless, we cling to the convenience, which often is some strange or dramatic feature representing the whole. And it isn't always a bad one. As Lawrence Hogue points out, the bighorn sheep is incorporated into the very name of Anza-Borrego Desert State Park, *borrego* being the word for sheep in Spanish, and the benign but mysterious creature with the weirdly spiraling horns who gazes down at us from the heights often is pictured as the logo on the park's publications.

What may serve well for publicity, however, having an official authority, may have little to do with everyday reality. In fact, behind the fetching symbol of this wild creature is an animal in rapid, some would say disastrous, decline, so rapid that the day may be near when the symbol lives boldly on while the animal itself has disappeared, thus leaving us entirely in our self-deception.

In this lies yet another danger in our comfortable grasping for simple handles on the world and the self-gratifying finger-pointing of blame. As Hogue develops his case, we see that the decline of the bighorn sheep is no simple matter of greedy hunters and the ousting of the gentle and curious creatures by the construction of new shopping malls but our very own romanticization of nature and our misguided, if sincere, efforts at preservation. In this we learn once more that thinking about the desert can be a dangerous thing, for at times the process challenges not only who we are but some of our deepest-held and most treasured perceptions of the world.

~~~~ **Lawrence Hogue,**
   from *All the Wild and Lonely Places:*
   Journeys in a Desert Landscape

The start of the 1997 Fourth of July bighorn sheep count at Anza-Borrego Desert State Park is not auspicious. It's seven o'clock in the morning, and my partner, Carl, and I have just arrived at our count site, a large boulder above Third Grove in Borrego Palm Canyon. The first thing we notice is a scatter of bones and tan hide under a slight overhang of the rock. I find another bone or two a short distance away. By the size of the bones, it's a small animal, and the hide looks like sheep—probably one of this year's lambs. We wonder what got it. Coyotes? A bobcat? Or perhaps one of the mountain lions that seem particularly numerous in these parts recently?

Mark Jorgensen, who organizes the annual sheep count, warned us that most lambs don't survive their first few months of life, falling prey to disease, predators, heat, drought, or a combination thereof. How many have actually survived their first three to five months? This is one of the questions the sheep count seeks to answer, beyond that of the simple trend in the number of sheep. How many lambs are there for every ewe? How many yearlings have survived their first full summer? By keeping track of the age and sex of every sheep we see coming down to drink at this water hole, we can help provide the answers to these questions, and to the ultimate question: are the Peninsular bighorn sheep, now recognized as a distinct subspecies of *Ovis canadensis*, on their way to recovery or moving further toward extinction?

In recent years, the number of sheep spotted at these annual counts has been down, as it has been on helicopter surveys operated by the California Department of Fish and Game (DFG). After the 1996 survey, Jorgensen and others estimated that there were 280 bighorns left in the Peninsular Ranges north of Mexico. This year, the second of two years of little rainfall, Jorgensen expects the count to be down even further. We're not keeping track of dead sheep, but the remains of this lamb are one data point that tends to confirm Jorgensen's suspicion.

Still, we are less dismayed by this finding than we could be. Early yesterday evening, on our way to our count site, we came across a band of eleven or twelve sheep at First Grove—three adult rams with half-curl horns, a yearling ram, several ewes, and two lambs. We didn't bother tallying them precisely because this wasn't our site. Instead, we just observed. Accustomed to the heavy foot traffic to First Grove, they showed no sign of bolting as we drew to within twenty-five yards of the boulder pile where they perched in safety. They did have a curious look about them, as if wondering who were these strange visitors who kept holding odd black instruments up to their eyes. Of course, you can't judge a sheep by its facial expression. Researchers suspect that even though bighorns can seem calm and alert when approached by humans, they may be experiencing great stress.

Most photographs of bighorn sheep show an adult ram, often the Rocky Mountain variety, with a three-quarter or full curl to its horns, a deep chest, and stout haunches, posed on a rock against the sky. Desert bighorns are not as large or as stout, and the ewes are more spindly still, with short, flared horns describing perhaps a quarter circle, elongated faces, and thin legs and necks. The rams appear to be lords of all they survey, but the ewes seem somehow out of place here in the desert environment, too dainty, almost otherworldly. Perhaps because nature photographers have made me accustomed to the appearance of the rams, the ewes have always seemed to me like strange beings.

As we set up our shade tarp and settle in for a long day of scanning the rocky slopes, I'm confident that we'll see more sheep today. Armed with lunch, a gallon of water each, Carl's spotting scope, binoculars, aluminum folding chairs, and spray bottles filled with water to keep us cool, we're all set. Carl, a middle-aged lawyer, has been doing the sheep count for eleven years now, though he's hardly in shape for summer backpacking in the desert. Struggling up the canyon yesterday, he kept saying, "I don't know why I do this—just for fun, I guess."

He seems to know what he's doing, though, when it comes to searching for sheep. The spot he's picked gives us a broad view up and down the canyon and up a drainage coming in from the north. I rig the shade tarp away from the rock so we can go out and scan the slopes behind us.

At eight o'clock, the sun rises over the eastern canyon wall and pounds its first rays at us. The sun will blast us all morning, but we should have some shade after noon, when the temperature will hit 115 degrees Fahrenheit or so. It's no accident that Jorgensen holds the count at water holes during the hottest time of year—it's the only sure way to know where the sheep will be. The sheep often drink twice daily but can go as long as two days without drinking, if necessary. Counting for three days, we should see most of the sheep that use the creek below us at least once. We're supposed to stay up here, away from the water, from seven in the morning to five in the afternoon. Our best chances of seeing the sheep are in early morning and late afternoon, but we need to scan the hillsides with binoculars or spotting scope virtually all day. We settle down and wait for the sheep.

The desert bighorn, *borrego cimmarón* to the Spanish, is the most visible and popular symbol of wildness in Anza-Borrego Desert State Park and probably in southern California. The park is best known for its spring wildflowers, its most popular attraction, but it was created largely to preserve the bighorn. Not only does it include the animal in its name, it also uses the image in most of its publications.

In the early 1800s, several thousand desert bighorn sheep are thought to have roamed the Peninsular Ranges down to the tip of Baja California. Those numbers declined rapidly on both sides of the border but especially in the United States, mainly a result of hunting and livestock grazing. The construction of Interstate 8 in the 1960s and poaching in northern Baja California seem to have cut off the U.S. population of Peninsular bighorns from their more numerous relatives south of the border. As recently as 1978, 1,200 bighorns remained in the Peninsular Ranges north of the border. But by 1994, that number had dropped to about 350, with 275 inhabiting Anza-Borrego itself and the remainder spread throughout the Santa

Rosa Mountains north to San Jacinto. By 1996, the total number had declined further, to 280 for the entire range.

The principal causes for the decline through the 1980s seem to be three: loss of habitat, mostly from golf-course and housing construction at the lower edge of sheep habitat; fragmentation of habitat by roads and highways; and respiratory diseases the bighorns picked up from domestic sheep and cattle. Normally, only about one-third of bighorn lambs survive their first year, but disease reduced that survival rate to about 10 percent—too few to maintain the species....

Instead of rebounding after respiratory diseases subsided, as the theory of natural regulation would predict, the number of Peninsular bighorns has been kept low by a sudden increase in the number of mountain lions and a change in their eating habits. Jorgensen is careful to point out that the situation is complex, with numerous interrelated factors such as habitat loss, forage and water loss, disease, drought, and predation all interacting to reduce the sheep population. But scientists studying mountain lions and bighorns agree that predation is a significant factor. Ironically, after so much disturbance by humans, it may be the mountain lion that finally does in the bighorn.

In 1998, the U.S. Fish and Wildlife Service listed the Peninsular bighorn as endangered (it was already considered threatened by the state of California). The listing was a sad milestone for the bighorn population, but it puts teeth into efforts to protect the animal's habitat from development and road building. It could bring more money from the federal government for bighorn and perhaps mountain lion research, as well as greater cooperation from federal agencies such as the Bureau of Land Management (BLM). The U.S. Fish and Wildlife Service, along with Jorgensen and other bighorn experts, is developing a conservation plan and a precise habitat map that will chart terrain, vegetation, and water sources.

Perhaps all this will turn things around for the bighorn, or maybe it's too late. The Peninsular Ranges, following at least a dozen other mountain ranges in California, could be the next to lose its bighorns, making the mountains one degree more lonely. But this particular population of *borrego* has induced a higher level of human concern. If writer Jack Turner is right in likening wildlife management to invasive medicine, then the Peninsular bighorn has just arrived in the emergency room....

To Rubin, that line was like a wall the sheep wouldn't cross. "We don't need to waste our time looking up that way," she told me. "That's good mountain lion cover, and the sheep don't usually go in there." In addition to food and water, the sheep need two things: steep, rocky slopes, known as "escape terrain," and open spaces where they can see predators approaching from far off. We spotted fourteen sheep that day—all of them out on the rocky slopes below us. Jorgensen agrees that bighorns won't go into chaparral. The brush has encroached on what used to be sheep habitat, even since 1967, when he began studying bighorns. Then, he saw forty-two sheep in one day at Fourth Cove. "Now I go there and it doesn't even look like sheep habitat," he said. That change is reflected in the annual counts at that site—zero for most of the 1990s and two in 1997.

If you've followed my argument so far, you may already be putting two and two together. The gears of my brain work slower. But over the years since that sheep count, I've begun putting together my own little grand theory, drawing from the area's environmental history as told by Florence Shipek and from Esther Rubin's and Mark Jorgensen's knowledge of sheep behavior. In a nutshell, it is this: One cause of the decline of the bighorn sheep is our own leave-it-alone-and-put-out-the-fires management of these public lands. The Indians used to burn off the chaparral, *creating* habitat for the bighorn as well as for deer and small game. By failing to continue that management, by viewing the chaparral as what should "naturally" be here and trying to preserve it through fire suppression, we have actually reduced sheep habitat, pushing the sheep farther down toward the desert floor and further toward extinction.

In the Vineyards: "Tío, I Need Some Work"

The history of the United States and Mexico has not been a happy one. Land grabs, banditry, and racial prejudice have typified the mutual distrust down through the decades as the two nations have glared at each other across their common border. Some factions would put this down to the strong-arm tactics of the powerful country to the north. There is much truth to this. In the history of nations the more powerful almost always try to coerce the weaker to do their will. Yet, however appealing, such relations rarely are so simple as to be reduced to clear cases of good versus evil. Those who have lived in Mexico may have seen things from quite a different perspective. They have seen a government lubricious with corruption, a backward economy, and a haughty oligarchy routinely cheating fellow citizens for blithe financial gain. This has resulted in a mass egress over the years of poor Mexicans happily giving up their wretched circumstances in search of a better life to the north. The conditions they must endure, as Susan Straight sharply describes in the vineyards of the Colorado Desert, are heart-wrenching in human suffering; yet still they come, one measure of the dismal lives they are escaping.

Susan Straight,
from *Highwire Moon: A Novel*

Mecca was a few stores, a few streets lined with trailers and small houses, and the grapes all around. The smell of burning sugary fruit, fermenting in the sun, nearly made Elvia sick when they got out of the truck at a row of trailers—faded pink, turquoise, and—the one where Hector knocked—pale green as a watermelon rind. But when a man came out onto the single metal step, his huge belly straining against his white undershirt so the material was nearly purple, he frowned at Hector. "Where the hell you been?" he said. "Your jefita gave up on you. In May."

Hector bit his lips. Elvia thought he looked like he would cry. Jefe. Boss. His little boss?

"Where'd they go?"

"She took two or three hermanos up to Watsonville for strawberries. Your pops said, 'Fuck fresas' and went to Washington. Apples, I guess."

His mother, Elvia thought. *She gave up on him.*

Hector said, "Tío, I need some work."

His uncle looked at the clipboard in his huge hands. "Show up when you feel like it? Damn, Hector. Everybody started at five. It's seven now. And it's Thursday. You crazy?" He glanced at Elvia and Michael. "It's 112 today. They picked before?"

"Yeah," Hector lied. "Orale, Tío, I need some money. Please."

"Go see Manuel at Block twelve, off Sixty-sixth," the uncle said. "Tell him I sent you, and don't fuck up. People here are feedin kids. Not just playin around." He handed Hector a bag and slammed the trailer door.

I'm feeding a kid, Elvia thought. She ate the spicy tamale Hector gave her, drank the manzana soda. Apple.

But Michael said, "Mano, if we're gonna sweat our asses off, I need something to keep me going. You know."

Hector said, "My uncle's cousin, Guapo. He does the fields." He looked at Elvia. "My moms doesn't do speed. But her and my pops—they drink a lot, smoke mota. This is where she's from. No nothing. That's why I left last year."

Cars lined Sixty-sixth, and the grapes stretched across the hot earth, all the way to the ash-colored mountains. Hector counted off the blocks, and when she parked he said, "Put a long-sleeve shirt over that. Put on some pants. Or you'll get sunburned and cut at the same time."

He and Michael stood by the truck doors while she struggled out of shorts and into her jeans. Her skin was grimy with two days of sweat and dirt. She couldn't button her jeans at all. She left them undone and let the baggy tee shirt fall over her belly. Then she kicked up white dust on the roadside to keep up with Hector, who was waving at a man under a bright beach umbrella at the end of a row.

It *was* hell. Elvia held the clippers Hector gave her and snipped each stem. Crouching alongside the wall of grapevines, breathing the dust that rose from everyone's steps, from the wheelbarrow's progress, from the trucks that rumbled down the dirt road with boxes, she thought, *Shit, I can do this. I run in the desert all the time.*

But Hector yelled at her after the first box she filled. "Like frosty green marbles, big ones. Not babies. Not yellow. We get our asses kicked if we mess up the box." She worked slowly, dropping the heavy dangles of fruit into the box at her feet. After an hour, she looked up to see the people around her, their faces obscured by bandannas, their heads covered with baseball caps, their hands reaching through the leaves like blackened mitts. She felt dizzy, her back aching already as if her father's acetylene torch prodded the muscles above her hipbones. She could barely breathe, the heat like a thousand fire ants on her scalp. Salt trickled into her eyes, and when she wiped it with her hands, dirt and blood stung even worse.

Hector came by with a water bottle. He poured water into her eyes, into her mouth. Then he and Michael cut and dropped bunches like machines, filling three boxes to her one. Michael carried the full boxes to the end of the long row, where the scale man waited under the umbrella.

Through the stems and leaves, she could hear people talking in Spanish. She tried to look at the women's faces—what if her mother was here, right now, picking grapes? Each pair of eyes squinted, dismissing her, searching for the grapes.

As she touched each woody stem, each bunch of frosty green marbles, she smelled the fermenting juices and breathed the dust. Each breath was sharpened, hot, as if the dust particles carried thorns, and her lungs burned. When she'd filled another box, she bent over, ready to faint, and someone laughed on the vine wall. *Melting—you wanted to melt away the baby. Fine. You'll die, too.* She was on her knees when Hector came again, pouring more water onto her head and face, whispering, "You okay?"

"I can't breathe," she gasped.

Hector said, "There's pesticides on the grapes. You can't gulp with your mouth. Breathe through your nose. Don't give up yet. Come on. At least fake it."

A hand thrust through the vines, giving her a bandanna. Elvia tried to see the face, but she heard only laughter. She tied the cotton square around her nose and mouth, thinking it would suffocate her, but she smelled menthol in the cloth. She panted for a few minutes, then began to pick again.

Lunch was more tamales from a truck, and water. Elvia poured it onto her chest, her neck. She lay in the sandy alley between rows, her head in Michael's lap, her eyes closed. Melting—was the baby hot inside her, glowing like a tiny doll? No—it didn't have hands yet. No feet. It was just cells. Cells that might be disappearing into her aching, pulsing muscles and skin.

She could barely lift herself off the sand when the work began again. The sky and sand and leaves were all white, blinding her as she reached for the grapes, rubbery hot. She panted inside the bandanna. Her mother could be picking beside her. Her mother could be washing these grapes and popping them into her other children's mouths. Elvia steadied herself against a pole until she could see again. Then she turned and followed Hector back down the row, where the late-season vines were sending tendrils across the sand to trip unwary feet.

The green hallways emptied out before dusk, and Elvia was still struggling with her last box.

"So who's your ruca, Hector?" someone said behind her.

"I'm nobody's ruca," Elvia answered, spinning around.

The girl laughed. "You look like nobody. Never seen nobody pick so damn slow."

Elvia thought, *It's not my fault, okay? I'm pregnant.* But the teenage girl came around the wall of vines, in stretch pants and old sneakers, her belly huge, as if she'd have the baby any day.

Elvia was so startled she dropped her clippers, and the girl laughed again. "Clumsy, too," she said. "I was gonna tell Marisela you married Hector so she'd kick your ass."

"Shut up, Tiny," Hector said, grinning. "I'm not here. You're not talking to me. I'm not really here. I'm headin back to Rio Seco. City college this year."

"Orale, schoolboy, Sally's still in love with you, too," Tiny said. Elvia stared at the woman coming down the row, waving at Hector. She couldn't believe he was a big deal here, with his neat ponytail and wide smile, his notebook of maps. He took her box down to the scale man, who was waiting impatiently, and then another girl came up behind Elvia.

"So that's your vato buying crystal?" she hissed. "Spending your money you ain't made yet."

Elvia saw Michael now, leaning into the window of a turquoise Mustang that had been cruising the avenue. Hector said, "Guapo. Michael was looking for him. And he's always looking for somebody like Michael."

Just like Dually, Elvia thought, tired, her feet swollen into her shoes. Suddenly she knew—*Michael's gonna sketch all day and night, like Callie and my dad. He hates the world slow and ordinary, one place you know. Like I wish it was.*

"Everybody looks like fuckin ghosts fadin away," Michael said beside her. The trampled sand, the bare vines limp and bedraggled, the piles of trash and pallets and boxes at the end of the rows—she stared at the retreating backs, and they did look haunted, covered with fine, pale dust and bent by the day. People walked toward town or loaded into trucks and cars.

"Come on," Hector said. "We won't have a place to sleep if we don't book up."

Every parking lot and sandy area was taken up with cars and trucks. People were stretched out on hoods and in truck beds, sleeping or talking, propped against tires, playing cards and starting small barbecues. Elvia jerked the truck into a small island of sand in the sea of cars and trucks and folding chairs in a vacant lot. Hector said, "We gotta wait for Rosario."

Elvia laid her head on the door frame, so tired she could hardly move. A carload of men next to them was listening to the radio. "Por que l'amor de mi alma, solito Mexico…." The song spilled from the open windows. "Viva Zacatecas!" someone in the back sang along.

"Sinaloa, Michoacan, Zacatecas," Hector said. "Where'd you say your moms was from?"

Elvia shrugged. "Mexico."

"Thirty-one states, so you better get a clue." Hector pointed. "There's Rosario. The tamale lady. From Cabazon Reservation. See the red truck? Every night she comes. Beef tamales like you never had. And apple empanadas. Like pies but better."

"From the rez, huh? She's Cahuilla," Michael said, peering at the old woman.

Hector shrugged. "She's a cook. She's been coming here since I was a kid. Summer for the grapes. Winter for the dates. Sometimes we lived in a station wagon."

"Well, I ain't sleepin with all these people," Michael said, scowling, three lines etched between his brows. "Cause I don't want to be around when they start fuckin and fightin." His eyes were shiny as night glass. "My moms met my pops here. Probably fucked me into the world in a fuckin parking lot. I ain't in the mood to think about whether my pops is sitting in the old-ass Dodge Dart right there."

"Life's a bitch," Hector said, his voice hard for the first time. "And then you die. But if you got a better place ... We gotta be back in the field at five, or Manuel ain't paying us, sabes?" He stalked over to the red truck and brought back a bag that smelled of chile and cinnamon.

Elvia felt the sweat and dust drying on her arms and face now that a breeze moved through the valley. "I need a shower, big time."

"Most people take a bath in the canal right there." Hector pointed to the drainage ditch under the bridge.

She shook her head. "Then let's go somewhere else."

Michael pointed her south on the highway, the sun red in the dust hanging over the fields. After a few miles, Elvia saw a glimpse of blue, a huge mirage of a lake. Then she smelled briny ocean. "Where are we?" she asked, at the expanse of water glittering against the sand.

"Salton Sea," Michael said. "Everybody used to fish here, but now the lake's all fucked up. Full of poison and salt from the fields. See the mountains?" He pointed to the purple riven range rising across the water. "Where those stripes are, that's where the real lake was. When my grandpa's grandpa lived here."

Elvia could see the marks, an ancient shoreline. "So this lake isn't real?"

Michael said, "He told me Lake Cahuilla was a hundred years ago, big water from Indio to Mexico. And people fished. Then this long drought came and there was just a puddle. The people went further in the desert or up to the mountains. My grandpa's people went to Desert Springs. Then in, like, nineteen hundred something, farmers came and pulled the irrigation water from the Colorado River. It flooded a few times and the whole river poured in here, till the railroad people dumped all this junk to dam it up. Now it's the Salton Sea. A fake lake." His voice was still sketch-fast, Elvia thought.

Hector said, "My grandpa used to come here all the time. He was from Veracruz. Lived on fish—tilapia and corvina, in salsa colorado. But now all the fish are dying off. Pull in there."

Elvia parked at the concrete shell of a two-story motel, with the front wall gone and a honeycomb of bare rooms—no windows, no carpet, no furniture, like square caves staring at the glowing water.

"Desert people took it all for their trailers," Hector said when they climbed into a room on the second floor, the cement floor and walls still warm. He opened the tamales.

Michael was restless, sweeping trash from the floor with a palm frond. "What would your pops do if he saw his truck right now?"

"He'd probably try to kick your ass. Both of you."

"What if we kicked his ass?" Michael said softly.

"What?"

"You ran, right?" Michael shrugged. "Like you never want to see him again. Was he treatin you bad? Messin with you? Is he your *real* dad?"

She remembered what Sandy's daughter, Rosalie, had called him, that day he came to get her. "Yeah—my bio dad. He never messed with me. He messed with everybody else."

Once, at the Tourmaline Market, a man had leaned into the truck window while she waited for her father. He asked what time it was, how hot it usually got. Her father came outside and punched the man in the face, then rubbed his skull in the hot sand. He said, "Get in your fuckin Honda and drive. If you can't drive cause your face hurts, I'll drive you someplace. My choice."

She couldn't say to Michael, *I left him because I was gonna get bigger and bigger from a baby with your eyes. Your skin. And I was scared of everything.*

"You seem like him sometimes."

"Maybe. Sometimes. When I'm driving."

Michael didn't smile. He took out a cigarette. "And who knows what you got from your moms, right? See, Hector can't figure out what he got from his parents. He's like alien boy."

"Look," Hector said, turning to Elvia. "There's twelve of us. A dozen eggs, okay? I'm number ten. My parents, they work hard wherever. Like today. You do that every day, and then you gotta have some beer. They get drunk, they fight, they have another baby, they move on. But you know what? My mom—she works all day in the field, and then she's gotta cook somethin for everybody, gotta wash out the clothes and hang em up. I don't blame her for gettin high. She's like, so tired. I don't know what she was when she was herself."

"So now they're gone?" Elvia said.

Hector nodded. "I miss my mom. But last year, I worked the grapes. And then they were going up north to Parlier and Dinuba for the rest of the grapes. I turned seventeen. I figured it's like my last chance to finish school. So I stayed in the arroyo with Michael and went to Tourmaline High. Now I want to go to college. Geography." He looked embarrassed, holding out his hands for the cornhusk tamale wrappers. The apple empanadas were doughy, spicy with cinnamon. When Hector went out with the trash, Elvia lay on her side. Every muscle ached, in her thighs and along her back and even her wrists. Inside her lungs, she felt a washing sting like Listerine. Poison. Dust. Heat. She couldn't do this every day, for the rest of her life.

36

Any August Day a Hundred Years Ago: In the Cool Pines

August hardly is a glorious time, in Palm Springs or in any of the other settlements dotting the Colorado Desert. They lie under the quivering resignation of the tortured accepting the endless punishment that is their inevitable summer lot. Except, of course, for the chance traveler who, for whatever extraordinary reason, is visiting and will be welcomed by the bored hotelier with open arms and get not only a lavish resort room at a cut rate, but have the golf courses and museums nearly all to himself. If he stays long at all, he soon appreciates why and begins slumping into listlessness along with the rest of the sun-stricken citizenry.

Yet the desert is not all desert, as the keen visitor with gumption and a moderately strong pair of legs can learn. Soaring thousands of feet above the shimmering wastes are pine forests with deer drinking from cool streams. They, too, are part of the desert's milieu in this land of alternating basins and ranges which seem to go on in endless succession. Perhaps these islands of coolness and greenery are not as rarely visited as we'd like to believe; yet given human aversion to exertion and the strict controls on wilderness hiking, these realms continue to hold the secrets of those who, for whatever reasons, sought out their sanctuary.

I'm not sure why Mary Jo Churchwell, who grew up on the Colorado Desert and continues to hike there, begins her mini-essay embodying such things by commenting on the misnaming of a meadow with potentially poisoning consequences. Perhaps it has something to do with the virtue of being "close to nature," at once a dangerous if highly rewarding adventure. Here, it was successfully undertaken by one George Law, who both knew what he was doing and, no phony, understood that living deeply into nature requires a large person wise and strong enough to be humble. Of one thing we're sure. While he lived above Skunk Cabbage Meadow, he did not eat the poisonous corn lily. And during her stay there, neither did Mary Jo Churchwell.

~~~ Mary Jo Churchwell
from *Palm Springs: The Landscape, the History, the Lore*

August in the San Jacintos is glorious, warm in the sun, cool in the shade. Stoking myself with sunflower seeds, I hike to my destiny at a steady mile per hour, load humped against my back, bare legs pasted with sun block, DEET, and mashed flies. The trail goes steeply up, which is bad, then steeply down, which is worse. Up. Down. Up. And then, by golly, down again. Skunk Cabbage Meadow beckons and the boots keep moving, putting a steadily increasing distance between me and civilization.

Someone named it Skunk Cabbage Meadow without looking skunk cabbage up. These are corn lilies, and they are virtually odorless and look nothing like cabbages. What is even worse, the misidentified corn lily continues to be misidentified as skunk cabbage because of the meadow's name, a mistake that has caused unfortunate consequences over the years. As a young shoot, the skunk cabbage, which is edible, looks like the corn lily, which is poisonous, or it looks enough like it to occasionally require the evacuation of a boy scout.

To the northeast of Skunk Cabbage Meadow lies a forested bench called Laws Camp in commemoration of George Law, a freelance journalist who built a cabin on the site in 1916. Law meant his cabin to be a part of the mountain, simple, primitive, just the bare-handed basics. The walls were stone slabs laid as flat as they had lain in the earth, thick or thin as the spot demanded, in varying shades just as they came to hand from the stacks. The ridgepole and rafters were hewed from nearby cedars and pines, so the roof fitted the walls in an irregular way. Meadow grass covered the roof, wild-sown with buttercups, so it turned yellow in June, further binding the cabin to the earth. To his everlasting credit, Law used no ready-mix, no window glass, no chinking other than grass. He didn't turn the meadow into a pasture for livestock. He didn't divert the creeks, so they continued to flow where they wished, and deer drank from them instead of cows.

Working alone, how long did it take Law to build the cabin? Three seasons? Six? Stonework isn't something that lends itself to hurry and speed. No doubt he muttered to himself the usual entreaties: There's no need to go at this great guns, working yourself to a bloody pulp. It isn't going to get finished in one summer, so you might as well come to understand the process. Like using the heavier stones first, down low, lifting them no higher than necessary. And using the flat stones on top and the square stones on corners. So okay, it was possible, stone cabins could be built. He could do it.

Although a mason's eye must follow a wall precisely, his thoughts are free to veer off in any direction. So with his pipe drawing nicely, Law was able to delve into life, letting subjects come and go at will. With some people, the busier their hands are somewhere else the better they work in their head—which fortunately was the part that earned Law a living. I imagine an entry in his journal might read, "I have had a productive day: twenty stones and two thousand words."

Cabin-building and wool-gathering. But that wasn't all that went on around there. Living steadily outdoors, Law was able to gain an intimacy with the place, to learn the habits and schedules of the deer who came daily to the creek, were admired, and perhaps named, and the jays who filched his bacon, and the chipmunks who whisked off his crumbs, and the squirrels who watched the strong shell of his cabin grow stone by stone.

Even with frequent breaks to relight, refill, or simply find his pipe, Law managed to finish the walls, the floor, and the roof before he ran out of energy. Besides that, the cabin looked like it was supposed to look, that is, as if it had been thrown out of the ground. The only hitch was that it stood on land that Law had leased from the Southern Pacific Railroad for ten dollars a year. So he never really owned the cabin, except in his head and by his sweat, and by that time the cabin owned him too, his affection.

Law lived in the San Jacintos for ten seasons—plenty of time for a literary democrat to become a narrow-minded property owner at odds with everyone who plucked *his* gooseberries, caught *his* fish, shot *his* deer. At some point, he must have caught an extreme case of wanderlust, for he left the San Jacintos and never returned, thus cutting short my favorite story. For years thereafter, his byline was found attached to Mexican travel yarns in the Automobile Club's *Westways*.

The wild creatures seemed not to miss him any more than they had minded him. As soon as he turned his back, the mice moved in and plundered the bedding for feathers. Time worked its mischief on the roof, and the swallows flew in with bugs in their beaks. The chinking lost its grip, and the stone walls, weakened by wayward roots, collapsed with neglect. So by the time the Forest Service got around to knocking the cabin down it didn't have all that far to fall. Thus what had been the focus of one man's life vanished off the face of the earth, giving no truth that anyone had ever lived there.

And yet... I wanted to find the truth of that cabin. Even in ruins it had to be here, a dooryard path, perhaps, or the posts of a porch or the crumbled remains of a chimney, where the smoke of many a pipe dream once rose. But there wasn't a ruin in sight. Maybe I was searching too far east. Maybe the creeks had changed course. Maybe too many years had stacked up between me and the press clipping I held in my hand. Then suddenly, on a bench above the confluence of Willow Creek and Tahquitz Creek, I had a cornerstone at my feet, a granite boulder that looked exactly like the one I had pictured in my hand. And there, almost hidden in bushes and ferns, where heaps of smooth flat stones lay in disorderly lines, lay George Law's cabin.

When on that day last August I pitched camp beside the cabin site, it was like any August day a hundred years ago. The smell of pines was the same. The spring where I knelt and plunged my head was George Law's sweet little spring, and I came away from it all fresh and glowing with the cold as he had. The sun I watched set, round and red, and the moon I watched rise, yellow and bright in the green twilight, were his as well. I settled there for three days and pretended nothing had changed.

37

Palm Desert, Rancho Mirage, La Quinta, Las Mentiras

If Anza's ragged colonists, staggering through snow, then heat, plagued by thirst, hunger, and Indians, suddenly stumbled into the modern Palm Springs, they would have thought that the miracles their priests kept promising them had more than come true. Even those of us who have worked digging uncounted fence-post holes in an endless August sun, without the succor of iced drinks at night or the blast of air-conditioning to lure us through the day, still find the coolness of hotel lobbies bathing the skin and the rattle of ice cubes somewhat otherworldly.

The blessings of modern prosperity should not be easily dismissed, given what others have suffered, sometimes fatally. Yet this comes down to more than a matter of degree. At a certain pivot, the quantitative becomes the qualitative. Man either changes the nature around him or he doesn't survive. On the other hand, to what extent should success be carried? At a certain point it becomes bizarre and ridiculous, even self-destructive.

It is one thing, enjoying the ease of our times, to sit in our desert home while the air conditioning whirrs and watch the quail outside feeding on the patio. It's quite another when tens of thousands, even hundreds of thousands, of people want to do the same thing in the same desert. And more than that. Want to zip around on free-ways, play golf on a green, water-wasting course, then eat at a fashionable restaurant. And perhaps wear a turquoise-studded bolo tie to show their fellows that they're part of the desert cognoscente.

Yet what has any of this to do with the desert? The people who built the Palm Springs Convention Center, the Riviera Hotel, and Maxim's de Paris are forward-looking, upbeat, and proud of their yardage. But what does it profit anyone that the "shops in the new Desert Fashion Plaza equal those of Rodeo Drive in Beverly Hills"? Haven't we had enough of that? Maybe Beverly Hills should stay in Beverly Hills. Some of us, perhaps a diminishing number, would prefer the desert as it was to its remake into glitz on the one hand and a poison lake on the other. There's a deathly irony in much current boasting and a chilling lack of vision in those shaping our future when they clap their hands that open space on the desert means building more golf courses. One wonders if the souls of such people have completely turned to tinsel.

—ₘₘ Frank M. Bogert,
from *Palm Springs: First Hundred Years*

For years, nothing but open desert existed between Palm Springs and Indio. A few date, grape and alfalfa ranches sprang up when a plentiful water supply was discovered in underground aquifers. Villages along Highway 111 like Cathedral City, Rancho Mirage, Palm Desert and Indian Wells expanded as locations for new golf courses and subdivisions were sought by developers. By 1982, all of these villages were large enough to incorporate.

Today, the Coachella Valley is composed of nine cities: Desert Hot Springs, Palm Springs, Cathedral City, Rancho Mirage, Palm Desert, Indian Wells, La Quinta, Indio and Coachella. The total permanent population numbers 180,000, with a seasonal rise to approximately 240,000.

Palm Springs can boast of only eight of the valley's sixty-nine golf courses. Its greatest attractions are the Aerial Tramway, Palm Springs Desert Museum, Oasis Water Resort, Moorten Botanical Gardens and the spectacular Indian canyons.

The Palm Springs Municipal Airport, two miles from the center of town, has eight major airlines offering direct service to all parts of the country. Several deluxe hotels have been added to an already fine roster: Maxim's de Paris, Marquis Hotel, Shilo Inn and Palm Springs Plaza. The Riviera Hotel is currently being remodeled, and the Canyon Hotel is adding over two hundred rooms. The Wyndham Hotel and the Palm Springs Convention Center are scheduled to open in early 1988. At that time, Palm Springs will have approximately 7,000 hotel rooms.

Excellent shopping facilities make this "sport" one of the city's great-est assets and one of the main delights for visitors. Shops in the new Des-ert Fashion Plaza equal those of Rodeo Drive in Beverly Hills. The Court-yard's many boutiques also provide a high-fashion image. Other centers, with more moderately priced merchandise, appeal to local residents.

In addition, excellent art galleries, antique stores and many specialty shops line Palm Canyon Drive. An abundant supply of gourmet restau-rants and many quaint eateries around town offer choices of Chinese, Jap-anese, Mexican, Italian and other types of cuisine.

Baseball fans have an opportunity to watch a game when Gene Autry's California Angels return to the desert for spring practice and exhibition games. Angels Stadium is open all summer, and the Palm Springs Angels play nightly games with other farm-league teams.

Desert Hot Springs, six miles north of Palm Springs, has many spas, several small hotels and a number of fine restaurants. Cabots Old Indian Pueblo Museum gives tourists a glimpse of life in early America, and the Mission Lakes Country Club offers an excellent golf course.

Cathedral City, bordering Palm Springs to the east, is the home of the Desert Princess Hotel and Golf Course, Cathedral Canyon Country Club and an adjoining hotel as well as several smaller hotels and restaurants.

Next is Rancho Mirage, a city that got its start with two golf courses, Thunderbird and Tamarisk, and now has eleven courses and plenty of land available for more development. The city's two largest hotels are Mission Hills Resort and Marriott's Rancho Las Palmas Resort. A beautiful new Ritz-Carlton hotel, under construction in the hills overlooking the city, will open in 1988. Many fine restaurants are located in Rancho Mirage on "Restaurant Row" along Highway 111.

The Eisenhower Medical Center, Betty Ford Center for Chemical Abuse, Barbara Sinatra Center for Abused Children and Annenberg Center for Health Sciences are Rancho Mirage's most outstanding achievements. The city is also home to Frank Sinatra and Ambassador Walter Annenberg, whose estate includes a private golf course. The Bighorn Sheep Reserve lies in the hills south of town.

Palm Desert, to the east, is one of the valley's fastest-growing cities. College of the Desert, a community college, was built in this location be-cause the city is geographically in the center of the valley. The new and tre-mendously successful Town Center, built by Ernie Hahn, includes an ice skating rink and many fine shops. El Paseo, too, has become a fine street for upscale shopping.

The Bob Hope Cultural Center, which will include the McCallum Theatre and several smaller theaters, opens in 1988. At that time, the valley will finally have proper facilities for staging operas, ballets and other theatrical events.

A major tourist attraction, The Living Desert, was established by the first mayor of Palm Springs, Philip Boyd.

Palm Desert has nineteen golf courses, more than any other city in the valley. With so much undeveloped land still available, more spectacular courses are already on the drawing board for the near future. The city's largest hotel is Marriott's Desert Springs Resort, with 900 rooms, two complete eighteen hole golf courses and superb convention facilities. Several smaller hotels and many excellent dining spots round out the visitor attractions.

Indian Wells started with Eldorado Country Club and Indian Wells Country Club. There are now six golf courses. Among the major hotels are Erawan Garden Hotel, Ramada Inn and the exclusive Grand Champions Resort. The latter resort also contains a 10,000-seat tennis stadium that has been the site of the annual Pilot Pen Tennis Tournament. A new 192-room Stouffer Hotel will open in 1988. The Indian Wells Racquet Club is located on the site of the old Indian well that gave the town its name.

In a beautiful cove next to Indian Wells lies the city of La Quinta. A charming Spanish hotel, built in 1921, has been a famous resort for many years. Today, the area is popular for its eight golf courses, four of which make up PGA West, where a fifth is under construction. From La Quinta, fine riding and hiking trails lead into the nearby hills and a palm-lined canyon.

Indio is now looking forward to becoming a tourist destination in its own right. Three golf courses have already been built and several new projects are in the planning stages.

The ninth city, at the southern end of the valley, is Coachella. Like Indio, it has been an industrial and agricultural center, but is now actively seeking a future as a resort area.

Large developers from other parts of the world tell us that the valley is only in its infancy. Local developers, such as Bill Bone and John Wessman, agree. It is predicted that by the year 2000 the valley will have a population of over 400,000.

Several of the valley's golf courses and large developments, such as Palm Desert Resort and Bermuda Dunes, are still part of the county, although most of them lie within the sphere of influence of future cities. A need to maintain open space will certainly require the construction of additional golf courses.

Epilogue: A Beam of Dawn Light

And yet. And yet. Yes, it cuts to the quick to see the Rodeo Drive of Beverly Hills, having years ago swept into the idyllic village of Palm Springs, now spreading victorious in a self-congratulatory, hubristic tide ever eastward across the desert. The little shack where humble Carl Eytel painted was long ago torn down and replaced by the arts and croissants crowd inhabiting the upscale Tennis Club; the Cahuilla Indians who once took comfort that their legends held the Cosmos together now dupe the tourists with the flash of their casinos but deceive themselves grandly in the process with their new riches. To the other extreme, some of us, at least, can't take the Ed Abbey approach. His sarcastically titled novel *Good News* reflects smug satisfaction in the ultimate cataclysm of a self-imploding society. Yet sarcasm hardly is stuff to feed the soul. Either way, what's lacking is reverence, both for the world around us and ultimately for ourselves.

` self-destructive population growth, now measured by increases of hundreds of thousands zipping around the Coachella Valley in BMWs in their desperate, rodentine search for the most dazzling restaurants that will fleece them in a mutual silent conspiracy, there are still places where you can disappear into the desert and forget what's behind you, perhaps catch your breath seeing a bighorn sheep high above gazing quizzically down at you; and I can take you to a cave where at the summer solstice a beam of dawn light pierces a crevice to march across dots inscribed on the wall, as that beam has done for centuries. If such things are refuge in a crazed world beyond our control, it's an exhilarating refuge.

Yes, if in the streets of downtown Palm Springs you stand quietly in the midst of the crowds and fashionable shops listening with a preternatural ear, you can still hear old Tahquitz rumbling far up in his nearby canyon, old Tahquitz who is far more destructive today than the trembling Indians ever imagined, for perhaps those stories are always metaphorical, reflecting the conflicts within society, and within ourselves. They are conflicts more critical now than in those days when the Cahuillas gathered in their ceremonial houses and with soft beatings of drums sent the souls of their dead, finally, off to an assured resting place.

For now, we have inherited a far different world, and that is our burden; yet we, too, have our comforts, although not as absolute as the Cahuilla enjoyed. Despite the wreckage, whimsical qualities remain in the nooks and crannies of Palm Springs, if one knows where to look for them. Some years ago there was a terrible fuss over who would pay for the pedestrian bridge now arcing over the town's main drag and linking two nudist enclaves. I took some comfort in that. And with less commotion, there's the local historical society, a marvel in the midst of green grass downtown, a refuge for contemplative people seeking the depth of the past and, perhaps, a key to the future.

If we derive other comforts from the nostalgia of looking backward at what once was, so be it; that's some solace nonetheless. And perhaps we need not squint too painfully into the future, for present whimsy remains for us to enjoy, if as I said, one knows where to find it, either in reality or in the soul. On both scores, two gentle concluding pieces by desert chronicler Ann Japenga offering her own kind of reverence.

~~~ Ann Japenga,
from "A Landmark Fades"

Last year about this time I was driving the old road to the Salton Sea when I started to crave shade and sugar. There's something about this stretch of Highway 86 south of Indio that invariably makes travelers yearn along these lines. Russell Nicoll realized this back in 1928 when he opened the Valerie Jean Date Shop, a wayfarers' refuge complete with the world's first date shakes.

I wasn't even thinking about Nicoll's place as I drove, but my Subaru seemed to find its way there of its own accord. Buried deep in my hot brain were vestigial memories of childhood road trips: My siblings and I seated backwards in a station wagon. A searing wind, childish tempers—and salvation in the form of a date shop.

Years later here I was again stepping into the coolness of the low-slung rustic building. As I bit into an ice cream bar and looked around, it registered that there wasn't much left of the place, just a few scraggly packs of dates and ghosts of tourists past.

What I was witnessing was the last days of a Coachella Valley landmark. You'll still find the name Valerie Jean on the map; and if you drive down to Thermal there's the Valerie Jean building, all right. But there'll be no friendly greeting and no date shakes. The place is barred and boarded up.

The news should come as a wrenching blow to the global community of highway travelers. From Rome to Des Moines, the name Valerie Jean has come to symbolize rest, relief and sustenance.

The only consolation for this loss is that we still have the memories of Valerie Jean herself, the girl the shop was named for.

Now 81, Valerie Jean Smart was nine years old when her father and mother, Russell and Mary Nicoll, opened the family business in a tiny shack on a curve of highway where Avenue 66 from Mecca meets what was then Highway 99.

At the time, there were hardly any stopping places from Indio all the way to El Centro. Road trips were grittier in those days. Blowouts were common and auto air-conditioning was unheard of. The heat and peril only increased the appeal of Nicoll's oasis.

As the business prospered, Nicoll replaced the original 12x16 shack with a new home and a more formidable shop built from old railroad ties, bridge timbers and telephone poles. Creeping vines soon took over the ramada, adding the winning touch: Shade.

In addition to coddling motorists, Nicoll earned celebrity status for the California date with his far-reaching mail-order business. Locals who grew up in Thermal remember a parade of UPS trucks backing up to the shop, especially at the holidays.

And the packages the trucks carried away looked like early California works of art. (Take note all you Ebay traders.) Nicoll must have had an artistic streak because he took exquisite care in packaging his products.

Like a typical kid, Valerie Jean both loved and hated the attention that came from having her name on date boxes that traveled all over the world. A little-known fact: She secretly longed for someone to call her just "Valerie" or "Val" which no one would do, it seemed, as long as her full name was emblazoned on the highway.

When she grew up and married, Valerie Jean left the desert for the Bay Area, where she raised kids and later worked as a nurse.

Eventually, she found her way to Tucson where she lives today ("I just had to get back to the desert"), with an oil painting of the Valerie Jean date shop hanging over her fireplace.

Whenever a new acquaintance asks her where she grew up, she says: "Eleven miles south of Indio and north of the Salton Sea. Maybe you've heard of a little shop called Valerie Jean...?"

If the listener is lucky, Valerie Jean might go on to tell about the time she was coming home on the school bus and there, strolling out of the date shop, she caught sight of a man with wild, fuzzy hair. It was Albert Einstein, one of many famous guests to visit Valerie Jean over the years.

Or she might tell about the time General George Patton came to the shop, or the day she and her Dad drove out to deliver dates to Mrs. Patton. "Lines and lines of army trucks would stop at the store when Patton's men were stationed in the desert," Smart says.

Fairly often, the listener will light up at the name Valerie Jean.

"Sure, sure," the new acquaintance says. "My parents used to drive us out to the desert and we stopped there all the time." Then he or she gets lost in remembering the cactus shakes or the tangerine juice or the delectable shade.

⁓ Ann Japenga,
from *"The No-Girls Club"*

On walks around my neighborhood, I have noticed something clandestine going on in a little adobe house not far from the rush of Indian Avenue. Most times of day the house is shuttered and vacant. But then every day at noon the house is mobbed by two or three dozen fancy cars. By two o'clock, the cars are gone again.

One day I spotted a bronze plaque affixed near the front door. No one was around so I walked up the manicured path and studied the sign: The Palm Springs Club: Private.

Now I was convinced I had stumbled on a secret society. My suspicions gathered momentum when I asked around and found out this was a private men's club dating to 1956.

No women allowed? In 2003? My imagination went wild when I discovered the ostensible reason for the club: Dominoes. This was clearly a cover. How could a simple game draw all those expensive cars every day? I became determined to steal a glimpse behind the tan shutters.

Getting through the door proved easier than you might think. I simply phoned the club and talked to the president, Jack Oberle. A 65-year-old former general manager of the Desert Water Agency, Oberle politely told me that women were indeed not allowed at the daily lunch meetings.

So, I invited myself over after lunch.

The crowd had dispersed by the time Oberle greeted me at the front door of the bungalow. My first thought when he ushered me inside was: This is way too orderly. The place had the feel of a teenager's bedroom that's been hastily straightened up when Mom comes home.

The room was elegant and intimate, with a low, beamed ceiling of blonde wood. The space was dominated by a few dozen custom-made dominoes tables, with every chair tucked neatly in place and the dominoes (embossed with PSC, for Palm Springs Club) in perfect rows.

But there were clues all is not always so tidy and civilized: Miss January reigned over the bar, alongside an old poster of the Chi Chi Club. The clock over the bar announced the time in large letters: Who Cares?

If I had arrived a little earlier, I suspect I'd have seen beer bottles rolling across the floor and ties hanging from the ceiling beams. I sensed that this was a frat house for the local power elite, a place where deals were made the old-fashioned way—off the record.

Oberle was maddeningly discreet. When I asked him what goes on in the club he said, "We play dominoes. Sometimes we go on trips with our wives and girlfriends. That's it."

Figuring I wasn't going to get much more out of the club president, I asked to speak to one of the more talkative members of the gang and was referred to Ray Corliss, who was a member from the very start.

The founders were seven men who were movers and shakers in Palm Springs in the 1950s. Their leader, Arthur Bailey, was familiar with men's clubs in bigger cities such as L.A. and San Francisco. In that hallowed tradition, men met in dark-paneled rooms, ostensibly playing games but actually running the town's business. Bailey decided Palm Springs was getting big enough that such a club was called for here.

"Arthur Bailey decided what we needed was a lunch club where we could go hide," Corliss recalls. "Seven of us met at Art's call in the dining room of the Desert Inn. The dominoes came from Art's influence. He was just a tiger for dominoes and the game sort of crept in and took over the conversation."

Club members play a game called Double Six which is apparently addictive and difficult to master. Theoretically, you only have to be able to add to five to play the game, but the subtleties are so confounding that Jack Oberle has seen CPAs, who have worked with figures all their lives, quit in frustration.

The club grew quickly. In the early days they met in the employees' dining room at the Desert Inn, then at the Oasis Hotel. They purchased their current Movie Colony headquarters in 1973. Today the group consists of 85 full-time members and a core of 40 or so who meet for lunch as often as six days a week.

The club has a chef and waiter on staff so the guys can concentrate on dominoes and talking. What do they talk about?

Jack Oberle says vaguely, "Mostly dominoes and telling jokes and doing what guys do. It's like a locker room thing. You don't have to worry about offending anybody."

"It's our tree house," Corliss adds. "No girls allowed." (Though women are allowed to attend special events.)

The tree house is closed on Sundays but here's a tantalizing fact: All the members have keys and can hang out any time they wish, day or night.

Corliss says, "There are no secret rituals. We don't have a special grip. We're really kind of innocuous."

I ask Corliss if there is actually more to it. "In the old days they used to accuse us of running the city," he says. "I wish it was true."

I realize the club has not survived all these years because they admit blabbermouths. I'm never going to know exactly what goes on in that little adobe house. But I'm more sure than ever the No-Girls Club has played a behind-the-scenes role in Palm Springs' history and politics.

Once more before leaving, I try to nudge Oberle into a confession, "If these walls could talk..."

"Yeah," he answers. "but they won't."

Notes and Source Credits

INTRODUCTION

1. One can hear the ancient god's name tortured into any number of bizarre sounds. However, if you say Táhquits, almost everyone will know what you mean.

2. This one is much easier. Cahuilla is pronounced Kah-wée-ah. Specifically, we're referring to the Agua Caliente band of the large desert tribe.

3. The figures are taken from Berlo, 384–85.

4. Ann Japenga, "Bloomsbury, P.S."

CHAPTER 1

From *Stories and Legends of the Palm Springs Indians*, by Francisco Patencio, as told to Margaret Boynton (1943; Palm Springs: Palm Springs Desert Museum, 1970), ix, 40–41, 44–45, 45–50.

CHAPTER 2

From *The Forgotten Artist: Indians of Anza-Borrego and Their Rock Art*, by Manfred Knaak (Borrego Springs, California: Anza-Borrego Desert Natural History Association, 1988), 36–39, 79.

CHAPTER 3

From *Anza's California Expeditions: Volume 3*, by Herbert Eugene Bolton (Berkeley: University of California Press, 1930), 57–60, 61–64.

CHAPTER 4

From *The Personal Narrative of James O. Pattie, of Kentucky*, by James O. Pattie, Ed. Reuben Gold Thwaites (1833; Cleveland: The Arthur H. Clark Company, 1905), 212–13, 215, 216, 219.

CHAPTER 5

From *Six Horses*, by Captain William Banning and George Hugh Banning (New York: The Century Company, 1930), 121–25.

CHAPTER 6

From *Report of a Geological Reconnaissance in California*, by William P. Blake (New York: Baillière, 1858), 92–93, 94–96.

CHAPTER 7

From *Report upon the Colorado River of the West*, by Lieutenant Joseph C. Ives (Washington, D.C.: U.S. Government Printing Office, 1861), 33–34, 45–46.

CHAPTER 8

From "To the Colorado Desert," by Madge Morris Wagner, in *A Literary History of Southern California*, by Franklin Walker (Berkeley: University of California Press, 1950), 184.

CHAPTER 9

From *The Desert: Further Studies in Natural Appearances*, by John C. Van Dyke, with an introduction by Peter Wild (1901; Baltimore: The Johns Hopkins University Press, 1999), 44–46, 52–53, 54–61.

CHAPTER 10

From *The Desert: Further Studies in Natural Appearances*, by John C. Van Dyke, with an introduction by Peter Wild (1901; Baltimore: The Johns Hopkins University Press, 1999), 121–22, 123–27.

CHAPTER 11

From "I Remember John Muir's Visit," by Helen Lukens Gaut, in *Palm Springs Villager* 3.2 (October 1948): 28–32, 36.

CHAPTER 12

From *The Water Seekers*, by Remi A. Nadeau (1950; Santa Barbara: Peregrine Smith, 1974), 152–54.

CHAPTER 13

From *The Wonders of the Colorado Desert*, by George Wharton James (Boston: Little, Brown, and Company, 1906), 2: 453–56.

CHAPTER 14

From *The Winning of Barbara Worth*, by Harold Bell Wright (Chicago: The Book Supply Company, 1911), 73–74, 77, 506–11.

CHAPTER 15

From *Palm Springs: The Landscape, the History, the Lore*, by Mary Jo Churchwell, ([Palm Springs]: Ironwood Editions, 2001), 90–91.

CHAPTER 16

From *Palm Springs: The Landscape, the History, the Lore*, by Mary Jo Churchwell ([Palm Springs]: Ironwood Editions, 2001), 26–31.

CHAPTER 17

From "Imperial Earthquake, Million Damage Done," *Los Angeles Times*, June 23, 1915, pp. 1, 5.

CHAPTER 18

From *Our Araby: Palm Springs and the Garden of the Sun*, by J. Smeaton Chase (1920; Palm Springs, California: City of Palm Springs Board of Library Trustees, 1987), 17–21.

CHAPTER 19

From "Of Such As These Is the Spirit of the Desert," by Elwood Lloyd, *Desert Magazine* 11.11 (September 1948): 18.

Letter to Edmund Jaeger from Carl Eytel, April 16, 1917 (Carl Eytel Archive, Palm Springs Art Museum).

Letter to Edmund C. Jaeger from Carl Eytel, June 7, 1917 (Carl Eytel Archive, Palm Springs Art Museum).

Letter to Edmund C. Jaeger from Carl Eytel, no date; likely the early 1920s (Carl Eytel Archive, Palm Springs Art Museum).

CHAPTER 20

From *The North American Deserts*, by Edmund C. Jaeger (Stanford, California: Stanford University Press, 1957), 85–103.

CHAPTER 21

From *The White Heart of Mojave: An Adventure with the Outdoors of the Desert*, by Edna Brush Perkins, edited by Peter Wild (1922; Baltimore: The Johns Hopkins University Press, 2001), 22–29.

CHAPTER 22

From *California Desert Trails*, by J. Smeaton Chase (Boston: Houghton Mifflin Company, 1919), 20–27, 256–57, 259–60, 351–53.

CHAPTER 23

From "Stephen H. Willlard: Photography Collection and Archive," brochure by Christine Giles (Palm Springs, California: Palm Springs Desert Museum, 2004).

CHAPTER 24

From *Hollywood Saga*, by William C. deMille (New York: E. P. Dutton, 1939), 215–19.

CHAPTER 25

From *California: A Guide to the Golden State* (New York: Hastings House, 1939), 628–29.

CHAPTER 26

From *Patton's Desert Training Center*, by John S. Lynch, John W. Kennedy, and Robert L. Wooley (Fort Myer, Virginia: Council on America's Military Past, 1982), 8–11.

CHAPTER 27

From "Desert Refuge," by Marshal South, *Desert Magazine* 8.11 (September 1945): 25, 26.

CHAPTER 28

From "Black Nuggets in the Valley of Phantom Buttes," by John D. Mitchell, *Desert Magazine* 14.4 (February 1951): 5–8.

CHAPTER 29

From "Ships That Pass in Desert Sands," by Choral Pepper, *Desert Magazine* 43.10 (November 1980): 12–13.

CHAPTER 30

From *The Man from the Cave*, by Colin Fletcher (New York: Alfred A. Knopf, 1981), 297–300, 305, 307–08.

CHAPTER 31

From *Poodle Springs*, by Raymond Chandler and Robert B. Parker (New York: G. P. Putnam's Sons, 1989), 9–12.

CHAPTER 32

From *Salt Dreams: Land and Water in Low-Down California*, by William deBuys, photographs by Joan Myers (Albuquerque: University of New Mexico Press, 1999), 223–25, 226–27, 232–33, 234.

CHAPTER 33

From *All the Wild and Lonely Places: Journeys in a Desert Landscape*, by Lawrence Hogue (Washington, D.C.: Island Press, 2000), 149–54.

CHAPTER 34

From *All the Wild and Lonely Places: Journeys in a Desert Landscape*, by Lawrence Hogue (Washington, D.C.: Island Press, 2000), 189–92, 193–94, 198.

CHAPTER 35

From *Highwire Moon: A Novel*, by Susan Straight (Boston: Houghton Mifflin Company, 2001), 107–14.

CHAPTER 36

From *Palm Springs: The Landscape, the History, the Lore*, by Mary Jo Churchwell ([Palm Springs]: Ironwood Editions, 2001), 204–08.

CHAPTER 37

From *Palm Springs: First Hundred Years*, by Frank M. Bogert (1987; Palm Springs, California: Palm Springs Public Library, 2003), 263–67.

EPILOGUE

From "A Landmark Fades," by Ann Japenga, *Desert Magazine* 1.6 (June 2002): 98.

From "The No-Girls Club," by Ann Japenga, *Desert Magazine* 2.4 (April 2003): 114.

Bibliography

INTRODUCTION: TEETERING ON THE EDGE

Ainsworth, Katherine. *The McCallum Saga: The Story of the Founding of Palm Springs.* 1973. Palm Springs, California: Palm Springs Public Library, 1996. As pointed out, there are no documented histories of Palm Springs and its desert; because of that, caution is in order when reading this account and others that follow, for some of them, charming as they are, offer questionable information.

Berlo, Robert C. *Population History of California Places.* Livermore, California: No publisher, 2001.

Bogert, Frank M. *Palm Springs: First Hundred Years.* 1987. Palm Springs, California: Palm Springs Public Library, 2003.

Brigandi, Phil. *Borrego Beginnings: Early Days in the Borrego Valley, 1910–1960.* Borrego Springs, California: Anza-Borrego Desert Natural History Association, 2001.

Bright, Marjorie Belle. *Nellie's Boardinghouse: A Dual Biography of Nellie Coffman and Palm Springs.* Palm Springs, California: ETC Publications, 1981.

Carr, Jim. *Palm Springs and the Coachella Valley.* Helena, Montana: American Geographic Publishing, 1989.

Churchwell, Mary Jo. *Palm Springs: The Landscape, the History, the Lore.* [Palm Springs, California]: Ironwood Editions, 2001.

deBuys, William. *Salt Dreams: Land and Water in Low-Down California.* Photographs by Joan Myers. Albuquerque: University of New Mexico Press, 1999.

Hogue, Lawrence. *All the Wild and Lonely Places: Journeys in a Desert Landscape.* Washington, D.C.: Island Press, 2000.

Imperial County, California. [El Centro, California]: Imperial County Board of Supervisors, 1925.

Jaeger, Edmund C. *The North American Deserts.* Stanford, California: Stanford University Press, 1957.

Japenga, Ann. "Bloomsbury, P.S." *Desert Magazine* 3.4 (April 2004): 48.

Laflin, Patricia B. *Coachella Valley California: A Pictorial History*. Virginia Beach, Virginia: The Donning Company, 1998.

Lee, W. Storrs. *The Great California Deserts*. New York: G. P. Putnam's Sons, 1963.

Lindsay, Diana. *Anza-Borrego A to Z: People, Places, and Things*. San Diego, California: Sunbelt Publications, 2001.

———. *Our Historic Desert: The Story of the Anza-Borrego Desert, the Largest State Park in the United States of America*. San Diego, California: Copley Books, 1974.

Lindsay, Lowell, and Diana Lindsay. *The Anza-Borrego Desert Region*. Berkeley, California: Wilderness Press, 1978.

Mitchell, Kathleen Ann. *Submarines, Salsa and Pottery Shards: A Narrative History of Coachella, California*. Riverside: University of California, Riverside, 1991.

Nelson, Jack. "A Diligent People Had Faith." *Palm Springs Villager* 2.9 (April 1948): 14–19. This and the following three articles by Nelson form about as solid a history of the personal dynamics and conflicts shaping Palm Springs as one is likely to find. Serious students of the area will find the four pieces well worth digging out from the archives of the Palm Springs Public Library.

———. "The History of Palm Springs." *Palm Springs Villager* 2.7 (February 1948): 11–15.

———. "A Path Was Beaten to the Door." *Palm Springs Villager* 2.10 (May–June 1948): 16–21.

———. "With Toil and Planning a Desert Village Grows." *Palm Springs Villager* 2.8 (March 1948): 14–19.

Niemann, Greg. *Palm Springs Legends: Creation of a Desert Oasis*. San Diego, California: Sunbelt Publications, 2006.

Nordland, Ole J. *Coachella Valley's Golden Years: The Early History of the Coachella Valley County Water District and Stories about the Discovery and Development of This Section of the Colorado Desert*. 1968. [Coachella, California]: Coachella Valley County Water District, 1978.

Pepper, Choral. *Guidebook to the Colorado Desert of California*. Los Angeles: Ward Ritchie Press, 1972.

Postlethwaite, R. H. *The Coachella Valley and Its Date Industry*. Coachella, California: V. V. Green, 1938.

Shumway, Nina Paul. *Mountain of Discovery: Homesteading in the Santa Rosas above the Coachella Valley*. West Los Angeles: Westside Printing and Publishing Company, 1992.

———. *Your Desert and Mine*. 1960. Palm Springs: ETC Publications, 1979. A highly personal version of the history of the Palm Springs area.

Simon, Hilda, and Henry Simon. *The Date Palm, Bread of the Desert*. New York: Dodd, Mead, 1978.

Steere, Collis H. *Imperial and Coachella Valleys*. Stanford, California: Stanford University Press, 1952.

Tout, Otis B. *The First Thirty Years, 1901–1931*. San Diego: Otis B. Tout, 1931.

Walker, Franklin. *A Literary History of Southern California*. Berkeley: University of California Press, 1950.

Wilhelm, Paul. "One Hundred Years in the Coachella Valley." *Palm Springs Villager* 4.5 (December 1949): 16–20. How the coming of the railroad, the discovery of water deep beneath the desert sands, and other factors evolved into the present agricultural/resort empire of Palm Springs' valley.

CHAPTER 1. FOR MY OWN PEOPLE

Bean, Lowell John. "Cahuilla." *Handbook of North American Indians: California*. Robert F. Heizer, ed. Washington, D.C.: Smithsonian Institution, 1978. 8: 575–87.

———. *Mukat's People: The Cahuilla Indians of Southern California*. Berkeley: University of California Press, 1972.

Bean, Lowell John, Jerry Schaefer, and Sylvia Brakke Vane. *Archaeological, Ethnographic, and Ethnohistoric Investigations at Tahquitz Canyon, Palm Springs, California*. Menlo Park, California: California Cultural Systems Research, 1995.

Bogert, Frank M. *Palm Springs: First Hundred Years*. 1987. Palm Springs, California: Palm Springs Public Library, 2003. 25–51.

Brumgardt, John R., and Larry L. Bowles. *People of the Magic Waters: The Cahuilla Indians of Palm Springs*. Palm Springs, California: ETC Publications, 1981.

Churchwell, Mary Jo. *Palm Springs: The Landscape, the History, the Lore*. [Palm Springs, California]: Ironwood Editions, 2001. 209.

Dozier, Deborah. *The Heart Is Fire: The World of the Cahuilla Indians of Southern California*. Berkeley, California: Heyday Books, 1998.

Japenga, Ann. "A Bewitching Realm Reopens." *Los Angeles Times*, January 14, 2001: Magazine Section, pp. 18–21, 45. Surveys the complex history of the evil Tahquitz and the ominous canyon named for him.

Kroeber, A. L. *Ethnography of the Cahuilla Indians*. Berkeley, California: The University Press, 1908.

———. *Handbook of the Indians of California*. Washington, D.C.: U.S. Government Printing Office, 1925. 689–708.

Patencio, Francisco, as told to Margaret Boynton. *Stories and Legends of the Palm Springs Indians*. 1943. Palm Springs, California: Palm Springs Desert Museum, 1970.

CHAPTER 2. LIFE FROM THE ROCKS

Dozier, Deborah. *The Heart Is Fire: The World of the Cahuilla Indians of Southern California*. Berkeley, California: Heyday Books, 1998. 109–114.

Knaak, Manfred. *The Forgotten Artist: Indians of Anza-Borrego and Their Rock Art*. Borrego Springs, California: Anza-Borrego Desert Natural History Association, 1988.

Schaafsma, Polly. *Indian Rock Art of the Southwest*. 1980. Santa Fe, New Mexico: School of American Research, 1986.

CHAPTER 3. THE SPANISH LEWIS AND CLARK:
INTO THE SWALLOWING WILDERNESS

Bolton, Herbert Eugene. *Anza's California Expeditions: Volume 3*. Berkeley: University of California Press, 1930.

Garate, Donald T. *Juan Bautista de Anza: Basque Explorer in the New World*. Reno: University of Nevada Press, 2003.

Japenga, Ann. "The Other Lewis and Clark." *Desert Magazine* 3.6 (June 2004): 66. On a cold day, a journalist explores sites of Anza's desert journey.

Lee, W. Storrs. *The Great California Deserts*. New York: G. P. Putnam's Sons, 1963. 37–46.

CHAPTER 4. WE TOOK OUR BULLETS IN OUR MOUTHS

Batman, Richard. *American Ecclesiastes: The Stories of James Pattie*. San Diego: Harcourt Brace Jovanovich, 1984.

———. *James Pattie's West: The Dream and the Reality*. Norman: University of Oklahoma Press, 1984.

Pattie, James O. *The Personal Narrative of James O. Pattie, of Kentucky*. 1833. Ed. Reuben Gold Thwaites. Cleveland: The Arthur H. Clark Company, 1905.

CHAPTER 5. STUCK IN THE YUMA DUNES:
A SANDSTORM ENVELOPS A STAGECOACH

Banning, William, and George Hugh Banning. *Six Horses*. New York: The Century Company, 1930.

Beattie, George William, and Helen Pruitt Beattie. *Heritage of the Valley: San Bernardino's First Century*. 1939. Oakland, California: Biobooks, 1951. 341–48.

Lee, W. Storrs. *The Great California Deserts*. New York: G. P. Putnam's Sons, 1963. 83–105.

Ormsby, Waterman Lilly, Lyle Henry Wright, and Josephine M. Bynum. *The Butterfield Overland Mail*. San Marino, California: The Huntington Library, 1942.

Warren, Elizabeth, and Ralph Joseph Roske. *Cultural Resources of the California Desert, 1776–1880: Historic Trails and Wagon Roads*. Riverside, California: Bureau of Land Management, California Desert District, 1981.

CHAPTER 6. SEEING WITH NEW EYES: WILLIAM P. BLAKE, GEOLOGIST

Blake, William P. *Report of a Geological Reconnaissance in California*. New York, Baillière, 1858.

Blake Papers—1847–1910. Four boxes of notes and diaries of the geologist written throughout his wide travels. Arizona Historical Society, Southern Division.

Hoyt, Edward. "He Discovered the Dead Sea of the Cahuillas." *Desert Magazine* 19.7 (July 1956): 19–22.

Lee, W. Storrs. *The Great California Deserts*. New York: G. P. Putnam's Sons, 1963. 133–34.

Merrill, George Perkins. "Blake, William Phipps." *Dictionary of American Biography*. Allen Johnson, ed. New York: Charles Scribner's Sons, 1927. 1: 445–46.

CHAPTER 7. STEAMBOATING ACROSS THE COLORADO

Haworth, Al. "He Explored the Unknown Colorado." Part 1. *Desert Magazine* 13.3 (January 1950): 5–10.

———. "He Explored the Unknown Colorado." Part 2. *Desert Magazine* 13.4 (February 1950): 17–22.

Ives, Joseph C. *Report upon the Colorado River of the West*. Washington, D.C.: U.S. Government Printing Office, 1861.

Lingenfelter, Richard E. *Steamboats on the Colorado River, 1852–1916*. Tucson: University of Arizona Press, 1978.

Ross, Frank Edward. "Ives, Joseph Christmas." *Dictionary of American Biography*. Dumas Malone, ed. New York: Charles Scribner's Sons, 1932. 5, Part 1: 520–21.

CHAPTER 8. "THOU BROWN, BARE-BREASTED, VOICELESS MYSTERY": THE DESERT AS URBAN MELODRAMA

Wagner, Madge Morris. "To the Colorado Desert." In Franklin Walker, *A Literary History of Southern California*. Berkeley: University of California Press, 1950. 184.

CHAPTER 9. SEEING WITH NEW EYES: JOHN C. VAN DYKE, AESTHETICIAN

Van Dyke, John C. *The Desert: Further Studies in Natural Appearances*. 1901. Introduction by Peter Wild. Baltimore: The Johns Hopkins University Press, 1999.

CHAPTER 10. MORE ON VAN DYKE: THE NASTY YOUNG MAN ON THE IMAGINED TRAPEZE

Teague, David, and Peter Wild, eds. *The Secret Life of John C. Van Dyke: Selected Letters*. Reno: University of Nevada Press, 1997.

Van Dyke, John C. *The Autobiography of John C. Van Dyke: A Personal Narrative of American Life, 1861–1931*. Peter Wild, ed. Salt Lake City: University of Utah Press, 1993.

———. *The Desert: Further Studies in Natural Appearances*. 1901. Introduction by Peter Wild. Baltimore: The Johns Hopkins University Press, 1999.

Wild, Peter. *The Art of John C. Van Dyke's* The Desert. Johannesburg, California: The Shady Myrick Research Project, 2002.

———. Introduction. *The Desert: Further Studies in Natural Appearances*. By John C. Van Dyke. 1901. Baltimore: The Johns Hopkins University Press, 1999. xxiii–lxiii.

———. *The Opal Desert: Explorations of Fantasy and Reality in the American Southwest*. Austin: University of Texas Press, 1999. 75–87.

CHAPTER 11. JOHN MUIR ON THE COLORADO DESERT: IN A FLOWERED BATHROBE

Bogert, Frank M. *Palm Springs: First Hundred Years.* 1987. Palm Springs, California: Palm Springs Public Library, 2003. 66, 84.

Churchwell, Mary Jo. *Palm Springs: The Landscape, the History, the Lore.* [Palm Springs, California]: Ironwood Editions, 2001. 88–90.

Fox, Stephen R. *The American Conservation Movement: John Muir and His Legacy.* Madison: University of Wisconsin Press, 1985.

Gaut, Helen Lukens. "I Remember John Muir's Visit." *Palm Springs Villager* 3.2 (October 1948): 28–32, 36.

Miller, Sally M., ed. *John Muir: Life and Work.* Albuquerque: University of New Mexico Press, 1993.

Wolfe, Linnie Marsh. *Son of the Wilderness: The Life of John Muir.* 1945. Madison: University of Wisconsin Press, 2003.

CHAPTER 12. THE RUNAWAY RIVER

Duke, Alton. *When the Colorado River Quit the Ocean.* Yuma, Arizona: Southwest Printers, 1974.

Fradkin, Philip L. *A River No More: The Colorado River and the West.* 1981. Berkeley: University of California Press, 1996.

Lee, W. Storrs. *The Great California Deserts.* New York: G. P. Putnam's Sons, 1963. 137–53.

Nadeau, Remi A. *The Water Seekers.* 1950. Santa Barbara: Peregrine Smith, 1974.

Woodbury, David Oakes. *The Colorado Conquest.* New York: Dodd, Mead, and Company, 1941.

CHAPTER 13. THE WONDERLAND: GHOSTS AT THE WELL

James, George Wharton. *The Wonders of the Colorado Desert.* Two volumes. Boston: Little, Brown, and Company, 1906.

Parker, Horace. "Brush Country Journal: Indian Wells, Part I." *Press-Enterprise* [Riverside, California], January 27, 1957, p. C10. The history, along with more ghost stories, of the well where George Wharton James trembled.

Wild, Peter. *George Wharton James.* Western Writers Series #93. Boise, Idaho: Boise State University, 1990.

CHAPTER 14. LOVE ALONG THE IRRIGATION DITCHES

Japenga, Ann. "The Gospel of Barbara Worth." *Desert Magazine* 3.2 (February 2004): 178. "It's not well-known that Barbara Worth's creator had a house here in Palm Springs."

Tagg, Lawrence V. *Harold Bell Wright.* Western Writers Series #115. Boise, Idaho: Boise State University, 1994.

————. *Harold Bell Wright, Storyteller to America.* Tucson, Arizona: Westernlore Press, 1986.

Wright, Harold Bell. *The Winning of Barbara Worth.* Chicago: The Book Supply Company, 1911.

CHAPTER 15. A TREACHEROUS CAMEL AT THE TRAIN STATION

Bogert, Frank M. *Palm Springs: First Hundred Years.* 1987. Palm Springs, California: Palm Springs Public Library, 2003. 14–15, 58–79.

Churchwell, Mary Jo. *Palm Springs: The Landscape, the History, the Lore.* [Palm Springs, California]: Ironwood Editions, 2001.

CHAPTER 16. OUT OF REVOLUTIONARY MEXICO: THE THREE WEALTHY WHITE SISTERS

Bogert, Frank M. *Palm Springs: First Hundred Years.* 1987. Palm Springs, California: Palm Springs Public Library, 2003. 37, 63, 84, 88, 93, 110, 111, 121, 279.

Churchwell, Mary Jo. *Palm Springs: The Landscape, the History, the Lore.* [Palm Springs, California]: Ironwood Editions, 2001.

Wild, Peter. *J. Smeaton Chase.* Johannesburg, California: The Shady Myrick Research Project, 2005.

CHAPTER 17. BARBARA WORTH ON THE RAMPAGE

Churchwell, Mary Jo. *Palm Springs: The Landscape, the History, the Lore.* [Palm Springs, California]: Ironwood Editions, 2001. 209–12.

Fradkin, Philip L. *Magnitude 8: Earthquakes and Life along the San Andreas Fault.* New York: Henry Holt, 1998.

Heppenheimer, T. A. *The Coming Quake: Science and Trembling on the California Earthquake Frontier.* New York: Times Books, 1988.

"Imperial Earthquake, Million Damage Done." *Los Angeles Times,* June 23, 1915.

Lee, W. Storrs. *The Great California Deserts.* New York: G. P. Putnam's Sons, 1963. 288–90.

CHAPTER 18. A DESERT VILLAGE

Chase, J. Smeaton. *Our Araby: Palm Springs and the Garden of the Sun.* 1920. Palm Springs, California: City of Palm Springs Board of Library Trustees, 1987.

Churchwell, Mary Jo. *Palm Springs: The Landscape, the History, the Lore.* [Palm Springs, California]: Ironwood Editions, 2001. 38–44.

Wild, Peter. *Desert Literature: The Middle Period.* Western Writers Series #138. Boise: Boise State University, 1999. 12–25. A positive evaluation of J. Smeaton Chase and his work.

————. *J. Smeaton Chase.* Johannesburg, California: The Shady Myrick Research Project, 2005.

———. *The Opal Desert: Explorations of Fantasy and Reality in the American Southwest.* Austin: University of Texas Press, 1999. 116–30.

CHAPTER 19. A DESERT SAINT—WITH CRACKS: CARL EYTEL

Bogert, Frank M. *Palm Springs: First Hundred Years.* 1987. Palm Springs, California: Palm Springs Public Library, 2003. 17, 30, 85, 100–103, 105, 130, 131.

Hudson, Roy F. *Forgotten Desert Artist: The Journals and Field Sketches of Carl Eytel, an Early Day Painter of the Southwest.* Palm Springs, California: The Desert Museum, 1979.

Jaeger, Edmund C. "Art in a Desert Cabin." *Desert Magazine* 11.11 (September 1948).

Jennings, Bill. "Early Day Desert Artist Re-Emerging Folk Figure." *Desert Magazine* 41.9 (September 1978): 12–15.

Law, George. "Carl Eytel, Desert Painter." *Los Angeles Times*, January 28, 1923: Illustrated Magazine Section, pp. 7, 29.

Lloyd, Elwood. "Of Such as These Is the Spirit of the Desert." *Desert Magazine* 11.11 (September 1948).

Wild, Peter. "Carl Eytel: The Monk of Palm Springs." *Wildflower* [Canada] 13.4 (Autumn 1997): 22–25.

CHAPTER 20. JUST WHAT WAS NEEDED: EDMUND C. JAEGER

Bogert, Frank M. *Palm Springs: First Hundred Years.* 1987. Palm Springs, California: Palm Springs Public Library, 2003. 18, 120.

Japenga, Ann. "The Dean of the Deserts: Edmund C. Jaeger." *Desert Magazine* 2.10 (October 2003): 98.

Jaeger, Edmund. C. *The North American Deserts.* Stanford, California: Stanford University Press, 1957.

Jones, Richard S. *Index to* Son of the Living Desert: Edmund C. Jaeger, 1887–1983. By Raymond E. Ryckman and James L. Zackrison. Riverside, California: Richard S. Jones, 2001. Index to the major work on Jaeger, below.

Lawton, Harry. "Edmund C. Jaeger Fills Role of Nature's Sherlock Holmes." *Press-Enterprise* [Riverside, California] October 13, 1957, pp. B-4, 8. This is the best brief summary of Jaeger's life and contribution.

Ryckman, Raymond E., and James L. Zackrison. *Son of the Living Desert: Edmund C. Jaeger, 1887–1983.* Redlands, California: R. E. Ryckman, 1998. This great tome represents a huge gathering of information about Jaeger.

Wild, Peter. "Edmund C. Jaeger: From the Classroom to Palavers." *Wildflower* [Canada] 15.3 (Summer 1999): 40–43.

CHAPTER 21. TWO WEALTHY FEMINISTS FROM CLEVELAND: A GREAT HOLE FULL OF BLUE MIST

Perkins, Edna Brush. *A Red Carpet on the Sahara.* Boston: Marshall Jones, 1925.

———. *The White Heart of Mojave: An Adventure with the Outdoors of the Desert*. 1922. Introduction by Peter Wild. Baltimore: The Johns Hopkins University Press, 2001.

"Perkins, Edna Brush." *National Cyclopaedia of American Biography*. New York: James T. White, 1937. 26: 448–49.

"Perkins, Roger Griswold." *National Cyclopaedia of American Biography*. New York: James T. White, 1937. 26: 448.

Wild, Peter. "Conclusion: The Life and Work of Edna Brush Perkins." *The White Heart of Mojave: An Adventure with the Outdoors of the Desert*. By Edna Brush Perkins. 1922. Baltimore: The Johns Hopkins University Press, 2001. 225–88.

———. *Desert Literature: The Middle Period*. Western Writers Series #138. Boise, Idaho: Boise State University, 1999. 25–39. An evaluation of Perkins, including discussion of her little-known second book, *A Red Carpet on the Sahara*, about her camel trip into the desert of Algeria.

CHAPTER 22. A TINY FIGURE WAVERING IN THE BLUE MISTS

Bogert, Frank M. *Palm Springs: First Hundred Years*. 1987. Palm Springs, California: Palm Springs Public Library, 2003. 30, 31, 35, 40, 41, 48, 84–85, 88, 121.

Buber, Martin. *I and Thou*. 1923. Translated, with prologue and notes, by Walter Kaufmann. New York: Charles Scribner's Sons, 1970.

Chase, J. Smeaton. *California Desert Trails*. Boston: Houghton Mifflin Company, 1919.

Wild, Peter. *Desert Literature: The Middle Period*. Western Writers Series #138. Boise, Idaho: Boise State University, 1999. 12–25.

———. *J. Smeaton Chase*. Johannesburg, California: The Shady Myrick Research Project, 2005.

CHAPTER 23. THE ANSEL ADAMS OF THE DESERT: STEPHEN H. WILLARD

Bogert, Frank M. *Palm Springs: First Hundred Years*. 1987. Palm Springs, California: Palm Springs Public Library. 17, 85, 94, 129, 142.

Castleberry, May, ed. *Perpetual Mirage: Photographic Narratives of the Desert West*. New York: Whitney Museum of American Art, 1996. Although this study does not discuss Willard, a chapter by Limerick and Yeoman covers the work of J. Smeaton Chase, a photographer contemporary with Willard in Palm Springs.

Giles, Christine. "Stephen H. Willard: Photography Collection and Archive" [brochure]. Palm Springs, California: Palm Springs Desert Museum, 2004.

Limerick, Patricia, and Sharyn Wiley Yeoman. "A Pleasant Fellow in a Not So Pleasant Place: J. Smeaton Chase and His Trail of Good Nature." *Perpetual Mirage: Photographic Narratives of the Desert West*. Mary Castleberry, ed. New York: Whitney Museum of American Art, 1996. 98–103.

Willard Collection and Archive. Palm Springs Art Museum, Palm Springs, California. This is a vast collection of Stephen H. Willard photographs, letters, articles by and about, and related materials, donated to the museum by Willard's daughter.

CHAPTER 24. THE EXCITEMENTS OF CELLULOID: THE CAMEL'S NOSE

Bogert, Frank M. *Palm Springs: First Hundred Years*, 1987. Palm Springs, California: Palm Springs Public Library, 2003. 136–39.

deMille, William C. *Hollywood Saga*. New York: E. P. Dutton, 1939.

Lee, W. Storrs. *The Great California Deserts*. New York: G. P. Putnam's Sons, 1963. 227–51.

CHAPTER 25. THE EXCITEMENTS OF CELLULOID: THE CAMEL VICTORIOUS

Bogert, Frank M. *Palm Springs: First Hundred Years*. 1987. Palm Springs, California: Palm Springs Public Library, 2003. 83–163, 277–83.

California: A Guide to the Golden State. New York: Hastings House, 1939.

CHAPTER 26. AFTER GOD...GEN. GEORGE S. PATTON!

Henley, David C. *The Land That God Forgot: The Saga of Gen. George Patton's Desert Training Camp*. Fallon, Nevada: Lahontan Valley Printing, 1989.

Hirshson, Stanley P. *General Patton: A Soldier's Life*. New York: HarperCollins, 2002.

Lynch, John S., John W. Kennedy, and Robert L. Wooley. *Patton's Desert Training Center*. Fort Myer, Virginia: Council on America's Military Past, 1982.

CHAPTER 27. Desert Magazine and Marshal South: Living like Indians

Lindsay, Diana, ed. *Marshal South and the Ghost Mountain Chronicles: An Experiment in Primitive Living*. San Diego, California: Sunbelt Publications, 2005.

South, Marshal. "Desert Refuge." *Desert Magazine* 8.11 (September 1945): 25, 26.

Wild, Peter. *Desert Magazine: The Henderson Years*. Johannesburg, California: The Shady Myrick Research Project, 2004.

———. *Marshal South, of Yaquitepec*. Johannesburg, California: The Shady Myrick Research Project, 2005.

CHAPTER 28. PEGLEG SMITH: A LEGEND FOUND—THEN LOST AGAIN

Campa, Arthur L. *Treasure of the Sangre de Cristos: Tales and Traditions of the Spanish Southwest*. Norman: University of Oklahoma Press, 1963.

Dobie, J. Frank. *Apache Gold and Yaqui Silver*. 1939. Austin: University of Texas Press, 1985.

———. *Coronado's Children: Tales of Lost Mines and Buried Treasures of the Southwest*. 1930. Austin: University of Texas Press, 1978.

Humphreys, Alfred Glen. "Thomas L. (Peg-Leg) Smith." *The Mountain Men and the Fur Trade of the Far West*. LeRoy R. Hafen, ed. Glendale, California: The Arthur H. Clark Company, 1966. 4: 311–30.

McKenney, J. Wilson. *On the Trail of Pegleg Smith's Lost Gold: Legend and Fact Combined* to Provide Fresh Clues to the Location of Pegleg Smith's Famous Lost Mine. Palm Desert, California: Desert Press, 1957.

Mitchell, John D. "Black Nuggets in the Valley of Phantom Buttes." *Desert Magazine* 14.4 (February 1951): 5–8.

———. *Lost Mines of the Great Southwest, Including Stories of Hidden Treasures.* 1933. Glorieta, New Mexico: Rio Grande Press, 1970.

Simmons, Marc. *Treasure Trails of the Southwest.* Albuquerque: University of New Mexico Press, 1994.

CHAPTER 29. SANDS THAT BLOSSOM INTO VIKING SHIPS

Fierro Blanco, Antonio de [Walter Nordhoff]. *Journey of the Flame.* Boston: Houghton Mifflin, 1933. Best-known fictional account of lost ships.

Henderson, Randall. "Old Iron Boat on the Colorado." *Desert Magazine* 5.3 (January 1942): 5–10. The modern discovery of Lt. Ives' steamboat, *Explorer*, abandoned in the sands of the Colorado River delta in Mexico.

Japenga, Ann. "The Glamorous Galleon." *Desert Magazine* 4.6 (June 2005): 74. The legends of lost ships have a deep grip on the imagination, continuing to fluoresce in novels and movies, as well as in bars.

Pepper, Choral. "Ships That Pass in Desert Sands." *Desert Magazine* 43.10 (November 1980): 12–13.

Weight, Harold O. *Lost Ship of the Desert: A Legend of the Southwest.* Twentynine Palms, California: Calico Press, 1959.

CHAPTER 30. THE DEATH OF CHUCKAWALLA BILL

Fletcher, Colin. *The Man from the Cave.* New York: Alfred A. Knopf, 1981.

CHAPTER 31. MURDER IN FRU-FRU LAND

Chandler, Raymond, and Robert B. Parker. *Poodle Springs.* G. P. Putnam's Sons, 1989.

MacShane, Frank. *The Life of Raymond Chandler.* New York: E. P. Dutton, 1976.

———, ed. *Selected Letters of Raymond Chandler.* London: Jonathan Cape, 1981. 406, 464–65, 473–4, 478.

Moss, Robert F., ed. *Raymond Chandler: A Literary Reference.* New York: Carroll and Graf, 2002.

Widdicombe, Toby. *A Reader's Guide to Raymond Chandler.* Westport Connecticut: Greenwood Press, 2001.

CHAPTER 32. CONSEQUENCES: THE SEA OF POISONS

deBuys, William. *Salt Dreams: Land and Water in Low-Down California.* Photographs by Joan Myers. Albuquerque: University of New Mexico Press, 1999.

Garnholz, Brandon Derek. "The Salton Sea: A Narrative and Political History." Dissertation. San Diego State University, 1991.

MacDougal, Daniel Trembly. *The Salton Sea: A Study of the Geography, the Geology, the Floristics, and the Ecology of a Desert Basin.* Washington, D.C.: Carnegie Institution of Washington, 1914.

Salton Sea Atlas. Redlands, California: The Redlands Institute, University of Redlands, 2002.

Saving the Salton Sea: A Research Needs Assessment. [Washington, D.C.]: U.S. Fish and Wildlife Service, 1997.

Setmire, James G. *Detailed Study of Water Quality, Bottom Sediment, and Biota Associated with Irrigation Drainage in the Salton Sea Area, California, 1988–1990.* Sacramento, California: U.S. Geological Survey, 1993.

Shuford, W. David. *Ecology and Conservation of Birds of the Salton Sink: An Endangered Ecosystem.* Camarillo, California: Cooper Ornithological Society, 2004.

CHAPTER 33. THE PRESERVED LANDS: ECSTASY AND AGONY

Hogue, Lawrence. *All the Wild and Lonely Places: Journeys in a Desert Landscape.* Washington, D.C.: Island Press, 2000.

Japenga, Ann. *Monumental Treasure: A Celebration of Beauty and History in the Santa Rosa and San Jacinto Mountains National Monument. Palm Springs Life* 46.2 (October 2003). An insert printed as a special section of the magazine.

Lindsay, Diana. "The Creation of the Anza-Borrego Desert State Park." *Journal of San Diego History* 19.4 (Fall 1973): 14–26. Details the flying fur and the letting of blood in the long process of creating a park.

CHAPTER 34. BIGHORN SHEEP

American Desert Bighorn Sheep in California. Washington, D.C.: Bureau of Land Management, 1990.

Hogue, Lawrence. *All the Wild and Lonely Places: Journeys in a Desert Landscape.* Washington, D.C.: Island Press, 2000.

Jorgensen, Mark C. *A Survey of the Desert Bighorn Sheep (Ovis Canadensis) in the Anza-Borrego Desert State Park.* Sacramento: California Department of Parks and Recreation, 1972.

Peninsular Ranges Bighorn Sheep Research. North Palm Springs, California: Bureau of Land Management, Palm Springs—South Coast Field Office, 2001.

Rubin, Esther. *Recovery Plan for Bighorn Sheep in the Peninsular Ranges, California.* [Portland, Oregon]: U.S. Fish and Wildlife Service, Region 1, 2000.

CHAPTER 35. IN THE VINEYARDS: "TÍO, I NEED SOME WORK"

Conover, Ted. *Coyotes: A Journey through the Secret World of America's Illegal Aliens.* New York: Vintage Books, 1987.

Cozic, Charles P. *Illegal Immigration: Opposing Viewpoints.* San Diego, California: Greenhaven Press, 1997.

Diaz-Briquets, Sergio, and Sidney Weintraub. *Determinants of Emigration from Mexico, Central America, and the Caribbean.* Boulder, Colorado: Westview Press, 1991.

Gregory, Peter. *Undocumented Migration to the United States: Can the Flow Be Stemmed?* Albuquerque: University of New Mexico Latin-American Institute, 1989.

Ngai, Mae M. *Impossible Subjects: Illegal Aliens and the Making of Modern America.* Princeton, New Jersey: Princeton University Press, 2004.

Straight, Susan. *Highwire Moon: A Novel.* Boston: Houghton Mifflin Company, 2001.

CHAPTER 36. ANY AUGUST DAY A HUNDRED YEARS AGO: IN THE COOL PINES

Churchwell, Mary Jo. *Palm Springs: The Landscape, the History, the Lore.* [Palm Springs, California]: Ironwood Editions, 2001.

Ferranti, Philip, and Hank Koenig. *120 Great Hikes In and Near Palm Springs.* Englewood, Colorado: Westcliffe Publishers, 2003.

Jaeger, Edmund C. "Forgotten Trails." *Palm Springs Villager* 4.2 (September 1949): 12–13. Indomitable Jaeger sets out to find old trails in the Palm Springs area long ago fallen into disuse. Among them are Snow Creek, Gordon, Palms to Pines, Jack Meeks, and Vandeventer.

Japenga, Ann. *Monumental Treasure: A Celebration of Beauty and History in the Santa Rosa and San Jacinto Mountains National Monument. Palm Springs Life* 46.2 (October 2003). The insert to the magazine offers an especially beautiful and useful map.

Leadabrand, Russ. *Guidebook to the San Jacinto Mountains of Southern California.* Los Angeles: Ward Ritchie Press, 1971.

Maxwell, Ernie. *Pictorial History of the San Jacinto Mountains.* Idyllwild, California: Ernie Maxwell, 1988.

Stokes, Rick. *Trails Map, Santa Rosa Mountains National Scenic Area.* No place: Coachella Valley Trails Council, 1995.

Ulrich, Bob. *10 Day Hikes on Mount San Jacinto: Starting at the Tram Station.* No place: R. M. Ulrich, 1999.

CHAPTER 37. PALM DESERT, RANCHO MIRAGE, LA QUINTA, LAS MENTIRAS

Bogert, Frank M. *Palm Springs: First Hundred Years 1987.* Palm Springs, California: Palm Springs Public Library, 2003.

Lee, W. Storrs. *The Great California Deserts.* New York: G. P. Putnam's Sons, 1963. 292–98.

EPILOGUE: A BEAM OF DAWN LIGHT

Abbey, Edward. *Good News*. New York: E. P. Dutton, 1980.

Churchwell, Mary Jo. *Palm Springs: The Landscape, the History, the Lore*. [Palm Springs, California]: Ironwood Editions, 2001.

Japenga, Ann. "A Landmark Fades." *Desert Magazine* 1.6 (June 2002): 98.

———. "The No-Girls Club." *Desert Magazine* 2.4 (April 2003): 114.

Palm Springs: Brief History and Architectural Guide. [Palm Springs, California]: City of Palm Springs Historic Site Preservation Board, no date. A walking tour takes us into the historic nooks and crannies of downtown Palm Springs.

Index

Abbey, Edward, 192

agriculture, 10, 107, 114–15, 184. *See also* Imperial Valley; irrigation

Agua Caliente Reservation, 147

Agua Caliente Springs, 169

Alamo River, 69–70

Algodones Dunes, 111–12

All American Canal, 111

All the Wild and Lonely Places: Journeys in a Desert Landscape (Hogue), 10, 192–97, 199

Andreas Canyon, 66

animals, 100, 115, 118–121, 199–203. *See also* bighorn sheep

Anza, Juan Bautista de, 22, 24, 216

Anza-Borrego Desert, 5, 10, 20

Anza-Borrego Desert State Park, 112, 195, 198, 201

de Anza expedition, 22, 24–28

Anza's California Expeditions (Bolton), 25–28

Austin, Mary, 193–94

Banning, George Hugh & William, 34

Barbara Worth Golf Resort, 77

Barbara Worth Hotel, 76, 90–91

bighorn sheep, 3, 115, 199–203

"Black Nuggets in the Valley of Phantom Buttes" (Mitchell), 160–66

Blake, William P.: and Colorado Desert, 4, 107; and desert development, 49, 68; government funding of, 149; and railroad, 38–39

Bloom, Clark, 184

Bolton, Herbert Eugene, 25

Bogert, Frank, 9, 217

Borrego Springs, 27

Borrego State Park, 112

Botts, Myrtle, 169

Bureau of Land Management (BLM), 195–96

cactus, 41, 115, 116

Calexico (town), 70, 90–93

Caliente Reservation, 62

California Desert Trails (Chase), 128–36, 195

California: A Guide to the Golden State (1939), 146–48

Camp Young, 150

Carr, Jim, 10

Carver, Elmer, 171

caves and cave-dwellings, 51, 75, 128

Central Main Canal, 70

Chandler, Raymond, 181–82

Chase, J. Smeaton: early years of Palm Springs, 7; and flood in Andreas Cañon, 130–32; health of, 106, 127;

and marriage to Isabel White, 85,
99, 104; as travel writer, 128, 133–36,
194–95
Chocolate Mountains, 115, 162
Chuckawalla Bill (Anthony William
Simmons), 174–79
Chuckawalla Mountains, 115
Churchwell, Mary Jo, 9, 82, 85, 213
climate, 26, 41, 54
Coachella Valley, 4, 73, 109, 217
*Coachella Valley California: A Pictorial
History* (Laflin), 10
Coahuila Valley, 58
Colorado Desert: and adjacent deserts,
4–5, 116–17; as barrier to travel, 5, 29,
33; canyons of, 113–14; cities of, 4;
dunes of, 111; early geography of, 50;
fault lines running through, 89–90,
111, 115; location of, 3; as low desert,
4; and military installations, 149;
mountains surrounding, 112–15
Colorado River: and Colorado Desert,
108; course changes of, 68–69; flood
of, 69–70; and fossils, 168; geologic
importance of, 38; as source of water
for irrigation, 53, 68, 110; and Lake
LeConte, 109; navigation of, 43–45;
over-allocation of water resources
from, 3; as watershed for region, 3

deBuys, William, 10, 184
deMille, William C., 141
*Desert: Further Studies in Natural
Appearances, The* (Van Dyke 1999),
50–55, 57–59, 192
Desert Magazine, 7, 155
"Desert Refuge" (South), 156–59
deserts: aesthetic appreciation of, 9; for
agriculture, 37; colonial society of, 3;
geology of, 38–42; development of,
8, 53–55, 191–92, 196; government
influence on, 149; health benefits of,
5, 8, 156; legends of, 163; natural history of, 106; and off-road vehicles,

175, 195; preservation of, 53–54, 192,
194–97; towns of, 5–6. *See also* animals; climate; Colorado Desert;
plants; springs
Desert Training Center (DTC), 150
Devil woman, 15

earthquakes, 90, 169
El Centro (town), 90–93
Explorer (steamboat), 45, 167, 172
Eytel, Carl, 7, 98–105

First Thirty Years, 1901–1931, The (Tout),
10
Fletcher, Colin, 174
*Forgotten Artist: Indians of Anza-
Borrego and Their Rock Art, The*
(Knaak), 19–23
Fort Mojave, 43
forts, 33, 43–44
Fort Yuma, 44
fossils, 113, 168

Gaut, Helen Lukens, 61
geology. *See* caves and cave-dwellings;
dunes; fossils; gold and gold mining;
rock formations; springs
Ghost Mountain, 157–59
Giles, Christine, 138
gold and gold mining, 8, 33, 160–63,
165–66
Great California Deserts, The (Lee), 9

Henderson, Randall, 172
Herrington, Charlie, 174–79
Highwire Moon: A Novel (Straight),
204–11
Hogue, Lawrence, 10, 192, 199
Hollywood Saga (deMille), 141–45
Hubbs, Carl L., 110

"I Remember John Muir's Visit" (Gaut),
61–67
Imperial (town), 70

Imperial Dam, 111
"Imperial Earthquake, Million Damage Done" (*Los Angeles Times* 1915), 90
Imperial Valley: agricultural development of, 5, 68, 110; soil of, 38; flooding of, 69, 110
Indians: and de Anza expedition, 26; Apaches, 34; beliefs of, 12–13; and casinos, 11; Cahuillas, 1, 3, 12, 95; Cocomonga, 15–18; Cocopas, 44, 51; Comanches, 34; cultural remains, 21; Diegeno, 45; initiation ceremonies, 11, 13; legends of, 1, 168; living in desert, 2; Paiute, 193; and Reservation, 95; rock art, 19– 22; and tectonic shifts, 89; Torres, 73; sacred places of, 21; and springs, 40; villages of, 73; Yuma, 51
Indian Wells (town), 38, 219
irrigation: levee system, 92; reservoirs for, 53; runoff from, 183–84. *See also* agriculture; Colorado River; Imperial Valley; water and water resources
Iturbe, Juan de, 170
Ives, Joseph C., 44, 167

Jacobsen, Nels, 171–72
Jaeger, Edmund C., 4, 7, 106
James, George Wharton, 7, 72, 192
Japenga, Ann, 6, 222, 224
Jordan, Charlotte Hannahs, 123–26
Jorgensen, Mark, 199–203
Joshua Tree National Park (Joshua Tree National Monument): location of, 4, 114; and photography of Stephen Willard, 138; and establishment by Franklin D. Roosevelt, 138

Knaak, Manfred, 19
Kennedy, John W., 150

La Fiesta de los Monos, 147
La Puerta Real de San Carlos, 22

Laflin, Patricia B., 10
Laguna Mountains, 112
Land of Little Rain, The (Austin), 193–94
"Landmark Fades, A" (Japenga), 6, 222–24
Law, George, 213–15
LeConte, Lake, 109
Lee, W. Storrs, 9
Lindsay, Diana, 10, 156, 196
Little House (home of Cornelia White), 85
Lloyd, Elwood, 99
Lukens, T. P., 62, 66
Lykken, Carl, 86–88
Lynch, John S., 150

Man From the Cave, The (Fletcher), 174–79
Marcus, Willie, 83
Marlowe, Philip (fictional character), 180–82
McCallum, John Guthrie, 82–83, 88
Meighan, Tom, 142–145
mesquite, 74
Metropolitan Aqueduct, 116
Mexicali (town), 70–71, 90–93
Mexican War of 1846–1848, 33
military installations, 149–54
Miller, Robert L., 110
mirages, 52, 57–59
Mitchell, John D., 160
Mojave Desert, 4, 60, 149
Moraga, Alférez Don Joseph, 27
Muir, Helen, 60–67
Muir, John, 60–67
Murray, Welwood: and agriculture, 96; as founder of Palm Springs, 97; and Palm Springs Hotel, 61, 88; and theory of geological evolution, 63

Nadeau, Remi A., *The Water Seekers*, 10, 69
Native Americans. *See* Indians
Nelson, Jack, 9–10

New River, 53, 69
"No-Girls Club, The" (Japenga), 224–26
North American Deserts, The (Jaeger),
    107–21

"Of Such As These Is the Spirit of the
    Desert" (Lloyd), 99–101
Olmsted, Frederick Law, Jr., 195
*Our Araby: Palm Springs and the Gar-
    den of the Sun* (Chase 1987), 94–97
Our Historic Desert (Lindsay), 196

Palms-to-Pines Highway, 115
Palm Springs: creative people of, 6;
    development of, 82, 146–48, 216–20;
    early culture of, 7–8; famous visitors
    to, 60, 142, 180; and golf courses,
    217; and Hot Spring, 95; location of,
    4; and movie making, 141; nightlife
    of, 147; oasis of, 62; population, 1–2,
    95, 146; residents of, 84, 96, 98, 137;
    as rustic village, 94, 97; surrounding
    towns, 217; train stop, 82
Palm Springs: First Hundred Years
    (Bogert), 9, 217–20
*Palm Springs: The Landscape, the His-
    tory, the Lore* (Churchwell), 9, 82–
    83, 85, 213
Palm Springs and the Coachella Valley
    (Carr), 10
Palm Springs Art Museum (Palm
    Springs Desert Museum), 10, 85, 114,
    137–40
Palm Springs Historical Society, 88
Palm Springs Hotel, 61, 88
Palm Springs Municipal Airport, 148,
    217
palm trees: colonies of, 112, 117, 129–30;
    date palms, 115; fan palms, 113–14; at
    site of Palm Springs, 38, 40;
Palo Verde (town), 173
Parker, Robert B., 181–82
Parsons, Dick, 174–75

Patencio, Francisco (chief), 12
Pattie, James O., 29
Patton, George S. (general), 149–54
Patton's Desert Training Center (Lynch,
    Kennedy & Wooley), 150–54
Patton's Principles (Williamson), 151
Pegleg Smith. *See* Smith, Thomas L.
Pegleg mine, 160–62, 165
Pepper, Choral, 168
Perkins, Edna Brush, 123–26
*Personal Narrative of James O. Pattie, of
    Kentucky, The* (Pattie), 29–32
plants, 107–8, 111–13, 117–18. *See also*
    cactus; mesquite; palm trees
Poodle Springs (Chandler and Parker),
    181–82

railroads: and changing the desert, 37;
    early travel between San Diego and
    Yuma, 33; as means of supplying
    Camp Young, 153; transcontinental,
    37. *See also* Southern Pacific Railroad
*Report of a Geological Reconnaissance in
    California* (Blake), 38–42
*Report upon the Colorado River of the
    West* (Ives), 44–46
rock art: of de Anza expedition, 22;
    dating of, 21–22; petroglyphs, 20–21,
    109; pictographs, 20, 22; and sol-
    stices, 22–23
rock formations, 38–39
Ruhlen, George, 154

*Salt Dreams: Land and Water in Low-
    Down California* (deBuys), 10,
    184–90
Salton (town), 110
Salton Basin (Salton Sink), 50–51, 108–15
Salton Sea: and deaths of birds and fish,
    185–86; and flooding from Colorado
    River, 68, 108, 110; and irrigation
    runoff, 183–84, 186; pre-existence of,
    50; and selenium, 189

Salton Sea National Wildlife Refuge, 184–90

Salton Sea State Park, 113

San Bernadino Mountains, 51

San Gabriel Mission, 22

San Gregoria, 27

San Jacinto, Mount (San Gorgoño), 6, 38

San Jacinto Mountains, 51

sandstorms, 35

ships in the desert, 167, 168–72

"Ships That Pass in Desert Sands" (Pepper), 168–72

Six Horses (Banning & Banning 1930), 34–36

Smith, Thomas L. (Pegleg Smith), 160

Sonoran Desert (Arizona), 4

South, Marshall, 155–56

Southern Pacific Railroad: and containment of Colorado River, 69, 110; and Seven Palms Station, 83; excursion train to Palm Springs, 83

Spielbergen, Joris van, 170

Spiess, F. G., 150

springs: hot, 38, 40, 66, 115, 147; mud pots, 111; and fault lines, 111, 115

stagecoaches: Butterfield Overland, 33, 113; and mail delivery, 33; stations of, 5, 33, 35; travel on, 34–36; and wells, 33

steamboats, 43–46, 167, 172

"Stephen H. Willard: Photography Collection and Archive" (Giles), 138–40

Stories and Legends of the Palm Springs Indians (Patencio, as told to Margaret Boynton), 12–18

Straight, Susan, 204

Sulphur Springs, 147

Swinnerton, Jimmy, 7

Tahquitz (evil spirit), 1, 11, 14–15, 89, 222

Tahquitz Canyon, 65, 99

"To the Colorado Desert" (Wagner), 48

Tout, Otis B., 10

trappers, 29, 161

Travertine Point, 109

Valerie Jean Date Shop (local business), 222–23

Van Dyke, John C.: and desert as dreamscape, 9, 89; preservation of desert, 49, 56

Village Green (of Palm Springs), 88

Wagner, Madge Morris, 48

water and water resources: swimming pools, 3; water table, 3; availability of, 30–31; wells at stagecoach stations, 33; and "Pozo hondo" (Deep Well), 42; for towns and reservations, 65. See also Colorado River; irrigation; Salton Sea; springs

Water Seekers, The (Nadeau), 69–71

Weight, Harold, 171

Willard, Beatrice, 138

Willard, Stephen H., 137–40

Williamson, Porter B., 151

Winning of Barbara Worth, The (Wright), 77–81

White, Cornelia, 84–88, 104

White, Florilla (doctor), 84–85, 87, 104

White Heart of Mojave: An Adventure with the Outdoors of the Desert, The (Perkins), 123–26

White, Isabel, 85, 104

Wooley, Robert L., 150

Wonders of the Colorado Desert, The (Wharton), 73–75, 192

Worth, Barbara (fictional character), 76–81, 89

Wright, Harold Bell, 77

Yaquitepec (home of Marshall South), 157–59